60 037...1 3

D0864686

...DRAWN

SOCIAL WORK IN AN UNJUST SOCIETY

Bill Jordan
Reader in Social Studies
University of Exeter

NOTTINGHAM UNIVERSITY LIBRARY

HARVESTER
WHEATSHEAF

New York   London   Toronto   Sydney   Tokyo   Singapore

First published 1990 by
Harvester Wheatsheaf
66 Wood Lane End, Hemel Hempstead
Hertfordshire, HP2 4RG
A division of
Simon & Schuster International Group

© Bill Jordan, 1990

All rights reserved. No part of this publication may be
reproduced, stored in a retrieval system, or transmitted,
in any form or by any means, electronic, mechanical,
photocopying, recording or otherwise, without the prior
permission, in writing, from the publisher.

Typeset in 10/12 pt Century Schoolbook
by Photoprint, Torquay
Printed and bound in Great Britain by
Biddles Ltd, Guildford and King's Lynn

British Library Cataloguing in Publication Data

Jordan, Bill, *1941–*
  Social work in an unjust society.
  1. Welfare work. Ethical aspects
  I. Title
  174.93613   ✓C

  ISBN 0–7450–0896–8
  ISBN 0–7450–0897–6 pbk

---

3 4 5 94 93 92

6003769/3

CONTENTS

ACKNOWLEDGEMENTS

In writing a series of drafts of this book I have benefited from a stream of helpful and constructive comments by Martin Hollis, Nigel Parton and Sally Jordan. Collectively they have provided me with an excellent forum of philosophy, policy and practice to discuss the ideas I have been trying to develop, and I am extremely grateful to them all. In my experience, social work is fascinating and demanding because it requires its practitioners to reason with distressed people about the most contentious moral issues in their society, and to negotiate the most difficult aspects of human relationships. No longer myself a practising social worker, I have invented a number of situations which seem to require such reasoning and negotiation; it has been very rewarding to debate these with such acute critics. I would also like to thank Gill Watson for her expert typing.

PROLOGUE:
A QUESTION OF INJUSTICE

Outside, the demonstrators' chants were reaching a crescendo. The director shifted uncomfortably in his chair. His interrogator – he couldn't help thinking of her as such, despite her quiet, almost studied politeness – adjusted her glasses, and gave a little smile of reassurance that unnerved him all the more.

'Now that the opposition movement is entering upon the negotiation stage,' she explained, 'we are opening dialogue with all government agencies and institutions. We want to discuss your department's position on a number of issues.'

Of course he wasn't under arrest, he told himself. He had been invited to this meeting, and could leave at any time. As for his record on human rights, it was above question. His workers were among the best trained, the most professional in the country; the city was recognised as a centre of excellence for a whole range of services. He had no cause to feel defensive, let alone apologetic.

He tried to make his voice sound firm and authoritative as he asked, 'How can I be of help?'

'The opposition movement is calling for democracy, freedom and social justice. But a good deal of hostility has been expressed towards all the public services, including your social services department. The people are highly critical of the part your agency has played in the fifteen years since this government took power. Not so much the social workers themselves, you understand – the hostility is towards the department, its policies and practices. Some people blame the leadership . . .'

He felt slightly faint, suddenly more aware of the chanting outside, and for the first time it occurred to him that they might be calling his name. What if this woman were to

vii

denounce him to the crowd? He heard himself reciting a stream of empty official phrases.

'. . . the highest possible standards of professional integrity . . . value each client as an individual . . . do our best to promote human potential . . . thorough and rigorous assessment of need . . . support of all times for the family unit . . . of course, terrible constraints on resources . . . no longer the provider, just the enabling authority . . . difficult to monitor all the services we contract out through competitive tendering . . .'

'Yes, quite,' she said, not so much interrupting as putting his faltering speech out of its misery. 'None of us has been free to do what is right these past years. But what concerns us is the future, and the part that social services can play in building a better society. Do you, I wonder, share our values and aspirations?'

With the light behind her, he could amost forget that she was black. But not quite. Was she asking him about his department's stance on anti-discrimination, or was it a broader political question? He found it difficult to focus his mind because of the noise outside.

'Our professional ethics are quite clear. Every human being is of equal value, regardless of race, creed, age or abilities, and each has the right to self-fulfilment. Society should provide the greatest possible benefit for all individuals. The professional social worker should develop knowledge and skills to bring systematic and disciplined practice to his or her clients' needs, and each has an obligation to provide the best possible service. That is the basis of the international code of ethics, and of our own national code.'

'This sounds good,' she replied evenly, still with no trace of accusation or blame in her voice, yet for him all the more disturbing for this reason. 'Perhaps we could discuss a bit more what it means in practice. From the point of view of service users, it has often felt like being under the watchful eye of authority, being carefully monitored and controlled, and being jumped on as soon as they step out of line. This is what the parents and young people in the poor areas say. As for the women, they feel like they are being reminded of their responsibilities to care, for the children and the elders, and with little help or support. And as far as resources are concerned, for them all it has felt like being strictly rationed. First there are all these questions about how much money they have, and what relatives are available to help. Then there is the long wait – waiting for something to get worse, or to break down altogether, before they get a service. This is what the people with handicaps and the carers say.'

At last he began to see what she was getting at. 'You must understand,' he explained, 'that detailed assessment of each individual and family is the cornerstone of our professional skill, whether it is assessment for a statutory intervention or to provide a service. How can we tailor our intervention or our resources to the individual's needs, or give the right package of care, if we have not made a proper assessment? And of course, there is the budget. Central government is very strict on budgetary control, as you know, and its guidelines are firm on how we should spend in relation to the various priority groups and needs. We are required by law to test applicants' financial resources before we provide any form of service.'

'Do you think that this is just?'

He paused. 'I'm not sure that it's my part to say. Whatever I think, in the last resort it's the government – the *elected* government – that says what justice is about. It's a question for politicians, not officials. This government says, and lots of people agree with them, that people should be responsible for themselves, financially and morally, if they can. It says that any agency which undermines that kind of individual responsibility, for oneself or one's family, is doing harm. We can't simply ignore or overrule the government's view on social justice. So we have to try to target help to those in greatest need, the ones who are least successful, least able . . .'

'Yet the effect, you see, is that these people feel they are being regulated and controlled. They do not have any say or any choice. They are not in prison and they are allowed to speak, but they are not free. Like those people who have to wear electronic devices on their ankles, and report to the police every day.'

'Oh well,' he laughed with some relief, 'you'll have to talk to the Chief Probation Officer about them.'

'Yes, we are meeting him today,' she said, her small smile stopping his laughter in its tracks. 'We see his service very much like yours. They say they are for offenders' rights and freedoms, but the people see them differently. The whole machinery of the state, what we used to call the welfare state, seems to be treating the people as demanding and disruptive, and trying to keep them down. You both seem to be looking for the specially dependent and dangerous ones, to isolate or punish them, as an example to the rest, to make them work harder and for less. That's the way it seems.'

He paused, trying not to picture the probation chief as a fellow prisoner, confessing or blaming the social services department for his faults. Unsure of how to go forward, he strove to make sense of these criticisms from his own managerial perspective.

'Let me get this straight. You're saying that we don't respect people's freedom, or help them to get a decent life. But they're coming to us, more and more of them, for help. We're overwhelmed by people's needs, every day, in all our services, and I guess it's the same in probation – people begging for a hostel place, or a letter to help them get money from social security or whatever. From our point of view, we're doing the best we can, under very tight restrictions, and with legal duties to protect certain vulnerable people – the victims, if you like, of crime and abuse. What are we supposed to do?'

For the first time, he sensed a recognition of his dilemmas in her face. 'Yes, we have all struggled with these problems. It is not a question of blame – our society has been going along a wrong road, and we have all been going down that road together, getting lost and getting hurt. Now we are looking for another road. We want you to help in that process, and we want to find what your services have to offer to a new way.'

'Haven't I said enough about our values and objectives? Haven't we tried to do our best for those in need?'

She did not respond at once to his genuine perplexity, but looked towards the window. The crowd was quieter now, listening to a broadcast. When she spoke, it was slowly and with no trace of dogmatism.

'Let me tell you what we don't seem to see from your department or the probation service. First, we don't see clear statements or actions on injustice. I know you have taken positions on specific issues – racism in the criminal justice system, child sexual abuse, the rights of carers, and so on – but there isn't an *overall* position on injustice. We don't hear you say, quite clearly and unequivocally, that there should be no economic exploitation and no political domination in society. We don't hear you say that wealthy and powerful people, individuals and groups, should not be able to exclude or subordinate the poor and powerless, or coerce them against their will. And, as our movement has suddenly gathered strength and found a voice, we don't see you at our demonstrations, in the streets. We see more people from the churches than people from the state services, which is a shame. Are you afraid to speak out, or don't you recognise the injustice that I am talking about?'

He thought about it. 'Not afraid, exactly. No, more muddled really, and a bit compromised. But perhaps especially, not seeing an alternative. We were all radicals in our way, back in the 1960s and 1970s, but all that got sat on, and even the politicians on the left distanced themselves from it, and from us. We had to buckle down and accept change, things like privatisation and contracting out services. And some of it has been very good you know. Some very good quality care, and very satisfied customers, better than we could do when we ran the whole show. I guess we looked back to the time when we had our chance, when public services were growing, resources were expanding, and we thought . . . well, we blew it. So now we have to admit, we haven't got all the answers, we didn't do it so well, a lot of people run a mile from state services, they'd do anything rather than come to us, and I can't blame them. So, who are we to shout the odds? Something like that, maybe.'

'We've all had these doubts at times,' she responded. 'It's part of this government's success – to make us believe that everything else has been tried before and failed, to make us feel guilty, and to cut us off from everyone else who is feeling the same. To tell us that we can only be responsible for ourselves, to look after ourselves, and that doing right means keeping the rules it makes for us. Making us forget that we are all in the same boat, that we can support each other, can share and act together, can gain strength by depending on each other, rather than trying to stand alone. I always thought that those were the fundamental values of social work – to give support, to share, to listen to others' points of view, to get a fair deal for all, as members of the same community, because we all belong together.'

'Well, yes. But we don't belong together, do we? There are many things that divide us. Our roles, our legal responsibilities, our interests – as home owners, ratepayers, residents and whatever. And in some ways, I have to say, anti-racism and anti-sexism and all the other isms seem to divide us even more, or make us more aware of the divisions. So we just fall back on ourselves, and on keeping the rules, because it's safer that way.'

She didn't react, as he had expected, but looked thoughtful. 'It's true that for many of us the main block is a sense of isolation and helplessness. But if it's like that for you and your workers, what's it like for service users? Okay, you've had defeats for your unions, attacks on your resources, restructurings, changes in the law, privatisation, and all the rest of it. But poor people, black people, single parents, people with handicaps, they've been treated like the enemy. It's been like a war for them – a battle to keep their self-respect, their identity and some organisations to support each other, to stay in some control over their lives. And in the end, it's by seeing that we do belong together, that there is strength through co-operation and sharing, that we've come through, and the movement has grown.'

'I still don't understand,' he confessed.

'There's something else missing from your list of values, and from the way your department works. You don't say, or you've stopped saying, that it isn't all about individuals and their needs. All that stuff about individual assessments – what about people needing each other, not just in families, but in groups, associations, clubs, churches and communities? What about people having an equal voice in the running of their society, as a kind of club, because they're all members? What about democracy? What do you mean by democracy in your department? Sometimes it seems to us that you mean the same as the guy who said that local councils should meet once a year to hand out contracts for all their services. We mean that people should rule themselves, have a real say in those things that they share as citizens, or as service users. You can't privatise everything, you know; you can't give each person their own bit of the ozone layer, or the ocean; and why should you want to? Sharing things with other people is good – it's a benefit, not a cost, of being a member. Everybody for themselves is no way to run things. We all end up valuing nothing unless we own it, unless we can buy and sell it, unless we can keep others off it. So we end up putting no value on other people, as well as no value on the things we have to share with them. So we end up seeing nothing wrong with us having everything and them having nothing.'

He averted his eyes from hers, which were shining behind her glasses. 'That's not quite fair,' he said, 'because we've been trying all these years to see that poor people, the outsiders, the neglected and rejected ones, got something. It may not be much, but it's something.'

'That's true, but it's usually something they get at a terrible price. Not in money. To get it, they have to prove that they've failed, that they're desperate, that they're broke, that they've done something wrong, or they're deranged, or they just can't cope. And then what they get isn't what other people want. It's something for the other failures, or the other deviants, or deranged people. It isn't a way back into society, it's often a way out, and once they take it, it's even harder to get back.'

'But wait a minute. You know that we have deliberately been kept short of resources by this government. We've been put in a terrible position. Either we give adequate amounts to a few, and none to many, or we give everyone in need short rations. It's simply a question of the arithmetic. When *our* resources are at a desperately low level, our clients have to prove *they* are desperate to get anything. We don't want it to be like that – it's a straightforward consequence of the shortage of funding.'

'And this is helping them?' she asked quietly.

'You sound as if you want to abolish social work and social services,' he said wearily. 'It makes me feel that everything we've been trying to do all these years has been a waste of time, all wrong, more harm than good. Is that what you're saying?'

Her voice became more kindly again. 'They've been hard years, and some wasted years, for all of us, and we've all done things we regret, and that we wouldn't choose to do again. That's not the point. The only question is this: have we got something to offer to a better society, and to the search for justice for all?'

'What is justice?' he muttered, faintly aware that someone had asked this question before.

'Our movement doesn't pretend to have a ready-made answer to that question,' she replied. 'The important issue for us is whether you are willing to ask it, and to listen to those people out there when they try to answer.'

1

INTRODUCTION

Moral issues haunt social work; social workers stalk moral problems. If we try to think of a situation containing a serious ethical dilemma – a woman choosing between her husband and her child, an old person trying to decide whether she has become too much of a burden to her family, a teenager torn between parental standards and loyalty to delinquent friends – we immediately come up with one in which a social worker is likely to be involved. Most modern television dramas based on such dilemmas have a social worker or two (usually portrayed rather unsympathetically) hovering on the fringes of these crises in their characters' lives.

But social workers also face moral choices of their own. Should the young residential care assistant blow the whistle on her sadistic senior colleagues? Should the black probation officer turn a blind eye to racism in the police force and courts? Should the experienced social worker go on taking away children from single parents whose main problems are poverty, bad housing and lack of support?

The dilemmas facing the people who become clients are characteristically about their relationships with family, friends and neighbours. The dilemmas facing social workers are characteristically about power. The social workers in television dramas who hover on the edge of domestic crises (like those involved with Yosser Hughes's family in *The Boys from the Blackstuff*) are often eventually drawn into the use of their power, and this process can seem crude, clumsy, or callous (as it did when they removed Yosser's children – and got a head-butt for their trouble). As observers of the drama, we are often struck by the failure of their actions to take full account of the wider context of human tragedies (Yosser's loss of his job, and his slide into madness), or to communicate and share feelings with those struggling with profound problems.

1

If moral issues are so central to social work, it would seem equally obvious that they should be a major topic in training. They do indeed appear on the Central Council for Education and Training in Social Work's required curriculum. Yet – to judge by the texts available – there is a problem in relating moral philosophy to practice, skill, knowledge, technique and hence usefulness. Although social workers readily acknowledge that their work has moral implications, they seem seldom to draw on academic theory for guidance, and appear to make judgements in a way that is either intuitive or else relies on humbler rules-of-thumb.

I was therefore interested to hear a recently-qualified social worker talk about the reality of social services and probation work today as 'the ethically-informed use of power'. He was distinguishing the predominant 'heavy-end' activity (child protection, surveillance of serious offenders) from the counselling and enabling work which is the professional aspiration of social workers, and the major preoccupation of the skills-orientated sessions of training courses.

What are the implications of recognising this increasing responsibility of qualified social workers for coercive or restrictive intervention in the lives of their clients? And why should ethics (rather than the more precise and tangible disciplines of law and policy) be seen as especially relevant to these tasks?

It is quite possible to answer both these questions dismissively. In the first place, it may be that social work *in general* is no more coercive and restrictive than it has been in the past. Social workers have always had statutory powers to make people do things they do not want to do – to remove children from parents, to apply for compulsory admission to mental hospital, and so on. It could simply be that more of the everyday welfare work of practical assistance and routine visiting is being done by unqualified workers or voluntary agencies, while more of the counselling and enabling is being done by specialists – either non social workers or people who choose to specialise in these tasks later in their careers. So the more coercive nature of these workers' tasks is just a reflection of how the work is now divided up.

As for ethics, its notorious failure to provide precise

guidance for practical action seems to make it particularly unsuitable as a discipline to inform the practice of these tasks. Hawkish critics of social work are constantly attacking its lack of decisiveness in dangerous situations; the last thing they would prescribe would be further woolly-minded agonising when common sense demands clear-cut interventions. Radical critics bemoan its short-sighted concern with personal and relationship problems; preoccupation with moral issues would appear to drive it further in the direction of conservatism and introspection, when what is needed is a broader political vision.

I argue in this book that both these dismissive retorts are wrong. First, social work as a whole *is* more coercive and restrictive. In the field of criminal justice, in spite of the fact that probation officers have a much wider range of possible recommendations to make in their reports than in the past, the prison population in Britain is the highest this century. Furthermore, the government's response to this situation is to increase the scope for 'punishment in the community' – various forms of compulsory conditions and restrictions on offenders which fall short of imprisonment but which are intended to increase the scope of surveillance and reduce their freedoms. The probation service has protested about these proposals, but has been told that it must either participate in them or see them implemented by another agency. In child protection, although the total number of children in care is falling from the record figures of the early 1980s, the pressure for compulsory orders continues to grow, as new forms of child abuse (notably sexual abuse) are identified and new legal interventions are required. These developments outweigh minor reductions in the compulsory hospitalisation of people with mental illnesses and handicaps.

Second, moral reasoning is not an alternative to knowledge of the law and social policy, but it is an essential addition to them. The law provides the framework of rules under which social workers operate; policy provides an interpretation of these rules, and a commentary on their purposes. But there would be no point in using social workers to do these tasks if laws and policies could be precisely and unambiguously stated; it is because situations are complex and susceptible to a number of interpretations that the judgement, discretion and skill of a trained person are required. As Harris and Webb have remarked, 'professionals do not create discretion; rather the inevitability of discretion creates the need for professionals'.[1] But what needs to be interpreted, discussed, negotiated and communicated has an inescapable moral content. It concerns the issues about which people feel most deeply, and inter-personal bonds they take most seriously (family relationships, friendship, neighbourliness and mutual trust, communal membership, for example). It involves suspension or restriction of ordinary decision-making processes in such relationships, and the use of power. And it raises issues about equality and inequality of choices and resources. To try to avoid or deny these issues is to invite at best personal confusion and discomfort, at worst professional burn-out, leading to dangerous incompetence.

Suppose, though, that we recognise that social work is more coercive and does raise these moral issues: it could still be argued that ethical reasoning is of little practical use for social workers. If society decides to pass laws and implement policies which require more use of compulsory power, then even though social workers will have the duty to decide which particular individuals are to be compelled or punished, they have no control over how coercive or punitive these measures are. The real ethical issues about power are for politicians and policy-makers rather than for those officials who make the specific decisions. Social workers may debate these issues on courses or at political meetings, but they can only give themselves more distress and mixed feelings by dwelling on their implications for their day-to-day practice.

This objection is in many ways the most serious and difficult of the three raised so far against the subject matter of this book. It argues that both social workers and their 'heavy-end' clients are, in a sense, victims of the injustices perpetrated by powerful groups in society. Decisions about quite different issues – allocation of economic resources, taxation, public spending and so on – determine the life-chances and oppor-tunities of the people who constitute social work's clients. Because these same decision-makers also determine the powers and resources of social workers, their numbers on the ground, pay and conditions, the scope for real (as opposed to marginal or illusory) influence on their most-disadvantaged clients' lives is minimal. The really important moral questions are, therefore, located elsewhere, and social work becomes a largely technical activity of trying to get the best possible deal (for clients and workers alike) within very narrow options.

In my opinion, and as I argue in this book, present-day British society is unjust in its basic organisation and distribution of roles and resources. It is no coincidence that the vast majority of 'heavy-end' clients are poor, and that poor areas produce higher rates of all social problems than wealthier ones. Nor is it a coincidence that black people are over-represented in the proportions of people in prisons and children in care, and under-represented among people using resources which clients see as desirable and helpful. Nor yet is it a coincidence that women provide disproportionate numbers of social workers' most needy clients – especially single parents and people with mental health problems. All these facts reflect the way in which power is held and used by better-off white males, and the advantages and disadvantages that accrue from unequal holdings of assets in British society.

However, my intention is to put forward a view of morality and moral problems which rejects the distinction between political or structural problems on the one hand and personal or relationship problems on the other. I argue that political and structural injustices are not separate from the decisions that face us in everyday life, whether as social workers or in our other roles. This is because in all these roles (including that of citizen) we are jointly responsible for the choices we make about what happens to each other, as well as what happens to ourselves.

Social work in Smortham

David Jackson is a senior social worker in the deprived inner-city borough of Smortham. His team's area is characterised by high rates of unemployment and homelessness, especially among young people of Afro-Caribbean origin. Most of the social workers in his office are women; several of them are employed on a part-time basis or on short-term contracts (for example, covering maternity leave). He himself lives outside the borough, in a comfortable semi-detached house which is being paid for through a mortgage. His wife Sarah, who is employed as a part-time housing officer in another nearby borough, provides most of the care of their two young children, and also does most of the housework.

Although he could scarcely be described as privileged, David Jackson (as a white, male senior social worker) is at an advantage (in terms of income and power) in all the relationships mentioned in this brief pen-picture. The origins of his advantages may lie in the economy and the political system, but their daily outworkings are in these relationships. There are some moral issues for him to consider with his wife, with his colleagues and with his clients; they are all interlocked in a complex way. Suppose he starts at home by asking his wife whether she would prefer to work full-time, and for him to take major responsibility for the children and the housework, at least for a period of several years. She welcomes the chance, because there is a good opportunity for her to further her career by applying for a permanent, full-time post in her department. So there is a possibility that he might share his senior social work post. He discusses this with his team; they agree that their main priority is to increase the establishment of full-time jobs, but they also press the claims of Sonia Ridgeway, a young, black social worker, for the post of part-time senior. With some difficulty he is able to persuade the borough to agree to this unusual job-share, pointing out that it is in line with its declared (but largely unimplemented) anti-sexism and anti-racism policies. On her appointment, Sonia wastes no time in pressing for major changes in the way the office is run. She argues for a much more open and welcoming approach to clients, including them in discussions about priorities and policies, and as far as possible in all decisions affecting their lives. This in turn leads quickly to an important change in the way social work time is used: instead of being involved exclusively with individual (mainly statutory) case-work, the social workers make time for weekly excursions into the community, and especially the black community. They open up resources to neighbourhood groups, and offer support to residents in their attempts to gain control over aspects of their lives.

This highly idealised account is used to make the point that injustice penetrates all social relations, not just formal political and economic ones. It also helps us to recognise that principles like those generated by anti-sexist and anti-racist literature are not distinct from social work ethics, but are in fact related to them, and that both should inform good social work practice and good social relations. If we take moral issues seriously, we are required to recognise them in our relationships at home, at work, and in our communities. Doing something about them involves us in moral dialogues with others in all these spheres, and not just in lobbying, campaigning or voting.

The difference between the imaginary example of David Jackson and the real world is that things do not usually work out so neatly. In real life, the opportunity of a permanent job would be unlikely to present itself immediately to his wife, and she would, in any case, probably have mixed feelings about the role-switch (perhaps suspecting her husband of having ulterior motives for his suggestion, such as a covert cop-out). At the office, the social workers might regard him as reneging on his leadership and supervisory responsibilities and, no matter how clearly outstanding were Sonia Ridgeway's qualifications for the part-time senior post, some of them would probably resent and resist her appointment. As for the clients, many of them would refuse to become involved with a department they saw as alien and authoritarian, while others would quickly use the influence they gained for personal advantage or to settle old scores with others in the district.

All of these predictable problems would make life much more difficult for David Jackson and the others, but they would not invalidate the point of the example. If the course of action described can be regarded as a good one (by any reasonable and coherent criteria) then – as long as there is any chance of achieving some such results – David Jackson should try to embark upon these negotiations. This makes it important for him and the others to be able to reason together about the choices to be made, and to weigh the merits of various courses of action. To do this they must understand not only the structural origins of the injustices in their relations, but also what will constitute an improvement – a fairer and better set of relationships. This means having some ethical standards by which to assess them, and some criteria for choosing the steps which will lead towards new ones.

Lastly, of course, all of them will need ways of resolving conflicts of opinion and interest between them. There is no logical contradiction in saying that a certain course of action would be morally better than any other, but that I choose not to take it. Indeed, David Jackson might well read my story about the ethical improvements he could make in his relationships and say that, noble as these actions might be, he has not the slightest intention of following them. After all, they each involve him in giving up an advantageous position for the sake of a less advantageous one, so that he ends up as a part-time worker, more answerable to his colleagues and his clients, sharing managerial responsibility with a lively, radical, black woman, married to an independent and upwardly mobile housing officer, and spending a good deal of his time mopping up, fetching and carrying after his children at home. He could perhaps not be blamed for saying that the whole thing was at best very risky, and at worst directly against his interests.

This shows that moral issues cannot be considered in isolation from material ones, or ones of social choice (like those in the example) without also considering individual preferences. These questions are investigated in some depth in Chapters 5 and 6. What should be noted for now is that the structural inequalities and injustices which give some people (with the kinds of asset possessed by David Jackson) advantages over others make it more difficult to pursue moral objectives because they give individuals clear material investments in unjust social relations. But this does not exonerate those same individuals from moral accountability, nor does it displace ethical issues from the personal to the political sphere. It merely makes these issues much more difficult to resolve.

Our starting point, then, must be social relations in present-day British society, rather than a narrow consideration of the relationships between social workers and clients. This makes it a rather different book from the ones on social work ethics which have been the core texts for many years – analyses of the principles which should govern social workers' dealings with their clientele which take little account of the wider context in which these occur. I shall be casting my net much more widely, trying to understand how a moral analysis of the whole social system sheds light on the ethical issues of transactions in social services and probation offices.

The property-owning democracy

In Britain, Mrs Thatcher and her ministers have constructed just such a moral analysis of social relations, which they have grafted onto their economic and political philosophy. This view has become the ruling orthodoxy. Although few people are willing to swallow it whole, all are influenced by it. Social workers operate within the climate of ideas that it has fostered, and sometimes incorporate its assumptions unconsciously. Even when they totally reject the ruling orthodoxy, they are forced to take account of its effects on social institutions, including the workings of their own agencies. In order to combat it, I shall argue that an equally comprehensive alternative moral and political theory is needed.

According to this dominant view, individuals have a moral duty to look after themselves and those to whom they have special obligations – notably members of their households. Outside the household, no-one has any right to expect assistance from anyone else. But society is not a free-for-all; fortunately, a well-ordered market economy provides everyone with incentives to work and save, and hence to be independent of each other. Dependency – in childhood, sickness or old age – can be accommodated within household relationships. Families care for their own, either directly (through the unpaid work of a family member, usually a woman), or by paying for services. Thus self-reliance and family responsibility are the twin moral pillars of the system of social relations which sustains the majority of society.

However, the new orthodoxy does not expect all to be equally successful in their quest for self-sufficiency. It recognises that even people who make genuine efforts to provide for themselves and the rest of their household may fail – through bad luck, misjudgement or lack of skill. It caters for this minority of 'less fortunate' people through selective social services, given to those who can pass various tests of 'genuine need'. These 'targeted' services have gradually been expanding at the expense of the universal services which were characteristic of the post-war era, when state support was regarded as a right of all citizens.

Ideally, this would lead to a society in which the substantial majority of the population owned their own houses, had savings and shares, subscribed to private pension schemes, health insurance and perhaps also private education, and could afford to pay for the care they needed in extreme old age. They might also contribute to charities for the assistance of needy people at home and abroad, and offer voluntary help to local good causes. Social work would be carried on, both in state agencies and in charitable organisations, as part of the system for dealing with poverty and deviance. As well as giving conditional assistance to those who could prove that their need was no fault of their own, it would also be concerned with the identification and correction of anti-social behaviour – attempts to avoid self-responsibility (shirking, malingering) or failures of family responsibility (neglect, abuse), as well as the usual acts of violence, fraud, theft and irrational or destructive outbursts.

It can be seen at a glance that this view of the moral content of social relations is very different from the one set out in the example of David Jackson. It would suggest that David's first duty is to earn as much as he can in his post as senior social worker, so as to pay off the mortgage, provide for his children's upbringing, and save for his retirement. His higher salary as a senior would, of course, require him to take managerial and professional responsibility for his team, and to accept the leadership role in relation to other staff. As far as clients are concerned, we should expect him to see them either as unfortunates (through some inherent inadequacy or adverse event) or as deviants who require firm control and surveillance, backed up by threat of punishment.

Seen through the eyes of the women in the story, the new orthodoxy's perspective is also quite different. Sarah Jackson should be willing to postpone her career ambitions, at least until her children are older, so as to support her husband and help him improve his own professional prospects, and hence his salary. After all, it is through his job that she has a stake in the property-owning democracy – it allowed them to get their mortgage and to start payments to his occupational pension scheme. The other social workers are in much the same position as Sarah, so they too should be content with part-time or temporary posts, in the hope that these will eventually equip them for a full-time position: they should be pleased that these allow them to fulfil their roles as mothers so conveniently. As for Sonia Ridgeway, she is in fact a single parent, who has had the advantage of an access course at her local college and state support during her social work training. She should therefore be grateful for the opportunities supplied for her to gain professional status, rather than seeking premature promotion and undue influence on policies which should, in any case, be the prerogative of more senior officers.

Lastly, the clients' perspective too is rather different. They will not be unaware that the agency's philosophy is to categorise them in two ways (sheep and goats, deserving and undeserving poor). To qualify for the services that they want (cash assistance, home helps, day care, day nurseries) they must show that they have tried their hardest to work, earn and be thrifty, and to be responsible for each other in the family, but have been unsuccessful through no fault of their own. Yet they will not be unaware that some of the rules operating within the state system actually favour 'deviants'; for example, it is possible to get social security benefit as a 16- or 17-year-old if you are pregnant or a single parent, if you are mentally ill, if you have been in care recently, if you are on probation or under supervision for an offence, if you are in danger of physical or sexual abuse from your parents, if your parents are in prison, and so on. So, while presenting yourself as a deserving sheep may gain you some resources, presenting as an undeserving goat – committing a minor offence, getting pregnant, complaining of abuse or violence within the family, or acting plain crazy – although it is a high-risk strategy, may actually gain you more.

So the implicit incentives for clients often contradict the explicit morality of the new orthodoxy. For people with low earning-power, or living in economically depressed areas with

few employment opportunities, the chances of achieving the
goals of property-ownership, saving and security are minimal.
For black people, discriminated against in employment and
housing, they are often even less. So there are strong
inducements to break the law (by stealing or working while
claiming, for example) as the only way of breaking out of the
restrictions of their situation, and gaining some of the things
that most regard as part of their ordinary standard of living.
Even if they fail in this and are caught, the chances are that (in
the first instance) they will not lose their liberty, and may even
gain access to money or a flat, through rules like the ones just
mentioned.

All this means that relations between clients and social
workers in Smortham under the new orthodoxy are likely to be
opportunistic and mistrustful. Seeing that the rewards for
abiding by the moral injunctions of the system are strictly
conditional and limited, clients will probably alternate between
a shallow pretence of subscribing to majority values, and a far
more insistent and demanding assertion of needs arising from
crises like family break-up, trouble with the police, domestic
violence, mental illness, debt or intolerable personal stress.
This is one of the contradictions of the new British social
morality which is explored in Chapters 2, 3 and 4.

It will be argued that social work's loss of credibility, in the
eyes of the advantaged majority and the disadvantaged
minority alike, can be traced to such contradictions. To black
clients in particular, as the most systematically excluded
group, social work and the probation service are seen as forms
of 'soft policing', concerned with getting them to accept the
constrained, subservient and exploited role offered them by the
majority, and penalising them for refusing to accept it. To the
majority, social workers and probation officers are there to
discipline the excluded minority, and reduce the threat it poses
to prosperity, to property and to order. To both, claims of
benevolence and caring lack conviction, because agencies
whose main concern is with crime, mental illness and child
abuse can scarcely pretend to operate by consent. According to
the new orthodoxy, social workers and probation officers
should recognise the clash of interests between the moral
majority and the deviant minority, and act clearly and
decisively on behalf of the former against the latter.

Although these views have strongly influenced social work (not least by sapping its morale) they have not carried it with them. On the whole, social workers have tried to cling to other standards and values, often difficult to articulate and harder still to put into practice. Visiting students on placements, I am often struck by the courage and persistence with which individuals, projects, teams or whole areas have pursued their ideals of a more trusting, participatory and co-operative style of work, often in the most deprived districts and among the most disadvantaged client groups

These islands of hope have not always been well served by social work literature, still less by texts about social work ethics. The aim of this book is not to say what workers and projects like these should be doing, but to try to capture what they are already doing, and why. It seems to me that – as has often been the case – theory has failed to do justice to practice, and has rather clumsily and arrogantly presumed to dictate to practitioners not only how they should work, but also what rationale they should follow. Although the scope of this book – encompassing all social relations – may seem grandiose, the final aim is to clarify why so much good practice is good, so that others have a better chance of following it. It may also help students to recognise that a great deal of what they did as volunteers or unqualified workers was an excellent basis for what they will have to tackle as workers engaged in 'heavy-end' tasks.

Some case examples

As a way into the issues that are discussed in the next two chapters, here are some examples of situations in present-day social work which pose difficult ethical problems. I shall return to them from time to time in the rest of the book, and especially in the final chapter.

Michael

Michael is a black 17-year-old who is on probation for receiving stolen goods. Soon after the court case, his father (a railwayman) threw him out of the family home because he was 'keeping bad company' and making no effort to find a job. Since then he has failed to keep appointments with his probation officer and has virtually disappeared. On one occasion they meet by chance at the Afro-Caribbean Community Centre: Michael tries to avoid him, and is only reluctantly persuaded to leave the pool table for a brief conversation, in which he makes no eye contact. He insists that he is all right, that he is staying 'here and there' with friends, that he does not need the lodgings or hostel that his probation officer is offering to try to arrange. On the subject of money, Michael says that he 'can manage', even though he is not getting any benefits, and he evades questions about how he manages. Eventually the probation officer points out that Michael is in grave danger of getting into trouble again by trying to live in this way, and that if he accepts the offer of approved lodgings or probation hostel accommodation he will be able to get income support. At this Michael blazes back angrily that 'he doesn't want to live in no white places, or be watched over by no white police', that he is 'not interested in YTS or classes or any of the other shit' they try to make him take. The probation officer warns him that unless he keeps future appointments, breach proceedings will be taken against him. With an expression that conveys that this threat confirms all his worst opinions of the probation service, Michael returns to the pool table. What does the probation officer do next?

Donna

For the third night this month an out-of-hours social worker has been called to the police station about 14-year-old Donna. She keeps running away from home to be with her boyfriend, a 19-year-old labourer who is living in lodgings on the other side of town. She has been truanting from school, where her reports have been poor for the last two years, and she is not expected to pass any exams. Donna is refusing to return to her parents, saying she is unhappy at home, that they are always shouting at her, and that she will run away again anyway. Waiting at the police station are the parents, who immediately attack the

social worker and her colleagues for being 'too soft' with
Donna. Her father, a self-employed electrician who takes a
pride in his business success, insists that Donna needs a 'good
hiding', and that he will give the same to her boyfriend if he
meets him. He says he has no time for social workers, who have
no right to meddle in family matters that do not concern them.
Her mother says that Donna has had a wonderful childhood,
and that the family have a lovely home, and the chance of a
holiday abroad next month. She should be firmly spoken to and
told to stop this nonsense. The social worker points out that
this is the third time her department has been called in, and
that Donna is threatening to do the same again. Might it not be
better to consider a short period with foster parents, to try to
defuse the situation, get her settled back at school, and plan for
the future? The parents are outraged at the very suggestion,
and threaten to report the social worker for exceeding her
authority. What should she do next?

Louise

Louise is a young single parent with three children under the
age of five. She receives income support, but is deeply in debt to
various mail order firms, to the fuel companies and to the local
shop; money is being deducted from her weekly benefit to pay
off the fuel arrears and to repay a loan from the social fund. At
various times over the past two years the social services
department has been concerned about her care of the two
younger children, who have been left with 'unsuitable' baby-
sitters in the evening, and seem under-stimulated and rather
neglected. Now a neighbour is complaining that she is out all
hours again, that the children can be heard crying, and that
the house is being used for drinking and drug-taking by local
teenagers. When the social worker calls late in the morning,
Louise and the children are still in their night clothes, and the
house is cold, except for an unguarded paraffin heater. She
confirms that she has been going out in the evenings, saying
that she was getting depressed having to stay at home, and
that she was afraid of hitting the children if she goes on feeling
the same. She has been offered a job in a night-club, but cannot

afford to take it because of the babysitting costs. Her mother would look after the eldest, Vickie, who starts school next term, but is not well enough to cope with the other two. She is wondering whether to ask if they can come into care, as it would give them 'a better chance'. How should the social worker respond?

Brian

Brian is 28 years old and has spent twenty-one of those years in institutions of various kinds. Coming into care as a 2-year-old, he spent most of his childhood in – or running away from – children's homes, before graduating through detention centre and Borstal to prison, where he has spent most of his adult life. Now he is in The Laurels, a voluntary hostel for ex-offenders, where he has been making good progress. He has begun to take an interest in art, and is an enthusiastic member of the hostel gardening group. Recently he has started a part-time job washing up at a nearby hotel, even though he is able to keep only £5 a week of his wages under income support regulations. Sandra, his key worker, is so pleased with Brian's progress that she is discussing with him the possibility of finding lodgings or a flat. She is surprised to find that he is unenthusiastic, even nervous, about this prospect, and seems to regard it as a form of rejection. He explains that he is used to living in homes and hostels, and is happy at The Laurels. He is especially grateful to Sandra for the interest she has taken in him, and has been doing most of the things he has been doing to please her. If he left, he would miss her and the other staff. Brian points out that his income support for lodgings would be much more than he could expect to earn in his present job, or any other he was likely to get, so he has no financial incentive to leave. 'Independence' for him is another word for feeling lonely and lost. Later Sandra finds a notebook in which Brian has written of his despair at the prospect of leaving the hostel, and his plans to commit further offences and return to prison rather than move out. What should she do?

Samantha

The nursing staff find it difficult to understand why Samantha (aged 32) has made a second suicide attempt. She is attractive, intelligent and affluent, and her husband Nigel seems deeply concerned for her. They refer her to the hospital social worker, feeling that there must be a deeper problem that she is concealing. Perhaps she has a drink problem, or is a compulsive gambler? But a tearful Samantha eventually reveals that her dilemma is more basic. She is disillusioned with her life as Nigel's wife; he is endlessly kind in a paternal sort of way, but deeply unimaginative about her needs. Because she left school without proper qualifications, she has no prospect of interesting work – even though they could easily afford a nanny to look after their two young children – and so she can envisage no development for herself within their marriage. Yet she has too much to lose if she leaves Nigel – the wealthy lifestyle, car, clothes, pension, possibly even the children – and lacks the courage to strike out on her own, admitting that the prospect of poverty appals her. Samantha admits that her choice of affluent boredom and frustration is a cowardly one, and will probably mean that she will stay unhappy for much, if not all, of the rest of her life. But she cannot bear to choose impoverished autonomy as an alternative to wealthy dependence. How should the social worker counsel her?

Joan

Joan, a 57-year-old widow, looks after her mother who is suffering from senile dementia. She gave up her job as a school secretary to do so, and she receives an invalid care allowance of £24 a week, in addition to her mother's attendance allowance. She is applying to the social services department for day care for her mother, because she has begun to fear for her own mental and physical health – her mother is becoming incontinent, is unable to occupy herself, and repeats the same questions hundreds of times a day. Joan knows that her mother is eligible for private residential care, paid for by income support, but she also knows that her mother would be heartbroken to be separated from her, and would probably die immediately. Joan would really like to return to work, but even a part-time job would disqualify her for invalid care allowance. Would the department be able to offer five-day-a week day care so that she could take a full-time job? The social worker explains that shortage of resources does not allow the department to offer more than three days a week at the only centre that can take someone with her mother's needs. How can she advise Joan about the best way to conserve her flagging energy and commitment?

George

George is an old man who is in hospital following a stroke. He lives alone in a house which he owns but which is in need of major structural repairs which he cannot afford: he has a small occupational pension on top of his basic state pension, and almost no savings left. George is referred to the hospital social worker by the consultant, who wants him out of the hospital because his bed is needed for other stroke victims. The consultant is clear that George is not fit to go back to live alone, and should be placed in residential care. When the social worker sees him, he is tearful and distressed, insisting that he wants to go home. He says that he has a helpful neighbour, though on closer questioning it turns out that she is in her seventies and has mobility problems of her own. The home help and meals on wheels services in George's area are already overstretched, and operate on a nine-to-five, weekdays-only basis. The social worker explains all this to George, but he remains adamant that he wants to go home, that he is on the telephone, that he can call his neighbour if there are problems, and that he does not want residential care. The social worker feels that George may well be saying that he wants to die at home, and that he is willing to take the risk of doing so upon himself. What should he do?

These dilemmas have several features in common. Each can be read in a number of different ways, as issues about personal responsibility, structural disadvantage or legal duty. For example:

1. We can read the stories in terms of the moral obligations of their central characters. According to this reading, each has a clear duty which arises from his or her responsibility for self and to others. Our obligations are personal, and we have a moral imperative to fulfil them which is categorical. Michael should keep his promise to the court, and do as his probation officer requires; Donna should obey her parents; Louise should look after her children; Brian should at least try to look after himself; Samantha should make more effort to love Nigel; Joan should carry on caring for her mother; George should follow medical advice. The social worker's job is to reinforce and support these duties, and help their clients perform them.
2. We can read the same stories as illustrating the disadvantaged status of certain people in our society. Although each has a 'choice' about their predicament, their choice is structured so as to deny them the opportunities and incentives offered to others of their age. For Michael, Louise, Brian and Joan, the structure of means-tested benefits and the constraints of available casual, part-time employment combine to deny them any real autonomy or access to goods that bestow status. Donna, Samantha and George, by contrast, are subordinates in an otherwise prosperous and autonomous section of society; their status as dependants in the household, or their physical reliance on the help of others, makes them relatively powerless. The social worker might aim to raise the consciousness of all these clients about the structural origins of their problems, and involve herself and them in political campaigns to change society.
3. Neither of these first two readings conforms closely with social work practice in the real world. In reality, social workers and probation officers are more likely to muddle through in these situations, trying to use the limited and inadequate resources at their disposal. The third reading is therefore a legal/bureaucratic one which tries to fit these clients into categories of need and to 'solve' their problems

by proposing a finite offer of assistance on a 'take it or leave it' basis. For example, if Michael will not move into approved lodgings, he will be prosecuted for breach of probation; if Donna and her parents will not accept short-term care on a voluntary basis, then no more can be done; if Louise's children are not assessed as 'at risk', then they remain her responsibility; when Brian reaches the hostel's maximum stay period, then he will be discharged; if Samantha goes home to Nigel, then there is nothing more to be done; Joan will be offered the standard amount of day care for her mother, and she must decide how to adjust to it, and George's future will depend on exactly how many home help hours are available in his district. The social worker's legal responsibilities are defined and limited, and so, therefore, are her moral ones; she can provide only what is available from her department, and the rest is up to the client.[2]

There are various ways in which each of these ethical analyses of the stories can be made more impressive and sophisticated. We could develop the first reading into a complex account of interpersonal relationships, in which rights and duties are woven together into a tight-knit social fabric. But as shown in Chapter 2, this reduces social work to a mechanistic role. Intervention in people's lives consists of no more than an assessment that allows the social worker to calculate moral responsibility, apportion blame, or take decisive action. The stories are reduced to didactic moral tales, each with its too-neat and improving conclusion; social work becomes the smug reinforcement of a code designed for suburban self-sufficiency.

The second reading gives a far more convincing analysis of the social forces acting on the protagonists, and can provide an enlightening account of the injustices that infect all our social relations. It allows us to go behind the appearance of stark moral individualism and to question the assumptions on which the first analysis rests. But, as demonstrated in Chapter 3, it provides only hazy guidance as to what the social worker can actually do to help her clients. It offers a tempting intellectual escape route, leaving the practitioner with a clear conscience, and plenty of energy for after-hours political activism.

The third reading is the one most commonly adopted in practice. It has all the attractions of 'realism', of neutrality, and of official security. It can be bolstered by relating the particular actions of the worker to codes of professional ethics, in which the goals are stated so vaguely as to allow almost anything to be permissible, and the principles are hedged around with numerous qualifications and exceptions. Social work becomes an arm's length, rather impersonal activity, in which the worker is insulated from the client's dilemmas by a protective coat of law, regulations, resource controls and codes of professional conduct. It is not the worker's business to pass moral judgement or to experience these dilemmas as her own.

In the short-run, this insulation seems a necessary part of survival; social work teams cultivate an ethos in which members help protect each other from moral pain by telling each other, 'don't blame yourself', and 'don't take your problems home with you', and 'it's not your responsibility'. Research has charted the defensive strategies by which social workers distance themselves from clients' misery and justify the partial and incomplete solutions they offer to their problems.[3] The trouble is that this process can speed up rather than postpone 'burn out' (stress-induced, debilitating anxiety or depression, which ends with the worker having nothing to offer, and actually avoiding clients and their problems). It is as if more and more energy gets consumed in the defensive manoeuvre, in frantic attempts to exonerate the workers and shift the moral baggage elsewhere. This is developed in Chapter 4.

In the second half of the book, an alternative framework is proposed for looking at these dilemmas. It locates individual rights and responsibilities in a context of social relations which involve sharing and co-operation. Moral duties arise out of lives which are interdependent, commitments which are mutual, and communities with common interests. Hence we cannot hope to understand the dilemmas facing the characters in these stories without a far richer appreciation of the details of their personal lives, and the meanings for them of their relations with others. This is the subject of Chapter 5.

In Chapter 6, this analysis is broadened to include wider social relations and issues of conflict between larger groups and classes. Here we seek principles which allow choices about the shared environment and the distribution of resources to be made in ways that are accepable to all. It is democratic theory – in the broadest sense – that can provide the ethical basis for such social choices, and hence a framework for community social work practice. This chapter analyses the relationship between social work and the local political institutions in which most of it is embedded.

Moral responsibility is not like a bomb, to be passed around rapidly between unwilling holders until it finally explodes in the face of the last unlucky carrier. If we accept an analysis of society as a membership group based on shared commitments, then social work ideally expresses one aspect of mutual responsibility within the community. The process of sharing is especially difficult in examples like the ones already listed, where resources controlled by social workers are important elements in the possible easing of clients' problems. Chapter 7 considers how moral issues are negotiated, and how good practice can be a means both to better interpersonal communication and a more democratic society.

A note on the examples

This chapter has introduced two different sorts of example: David Jackson and the social workers of Smortham, and the cases of Michael, Donna, Louise, Brian, Samantha, Joan and George. The two serve contrasting purposes.

The Smortham story is intended as an example of the ethical principles and moral reasoning that are advocated in this book. The main characters in it espouse values and practices – fairness, sharing, democracy, negotiation, co-operation – which are put forward as the ones underpinning good social relations and good social work. In this sense, the purpose of the example is rhetorical rather than logical;[4] it is intended to persuade the reader that this is the way that social workers should behave, rather in the same fashion as Kant's examples were intended to motivate people to do their duty.[5] The story will be developed and embellished as the book proceeds.

The case examples are chosen as difficult but typical instances of current social work dilemmas, against which to test the arguments of the book. They do not illustrate principles, but instead pose problems, which are discussed in the light of the various concepts and theories advanced and analysed in each chapter. I explore how social workers who adopt a particular kind of ethical reasoning might approach each of these dilemmas, and hence how their moral thinking might affect their practice.

In this sense, the cases, although imaginary, are meant to be examples of real social work, not examples of the moral rules which apply to social workers and their clients – they will not, for example, conclude with a neat list of ethical principles for social workers. Instead, they allow me to tease out some of the moral reasoning implicit in what might be regarded as good social work practice, and to argue that making it explicit – especially among teams of social workers, in departments and in training – would promote good practice.

The relationship between the two sets of examples is therefore quite complex. The Smortham social workers are shown in the process of adopting a set of moral principles and starting to implement them in their own agency. The cases pose problems for which other social workers are glimpsed rehearsing various unsatisfactory solutions and then, near the end of the book, trying to apply the ethical reasoning that has been advocated. But there is no easy transition between the Smortham principles and the resolution of the case dilemmas. This is because the application of any form of moral reasoning requires training, judgement and experience.[6] Only after the Smortham team has worked for some time within the tradition it is shaping will it discover the most creative ways of applying its principles to particular situations. This is why the final chapter is in the form of a series of dialogues between Michael, Donna, Louise, Brian, Samantha, Joan and George and their social workers, who are seen trying out the way of thinking put forward in this work. The reader is left to decide whether these represent the best way to interpret and apply the book's reasoning to their problems.

References

1. Robert Harris and David Webb, *Welfare, Power and Juvenile Justice: The social control of delinquent youth* (Tavistock, 1987), p. 5.
2. George Gammack, 'Social work as uncommon sense', *British Journal of Social Work*, vol. 12, no. 1 (1982), pp. 3–22.
3. Carole Satyamurti, *Occupational Survival: The case of the local authority social worker* (Blackwell, 1980).
4. Charles Larmore, *Patterns of Moral Complexity* (Cambridge University Press, 1987), ch. 1.
5. Immanuel Kant, *Groundwork of the Metaphysics of Morals* (1797), translated H. J. Paton (Hutchinson, 1953), section 408, p. 75.
6. Larmore, *op. cit.*, pp. 19–20.

2

THE RIGHT AND THE GOOD

The case examples in Chapter 1 were chosen to illustrate how ethical issues arise in social work. Each describes a situation in which the worker is faced with a dilemma not just about *how* to help the client, but also about what the *right* thing is to do. The choices facing her are ones of morals as well as methods.

There are two reasons why ethical issues arise in such situations. First, the client faces decisions about how to act which involve his or her relations with family, friends, neighbours or strangers; the client's actions have important implications for the happiness, welfare or safety of others, as well as his or her own. Second, the social worker must decide how to use her professional discretion and official power (over resources and in terms of legal authority), so she must act in such a way as to express society's concerns and values. The issues at stake are ones in which the community, through the state and in the profession of social work,[1] has registered a public interest in the promotion of certain standards, and the avoidance of certain evils (crime, child abuse, suicide, etc.). The social worker's involvement, and her eventual actions, reflect a decision by society to use power and resources to promote certain outcomes which are valued, and avoid certain others which are disapproved.

Stated in this way, the complexity of the ethical issues in social work becomes immediately evident: there are two sets of problems, not one. On the one hand, the client's situation raises dilemmas about how he or she ought to behave, given that one person's actions can so fundamentally affect the lives of others. On the other, the social worker is not just one of those others, defending her corner; in some sense she is a 'generalised other', or the representative of all others. Her skill, status and power, and the resources she commands are all supposed to be marshalled on behalf of all those collectively interested in the way the client acts, because such actions are reckoned to be important for the welfare of society as a whole.

This dual nature of moral puzzles in social work has confused most writers about social work ethics. In the literature the standard lists of ethical rules for social workers consist of maxims about upholding the individual rights, choices and interests of potentially vulnerable clients, against the counter-claims of potentially powerful others, including the social worker herself.[2] These rules – such as respect for persons, self-determination, confidentiality, and so on – are supposed to ensure that the client is treated as an autonomous moral agent.[3] The client should be allowed to make choices in a way that reflects the status of a human being who understands right and wrong, and who can therefore only act morally if free to choose how to act.[4] However, the rules themselves are always qualified and limited by an enormous number of disclaimers and provisos, emphasising that others should not suffer harm as a result of the client's choices, and that society's dearest values should not be contaminated by the social worker's complicity in wrong-doing.[5] In other words, the client's status as a moral agent is severely limited by the social worker's responsibility to protect the public interest, and especially to avoid certain specific social evils.

The end result is usually an unhelpful mixture of contradictory messages. The literature is at one moment telling the well-intentioned social worker always to take seriously the client's wishes, feelings, fears and aspirations, so as to cherish his or her moral autonomy, which is the essence of individual humanity. Yet at the next moment it is telling her to keep an equally keen eye on the public interest, and specifically on the interests of certain others who are entitled to at least equal respect and protection. In any particular situation, therefore, there appear always to be two quite opposing arguments which must be given equal weight. This confusion is often seen in essays by students who, when asked about self-determination will wax eloquent in defence of clients' moral freedom, but when asked in the next question about whether care precludes control will assert equally firmly that it is the hallmark of a caring social worker not to be afraid of using her authority to override wrong choices for a deviant or distressed client's good.

Clearly this is not just a muddle that social workers have created, since many distinguished philosophers have bent their minds to these problems.[6] Rather it is a muddle that reflects the society we live in. There is a real contradiction between the ideals of personal freedom which are espoused by politicians, the clergy and economists, and the goals of social harmony, order and progress which are usually embraced by much the same people. It is by no means obvious that a society made up of individuals who are free to choose their own partners, friends, family life styles, careers, causes, hobbies, houses, holidays, fads, faiths and fantasies will be harmonious, co-operative fair, equal, orderly or even bearable.

The central problem for this way of thinking – and the one that defeated the optimistic eighteenth-century project for a modern age of personal liberty – is the idea that individuals can perhaps only be relied upon to know about what is good for them in a certain rather narrow sense, and to seek it in ways which are not necessarily conducive to the good of others. If we see the social world as made up of individuals acting from a set of material preferences (looking for bargains in the way of products and services) and subjective feelings (positive about some people, negative about others), then it is quite unrealistic to suppose that they know what is good for society as a whole, and impossible to imagine that they will seek it. So individual freedom needs to be curbed by moral rules, so that people learn about the rights and wrongs of personal relations, and the limits they should place on their pursuit of their own preferences and pleasures. But responsibility for the good of society passes into the hands of the state, as the guardian of the public interest, and justifies the use of power to bring about the kind of social world in which such individuals can thrive and prosper. In other words, morality becomes a matter for relationships between individuals, while social harmony becomes the sphere of politics.

So the clients in the case examples could be seen as learning about which moral obligations should restrain their personal freedom, and about the rights of other individuals, and of society as a whole, enforceable if necessary through the social workers' powers. Michael's freedom to move around and change jobs is limited by his duty to support himself through his own efforts and pay his way; Donna is free to pursue the high spending, fashion-conscious, pleasure-orientated life-style of a modern teenager, but not to flout her parents' authority or to run away with her boyfriend; Louise is free to do night work and choose her own friends, but only if she makes satisfactory arrangements for the care of her children; and so on. The social workers' authority to try to teach these clients about their responsibilities, and to overrule them if they default, comes from their role as duly appointed officers of the local or national government, and hence as upholders of the public interest.

I shall argue that there are not two conflicting sets of values – individual rights versus social harmony, freedom versus order, morality versus politics – at stake here, but a single set of interlocking issues. All the relevant actors – clients, their neighbours, their victims, social workers, moralists, media people, politicians – occupy the same, shared social environment. Within this, they belong to social units – families, firms, clubs, agencies, communities – which in turn require them to share certain resources. Yet because they move as individuals between these units, working, shopping, consuming, relaxing, they must make decisions as individuals also. So these two aspects of social life – the one involving social choices on behalf of groups who share the same social environment and the other involving individuals choosing for themselves – must somehow be co-ordinated. Individual decisions, whether about morality or the market-place, must somehow be reconciled with the common good – the good of the community.

Social workers are not concerned exclusively with individual choices or with social choices; they work on the borderlines between these, and are part of the process by which societies try to co-ordinate these two forms of decision-making. In the example of David Jackson and his colleagues in Smortham, his relationship with his wife Sarah, with his female team-members, and with his team's clientele, all raise issues of fairness over roles and resources, benefits and burdens, advantages and disadvantages, power and compliance. The concepts needed to analyse and reason about these issues are both moral and political, because personal and wider social relations intermesh in their lives as council employees and as citizens of Smortham. Neither in their domestic roles nor in their relationships with clients can the analysis provided by the dominant moral and political orthodoxy supply a convincing justification for some individuals' income and power advantages over others, or show how David's 'responsible choices' will promote the good of his wife, his colleagues or his clients.

This initial diagnosis of the problems to be addressed requires us to launch straight into some fairly broad theoretical discussion. The account of the issues and the possible solutions are kept as clear and simple as possible, and are regularly related back to the examples. However, we must start by looking at how major theoretical traditions, and recent political philosophers, have tackled the problem of reconciling the rights of the individual with the good of all.

The liberal solution

If there were one good life in which every individual could share then there would in principle be no conflict between the good of the individual and the good of society. Up to the seventeenth and eighteenth centuries writers about ethics thought there could be such a good life. Aristotle and his followers argued that there might be a secular society in which each individual citizen could recognise and follow his civic duties (though, of course, women, workers and slaves would not be included as full members of such a society of free and equal political animals).[7] Christians and Muslims, among others, argued that individuals who followed their religious duties could establish the Kingdom of God on Earth.[8] Even in modern times, Marx suggested that the transition from capitalism, through socialism, to communism would involve a transformation from alienated labour by individuals bearing class interests to free and voluntary co-operation for the sake of agreed social needs in a classless society.[9]

However, the dominant view in modern times has been that there is not one good life; there are potentially as many conceptions of the good life as there are individuals.[10] Hence the task of ethics is not to find ways of promoting and sustaining one secular or religious ideal community, but to find ways of reconciling a number of equally valid conceptions of the good life, in which each individual pursues his or her own chosen projects, through commitments involving certain relationships with others, and requiring certain resources for their fulfilment.[11]

Although there are many variants, the most widely accepted solution to this problem can be characterised as the liberal one.[12] Since everyone has an equally valid claim to pursue his or her good in their own way, the best means of reconciling competing claims is to carve out a sphere in which each can be free to live his or her life as they choose.[13] This involves creating individual rights which allow each person a space which is protected from others' interference and in which the invididual is a sovereign decision-maker. In return for this, each person is obliged to respect the corresponding protected sphere of all others.

These individual rights are of two quite different kinds.[14] The first are personal rights – freedoms from intrusive interventions in one's beliefs, opinions, political preferences, choices of associates, and so on. They are our civil and political liberties, which allow us to express the ideas, hold the religious views, support the political parties and join the pressure groups of our choice. The second sort are property rights – rules which allow us to sell our labour power, skills, expertise, products or possessions, and to accumulate money, land, houses, factories or offices. These rules give rise to freedoms to own, trade, produce and invest, and to establish holdings in the resources we require for our projects.

For some liberals, these two sets of individual rights amount to fundamental entitlements, and to interfere with these freedoms for the sake of any other goals – such as equality or social harmony – is to risk destroying the whole basis of a free society, the idea of each person pursuing their own good in their own way. No-one should ever be forced to do anything for the good of others, though people do have to be restrained from infringing others' freedom, and made to compensate for harming others.[15] This gives rise to a very narrow view of the state's role: as being concerned only with neutral arbitration between disputing individuals, and a responsibility for the very limited sphere in which all individuals share an interest in common action, though none has an individual interest in acting – notably external defence, social order and the policing of contracts. This version of the liberal solution is often called a libertarian one.

On the other hand, those liberals who are much more concerned with equality and fairness point out that personal and property rights are frequently in conflict with each other:[16] for example when someone who has immense wealth becomes the patron, employer or landlord of someone who is very poor. In this situation, someone who owns few resources is unlikely to have as much personal space in which to make choices as someone who owns many; indeed the latter is probably able to wield great power over the former, inducing or forcing him to act in certain ways, or even to worship, vote or live in accordance with his requirements. Hence personal freedom requires resources and opportunities if it is to be of use to anyone, and economic liberties can lead to inequalities of power which infringe the personal rights of those who have no property.

Egalitarian liberals point out that, despite the fiction that property rights stem from entitlements which are the results of free gifts, exchanges or labour, in practice they are as likely to be the results of historical conquests, forced appropriations, frauds or thefts, or of arbitrary distributions of talents, luck, looks, skills, strengths, etc. Hence there is a strong case for sharing out resources in a way different from the outcome of voluntary and market transactions: one which aims at something nearer to equality of resources as well as equality of personal rights. This obviously requires a much more interventionist state, redistributing various forms of income and wealth between its citizens.

A number of possible principles for doing this fairly have been proposed in recent years. The most famous of this is the 'difference principle', under which the only inequalities that can be justified are those that make the poorest group no worse off than they would be if resources were divided equally.[17] This tries to capture the notion that an unequal share-out may be for everyone's benefit if it allows some rather enterprising, talented and productive people to generate a larger national cake, from which even the poorest may derive a bigger slice. Another is the idea that people may want to 'auction off' some of their bundle of resources, because some will place a higher value on industry, accumulation, consumption or possession, while others may prefer leisure, relationships, art or study.[18] The auction would allow the latter to cash in their share of productive resources for the sake of a small but secure income on which to live while they pursue less lucrative or even unpaid activities. This principle tries to capture the notion that even an egalitarian society needs a mechanism – the market – through which people with different conceptions of the good life can trade some of their shares of resources and yet end up with bundles that are still equal in the sense that no-one envies anyone else's particular mix.

Both these principles offer an abstract idea of how a society might try to establish fairness in dividing up shares of the things people value, but neither can apportion shares in a way that stands for all time. Because both require a system of production and exchange which allows resources to be accumulated for private use, and both permit gifts and voluntary transfers, there must be a new share-out at intervals (either after a fixed number of years or between generations) in order to prevent unfair inequalities from being reinforced over time. Private property holdings allow national income to be maximised (more accurately 'maximinned'),[19] and also allow individuals to pursue their own goals in their own ways; but state intervention is continually called upon to correct the consequences of market and other transactions. So the egalitarian liberal solution requires a state which is as concerned with social justice as it is with upholding freedom.

A liberal society

Let us imagine the sort of society which might be set up according to these principles – concerned with the freedom of individuals to pursue a diversity of conceptions of the good life, and a fair distribution of resources. What sort of society would it be, and how would people relate to each other?

First of all, let us imagine a society in which each individual really does have a personal project for 'a good life which is identifiably different from every other individual's – as different, let us suppose, as those of a poet, a businessman, a scientist, a banker, a sportsman, a shopkeeper and a phil-anthropist.[20] All need personal liberties and a share of resources for their projects, but none can achieve them without the participation of some others (as audience, workers, experi-mental subjects, borrowers, competitors, customers and objects of benevolence). The obvious solution to the problem of how to reconcile their claims is to settle on some principle for shares of liberties and resources (equal freedom plus *either* property entitlements *or* the difference principle *or* equal post-auction resources), and then to allow them to conduct their relation-ships under a system of commercial contracts. Soon the businessman would find a workforce, the poet a publisher, the banker and the shopkeeper their customers, and so on. The state would then be necessary only to reinforce these contracts by law, and to redistribute as required by whatever principles were adopted. This does indeed approximate to the formal relationships that exist in advanced western societies, with rather strongly freedom-orientated ones like the United States and (increasingly) Britain following a more entitlement-based interpretation of property rights, and the more egalitarian ones (like Sweden) using mechanisms of redistribution to give individuals greater equality of shares.

But this does not account for informal relations in such societies. In particular, it does not explain why some people live together in households, why they join together to form associations (either clubs or friendships), why they choose to share certain resources, or bind together as members of the same church, political group or cultural community. None of these relationships is strictly contractual, and none can be regulated by that precise mechanism – the market price – according to which the exchange values of goods and services can be equated, so that millions of people with different projects and preferences can reach a mutually satisfactory accommodation. So what are we to make of these informal relationships, and how are we to judge them from the points of view of rights, freedom and equality?

Let us return to our original hypothesis of a society made up of individuals with entirely separate, non-overlapping personal projects. Under this assumption, no such informal relations are very likely to develop because each individual will spend all his or her time and energy either in direct pursuit of their project or in activities which give access to the resources which will enable their project (working for wages, advertising, training, practising, etc.). So anything they need from each other can probably best be secured by means of contractual or market relations, rather than in these relatively insecure informal ways.

The only difficulty about this is that such a society would not be able to reproduce itself. Since each individual pursues his or her project single-mindedly, without reference to the good of others, and certainly without reference to the good of any future generation, it makes little sense to think in terms of a future society which could develop out of this one. Perhaps this is less so in an entitlement-based version of liberalism (in which individuals could bequeath their property-holdings to their children) than in an equal-resources version (where each new generation's share-out would take place out of the resources left by the previous generation). But even in the former, an individual considering entering into a partnership with another for the purpose of producing children would have to bear in mind both the possible costs to his or her own project, and the likely problems of reconciling the tasks of parenting with the other's project.

Suppose that we build into the assumptions about individuals in our imaginary society an innate (biological) desire to reproduce the species by creating a new generation. How could this be reconciled with their individual projects and their social institutions? The obvious solution would be to treat parenting in the same instrumental way as other forms of labour not expended on personal projects. A man and a woman could agree to exchange parenting services for money on a contractual basis. Let us imagine, for example, that he is an artist and she is an accountant. He likes to work at home, is tolerant of mess, and might even find the presence of a child a source of inspiration. She works long hours in an office to earn a high salary, is fastidious, and finds the tasks of child care repugnant (though she quite likes the products). Accordingly, she could hire him to look after the child until such time as it can be independent, paying him out of her salary for his services. (Of course none of this contractual parenting would have anything to do with sexual services, or indeed with procreation, which could be the subject of quite separate contracts, either between the same partners, or with other individuals.)

Similar solutions could be adopted to other forms of temporary dependence, such as illness, injury and old age. Contract nursing, housekeeping and care attendance would be a considerably more reliable form of provision than informal help in a world of distinguishable non-overlapping projects. They would also be defensibly fair, since they could be regulated by the same combination of price mechanism and law which governed every other transaction between individuals, defined as free and equal according to the requirements of justice.

The reader, then, has been invited to imagine a liberal society constructed according to certain widely-accepted principles of fairness, and in which individuals have clear-cut rights and duties, defined by legally-enforceable contracts. In such a society there would be a clear way of settling many of the dilemmas which were posed in the previous chapter. What counted as child abuse or neglect, for instance, would be failure to carry out the contractual terms of an agreement with a legal parent. Men and women would be required to care for elderly persons neither more nor less than they had agreed to do for the wage stated. Samantha's duties to Nigel would be specified, and if she found some of them unacceptable she could either refuse to renew the contract when its fixed term expired or agree to settle for an earlier termination of the agreement. The rights of runaway teenager Donna would be clear: either she has reached the legal age of moral autonomy or she is still her parents' contractual responsibility. The state has merely to apply the rules in all these cases.

Obviously there would be little need for social work in such a society. The law could be applied rather precisely to these issues and disputes, leaving little room for disagreements except over the amount of penalties and compensations. There would, of course, still be the field of criminal justice – though a strong case could be made for fixed penal consequences for specific crimes in a society that aimed at precision in all other spheres. In other words, along with moral complexity, social workers would have been banished from this liberal utopia – except perhaps for a few individuals whose empathy and insight equipped them to sell their services on the market as counsellors to the distressed and lonely. Why, then, do moral perplexities of the kind used as illustrations arise in the real world, and why are social workers used to try to resolve them?

The problem of care

It is not difficult to detect the weaknesses of this model. First, although each individual starts with a bundle of resources relevant for his or her project, there are no guarantees of success or even survival. This is most obviously the case in the entitlement version, in which many people may start with no property at all, just their hereditary endowments of intelligence and aptitude, which for some may not be enough to earn them a subsistence living, still less to achieve their goals. Even in the maximin and auction versions, some individuals may embark on expensive projects which fail, others may suffer serious accidents or disabling illnesses, and others still may start with serious physical or mental handicaps. Of course there is always insurance as a way of guarding against these misfortunes, but nothing in the solution so far implies that individuals will always insure prudently, or know about the risks to be able to cover all possible eventualities.

Second, the contractual solution to personal relationships is unlikely to solve every problem. People with unpleasant personalities or habits would probably not be able to get regular companionship or care services at any price. The price of parental services for handicapped children would be exorbitant, and probably beyond the means of most of those responsible for them. Those who lived to a great old age in a condition of high dependency might well not have saved enough to pay for all the services they would need. Conditions like mental illness would not only disrupt existing contracts, but also create difficulties in negotiating new ones. People might insist on caring for themselves when incapable of doing so, to the great inconvenience of their neighbours, and with some danger to themselves and others.

These examples show why a liberal state might have an interest in the form and content of contracts between individuals over such relationships. Because people who are uninsured and destitute may perish as a consequence, this is a matter of public concern (if only because unburied bodies are a public health hazard). Because people who are especially deviant, disturbed or disabled may find themselves with no-one to care for them, the rest of society has an interest in taking some action. And even where an apparently satisfactory contract solution exists, there are certain issues – notably child care, education and health – over which the public is not indifferent to the quality of service that is being provided, since the outcomes of bad child care, bad education and bad health care are all likely to increase the amount of destitution, deviance, disturbance and disability in society.

One solution to these difficulties might be for the state to regulate personal contracts over such issues and to recognise a category of people for whom it has to take special responsibility. Not only would the state insist on certain standards of child care, education and health care, monitoring the terms of contracts and intervening when these standards are not met; but also it would subcontract the care of destitute, disturbed, deviant and disabled people to others, paying them out of the public purse. In other words, the state would come to express the public interest in these issues both by its regulation of contractual standards and by setting itself up as a contractor on behalf of people who could be shown to be incapable of contracting for their own needs. So the state would enter the arena of care in the dual role of monitor of standards and indirect provider of services. In this way, the liberal state becomes – almost by default – a kind of welfare state, and social work becomes one of its means of monitoring and contracting care.

So our ideal liberal solution begins to take on more of the characteristics of the real world, at least in the advanced western societies. But there is still the very important difference that all relationships remain contractual so that there are no families, friendships, associations or communities

as we would recognise them in ordinary society. This in turn
has odd consequences on the ethical issues for this ideal liberal
world. The only issues seem to be ones of formal justice –
whether each individual receives his or her fair initial share.
For example, the destitute, deviant and disabled people might
complain that their plight in an entitlement version of the
liberal society is the result of an unfair initial bundle of
resources, and they might argue for something much closer to
the maximin or auction bundle. But once they accept their
share as a fair one, they can have few grounds for disputing the
moral justification of state services designed to provide or
monitor their care contracts, so long as the state observes the
same standards in its own subcontracting as it imposes in
purely commercial contracts between individuals.

Relationships and sharing

One unrealistic assumption that was built into our ideal
liberal society was that each individual has a personal project
which is unique and distinguishable from all others. Clearly
this is not the case in the real world. Most of us have projects
which are similar to those of others, and most of us see this as
an advantage rather than a drawback. We want to do at least
some things with others – to enjoy their company, to benefit
from their support, to share the burdens and responsibilities,
to gain from their wisdom and experience, and so on. Most
projects are not lonely quests for pinnacles of solo performance
or personal achievement, they are humbler aspirations for a
comfortable and companionable existence. Furthermore, the
model outlined so far excludes commitments – regularities in
behaviour and relationships that stem from affection, faith,
passion, loyalty, bonds of kinship, mutuality, reciprocity,
obligation or habit, which tie people to the performance of
certain tasks, or to associating as members of certain groups.

So our initial assumptions need modifying to take account of
two things. First, most people do not have one, single,
individualistic project around which they organise their life:
they usually have several projects, which include rather
humdrum ones like making a convivial social environment for

themselves, having somewhere comfortable to eat and sleep, and enjoying a reasonable amount of healthy leisure activity. Far from being unique, these projects (if they can aptly be so called) are almost universal, even though people's tastes affect how they go about achieving them. Second, such general projects overlap with those of others, and are expected to do so. No-one supposes that they are unique in wanting these things, and few people want to create a solitary life-style in which their comforts and conveniences are attended to in isolation. In fact, it is part of what we mean by 'needs' (as opposed to projects) that we recognise that the same needs are present in other people, that this gives us something in common with other people and that one of our needs is to share certain aspects of our lives with other people.

So our model of a liberal society has to take account of overlapping projects concerned with meeting basic needs, including the need for companionship and a degree of sharing. Why should these not be subject to the same contractual relationships as those between individual project pursuers in an economic system? The answer to this is not easy. We have already seen that social reproduction could indeed be accomplished by contract as long as the state took a role as monitor and indirect provider of services. Presumably, then, people prefer informal arrangements for companionship, sharing and membership, or find them superior (in terms of efficiency) in some way.

There may be two sets of reasons for these arrangements. The first is to do with how we choose partners, friends and associates. We seem to want to be able to select these in a rather intuitive and idiosyncratic way, according to largely unspecifiable criteria, which include our feelings about them. We appear to value the non-rational (or at least inexplicable) elements in these choices, and the emotional interaction which we experience when our liking for others is reciprocated.[21] In other words, we put a high value on the fact that we enjoy the company of certain others, and they enjoy ours, for its own sake, rather than for any identifiable purpose. Our friends are simply the people we like to be with rather than the people who help us achieve our individual projects or our economic ends: so we want a personal, informal way of choosing them.

The second is that everyday living and the meeting of common needs requires considerable flexibility and adaptability to rapidly changing circumstances. Ordinary life is rather chaotic and unstructured, subject to discontinuities and incursions from unexpected quarters. It would be difficult to stipulate contractual terms for all its eventualities (as such employees as nannies and housekeepers notoriously discover). Hence the arrangements under which people share parts of their lives with family, friends and associates are best kept flexible and negotiable, based on a rough understanding of reciprocal roles and responsibilities, rather than closely defined rights and rules.[22] So reciprocity is generalised rather than balanced in most kinship relations (something done for someone is not expected to be paid back in a precise way within a specific time); there is a give-and-take approach in friendships; and even in more formalised associations, members help each other out in ways that are not required by the rule book.

This makes sense because such overlapping projects as sharing a household, or being members of the same network, club or church, involve placing a positive value on having certain resources which are common to all. They represent the choice of a shared life style, or at least of including certain others in a part of one's life where the fact that they use the same amenities is seen as an advantage.[23] When property is communal and goods are shared by members, then formal partitioning into exclusively owned bundles of resources is counter-productive. There would be little point in deciding to set up house together, and then dividing up the rooms and putting locks on all the doors; or in joining a club and then refusing to share the facilities with other members. Since the company of those others is part of the benefit of membership, it makes sense to have roles that allow points of contact to be informally negotiated within an overall understanding of individual as well as common needs and purposes.

So we come to recognise that once overlapping projects, common needs and shared lives are built into our assumptions about a liberal society, then new relationships appear, and with them new social institutions. These are based more on trust than contract, on promises or understandings more than legally binding agreements. We know roughly what we expect of our spouses, our friends and our neighbours, but we would be surprised if they asked us to write it down. Because we have chosen them, and they us, from a sense of mutual intrinsic value, we expect to treat them as ends in themselves rather than as means of achieving our projects. And we regard our mutual obligations to each other as having a moral rather than a legal sanction, because it is based on a personal commitment rather than an instrumental, impersonal undertaking.

Ethical implications

Once informal relations of this kind appear in our society, recognisable ethical issues arise with them. Instead of being concerned only with abstract but precise questions of justice, we see problems about how to create and sustain the quality of shared lives which allow people to meet their emotional and social needs. Since individuals must choose and negotiate their partnership and friendships, and try to enter particular associations, there is massive scope for rejection, disappointment and loneliness. Since the terms of relationships are implicit rather than explicit, and can change almost imperceptibly over time, there are enormous opportunities for misunderstanding, manipulation, mistrust and mystification. Since emotional needs vary, both between individuals and over time, there are endless occasions for cruelty, exploitation and domination within relationships.

It is impossible to enjoy the benefits of flexibility, informality, idiosyncrasy, spontaneity, emotional authenticity and sharing within a framework of precisely-stipulated rights and duties. While we need general rules to guide our conduct in personal relationships, a good and reliable partner, friend or associate is not someone who is super-conscious of his or her rights and duties, and punctilious in their performance; he or she is someone with the virtues of a good partner, friend or associate (empathy, patience, courage, humour, forgiveness, enthusiasm, commitment, and so on), and with the ability to judge how and when to apply these virtues to particular situations so as to sustain and enhance the relationship or to link it with wider aspects of the good life.[24] The quality of anyone's relations with others depends on this creative, *ad hoc* and personal interpretation of the bonds which connect them, on how decisions about action are communicated and negotiated, and on how the resulting feelings and experiences are shared.

The liberal tradition of moral philosophy has been strong on emphasising the unique individuality of each person, and how, therefore, he or she is entitled to respect and to be treated as an end rather than as a means.[25] Various justifications have been offered for the value placed on the human individual;[26] I argue in the final part of the book that it follows from a social system in which relations such as the ones described in the previous section are fundamental, and in which, therefore, people count for who they are rather than what they can do. Hence an important social work value – respect for persons – can be traced directly to the nature of informal social relations, overlapping projects and shared lives.

But the liberal tradition has had much more difficulty in making the connection between this basic ethical commandment – treat people as ends not means – and the characteristic relationships that its economic principles produce.[27] In particular, how can the self-interested, calculative and instrumental behaviour of market and contractual relations (seeking the best possible deal according to individual preferences) be reconciled with the moral rules of loyalty, fidelity, reciprocity, mutuality and sharing? This question arises most urgently in families, where individuals who earn and spend as economic beings try to negotiate the most intimate details of shared lives.

Take the example of Joan. She has a brother Christopher who lives fifty miles away. He has a good income from his job as a salesman, and his wife Helen also works as a secretary to the managing director of the same firm. Christopher expects to be consulted over decisions about the care of his mother, but not to be directly involved in providing that care. Because Joan has always been 'close' to her mother, both geographically and emotionally, because she lived alone, because she is a woman, because she has helped her mother through widowhood and the gradual loss, first of her faculties and then of her independence, Joan has been 'lined up' for years for the role of care-giver. Christopher and Helen drop in to see her about once a month.

Joan experiences her role as carer for her mentally confused mother partly as a 'natural' one for her as a loving daughter, and partly as a duty that arises from the love and support she received from her mother. She feels she has a moral bond with her mother, even though nowadays her mother often does not recognise her, and certainly does not show gratitude or appreciation. If pressed, Joan could express her obligation to her mother as an ethical duty to pay back all the kindness and affection she received, and stay true to the relationship with her mother that she has enjoyed all her life.

Yet Joan's role is clearly not fair if seen in terms of the roles of Christopher and Helen. The moral rule that she applies to herself seems to allow exceptions in the case of her brother (because he is a man) and his wife (because she is not 'close' to his mother). Behind it seems to lie an assumption that men should be the primary protagonists in the public life of economy and polity, while women should be the primary providers of care and unpaid labour in the domestic sphere; and the assumption that women should be prepared to sacrifice their personal development for the sake of other family members' need, even if men are not. Joan's 'moral duty' can be recognised as having little to do with sharing in family, and much to do with the economics of a particular system of production and the politics of a particular system of power.

To understand this, we need to be able to see how moral rules are made – who makes them, and for whom. We shall never be able to understand the situation so long as we analyse social relations purely in terms of individual choices, and transactions between individuals. On that method of analysis, Christopher's choice of his job and Joan's choice of the role of carer will both show up as free choices, made in the separate spheres of economy and morality, to which different standards apply. It may be able to say that Joan did not have a fair share of initial rights and resources as compared with Christopher, but it will not be able to show how a coalition of Christophers use their control over resources and power in relationships to make the 'moral rules' under which Joan has a duty to care for her mother.

In liberal theory, morality is a code of conduct which serves largely to make actions in the sphere of personal relationships predictable and reliable. Moral principles are sets of rules from which in turn are derived other, higher-level rules such as the one which underpins respect for persons.[28] But to understand the discriminatory nature of many moral rules (such as the one that Joan applies to herself) we need a systematic account of the connections between the economic and moral relations. This is further discussed in the next chapter.

Shared decisions

There is yet another weakness in the liberal account of ethical decisions which is just as important. This is its failure to show how individual choices relate to the good of whole social units. Since people live in families, associations and communities, we would expect that there would be a close connection between individual choices made under moral rules and the common good of all members of those units. But liberal theory, far from making those connections actually distinguishes between the rights of individuals to seek their own good, and the authoritative imposition of the goals of the association or society.

Going back to the Smortham example, we saw that David Jackson's choices were based on a series of discussions, first with Sarah about the implications of his job decisions for hers, then with the team about the implications of his job-share for them, and then between social workers, clients and members of the local community. All these discussions treated the choices to be made as shared decisions, not individual ones. They acted as if the standards which should guide their actions were not matters of private conscience (rules governing individuals' duties) but matters of common concern for the partnership, team or group.

This way of thinking reflects the idea that people are not self-sufficient but interdependent, so some form of joint decision-making is essential. David's good is inextricably linked with Sarah's; the team rely on each other; how social workers treat clients affects the quality of life of the whole community. This means that moral issues are not confined to a special sphere of personal conduct; they are pervasive and complex. They require David and his colleagues to think of themselves as partners, colleagues and members of various social units, and of their decision-making as having important implications for others. They can only know exactly what these implications are, and what considerations they should take into account, by debate and negotiation, and by trying to reach agreement.

The whole tendency of liberal theory is to obscure this, by trying to divide up and parcel out to individuals not only rights and resources but also duties, so as to emphasise individual choice at the expense of social choice. For example, in reasoning about why we should respect and value other individuals, it emphasises that they have morally sovereign wills like our own, and hence must be accorded similar rights. But a more binding moral reason for doing so is that we ourselves are members, along with those others, of a network of relationships in which everyone's good depends on everyone else's. So we actually experience our moral bonds with others most strongly when we are jointly at the mercy of over-whelming external forces (as, for example, in a disaster such as a shipwreck). Our concern for others, and our desire to help them, is greatest when we are 'all in the same boat' and must act or perish together.

Neither the subjective feelings of people in such situations nor their moral responsibilities to each other can be under-stood in terms of individual rights and duties; they only make sense as part of a shared experience of peril, and a common attempt to survive, through mutual concern. For instance, counsellors in the aftermath of large-scale tragedies like the Hillsborough disaster report that the most common question asked by survivors is, 'What happened to the people standing next to me?'

If social workers operate at the interface between the good of the individual and the good of social units like families and communities, then they cannot deal exclusively in the rights and responsibilities of individuals; they must also understand how groups of people make decisions about shared projects and their common good. This chapter started by tracing the complexity in the case examples to just this issue. All the people in the examples are making decisions about their relationships with others in which their own good is closely linked with the good of those others. Louise's decision about the night-club job, Samantha's about the future of her marriage, Joan's about work outside the home, are morally significant within networks of interdependence. But social workers' roles are also linked with public concern about decision-making in these social units, if possible mediating and conciliating to help the members co-operate and reach settlements which are agreed by all.

So the liberal approach to ethical issues seems one-sided and incomplete. If the task is to reconcile individual choices with the good of groups with shared lives, then the means must include both the equal autonomy of individuals (fair shares of rights and resources for each person) and the opportunity for all to share in joint decisions, leading to the best possible quality of their communal life. Modern liberalism is sometimes narrow in its concern for justice in terms of individual rights, and neglectful of the relationships which make a good society.[29] It does not deal much with justice in Aristotle's sense, as 'what tends to promote the common interest' because it allows 'each to attain a share in the common good'.[30]

It would be misleading to suggest that the whole liberal tradition has this weakness. The one-sidedness of the dominant version of present-day liberal philosophy comes from the American East Coast; as Michael Freeden has argued, this form of 'non-realisable, neutral, contractarian liberalism' has overwhelmed the far richer tradition of 'communitarian liberalism' which is concerned with human flourishing through membership, participation and sharing.[31] There are some signs that this older British version of liberalism may be re-emerging.[32]

The American liberal theorists (and especially Dworkin) have been looking for 'principles of justice' – decision procedures about rights and resources that are strictly neutral between every kind of claim, and can apply to every situation – which can function as a kind of supreme court to which every individual can appeal, and which can deliver decisions that are morally watertight. In their rights-based systems, 'arguments of principle are arguments intended to establish an individual right; arguments of policy are arguments intended to establish a collective goal';[33] it is always possible to reach a decision about what individuals' rights are according to principles, even in hard cases involving complexity and conflict. Rights provide individuals with trump cards or vetoes that they can use against collective decisions of all kinds.[34]

If justice is defined in terms of individual rights, the method of settling disputed claims must take a form rather like a court of law, and the outcome of applying principles must be to decide a 'winner' – someone whose rights prevail over others'. This view invites us to see social workers as informal judges, presiding over situations like the ones facing the clients in the examples, and reaching decisions in favour of one party or another according to their moral rights. Alternatively, social workers may be seen as having powers that stem from collective goals (such as public hygiene or universal schooling) against which clients have rights to defend a territory of individual choice. Although there are strong temptations to see social work in these terms, and those temptations are strongest in a very unequal liberal society such as present-day Britain, I intend to argue against this point of view. These themes are taken up again in Chapter 4.

Conclusions

If liberal principles were purely philosophical and confined to abstract speculation, then social workers would not have to worry too much about them. But there are good reasons for thinking that British society is in the midst of an enormous political experiment, to try to reconstruct our social institutions in line with these principles. The welfare state in particular is being remodelled as if society were made up of transactions between individuals, as in liberal theorists' 'thought experiments'. Social work itself is directly affected by these changes.

A good example of this trend is in the field of community care. The White Paper published in November 1989 aims to reorganise the care of people who are old and frail, or who have mental or physical handicaps, so that it can be seen as being made up entirely of moral rights and duties (family care) and contractual rights and duties (paid care).[35] Those individuals who need paid care will be neatly divided into ones who can pay for it themselves and ones who are to be paid for by the state. The assessment of needs and means will be done by 'case managers', many of whom will be social workers, and their task will then be to allocate each individual a 'package of care' – domiciliary assistance, day care or residential care – to be paid for out of a budget held by the local authority.

Community care will be funded by central government in the form of a grant, calculated as if it were the sum of the costs of all the individuals in need. So the task of the budget-holders and case managers is to translate this sum back into individual 'packages', and to buy the appropriate amount of care for each person's needs. They must spend the budget in such a way as to make 'the maximum possible use of private and voluntary providers'[36] and to secure the best 'value for taxpayers' money.'[37] They must use their own public services only where 'other forms of service provision are unforthcoming or unsuitable' – for example, 'for people with high levels of dependency, or particularly challenging patterns of behaviour'.[38]

This programme for change looks at care and the role of the state exactly in the way discussed in this chapter. Ideally, individuals come together in households and make morally binding agreements with each other for mutual assistance, which give rise to duties to care; they then accumulate resources out of which they can contract to buy extra care on the market. The role of the state is to monitor these arrangements, and to make contractual arrangements for those individuals who lack the resources to pay for their needs. Collective provision should only be for people who are too dependent, disturbed or deviant for their families to handle or for commercial caring companies to take on at any price.

This looks like a neat solution to the problems of individual and collective responsibility over care, and it is presented with much rhetorical emphasis on freedom and choice. But really it solves nothing. Joan's dilemma is still this: if she defines herself as a daughter with a duty to care for her mother, then her ration of services does not allow her any other role through which she can be an active member of society. Alternatively, the social worker can define her mother as in need of far more care than Joan can supply, which will allow Joan to work and have a social life, but only by defining Joan as no longer responsible for her mother in their previous relationship of interdependence. This is partly because of the rules of the benefit system (according to the conditions for invalid care allowance, Joan must either be a full-time carer or not a carer at all); but it is also because the mechanism of an 'individualised package' of care for her mother does not give the old lady any more say in the matter than she had before. The social worker still has exactly the same dilemmas about how much heed to pay to the old lady's (confused, dependent) views of her needs. She must either risk asking the question, and hearing that she wants to stay at home with Joan, or she must decide for her, on the grounds that Joan's needs have the stronger claims. If she takes the latter option, then the council's contract with a private company to provide weekly care for fifty old people at £200 a week does not increase Joan's mother's freedom and choice one iota.

Indeed we can imagine a community in which there are a hundred households like Joan and her mother's, fifty of whom get allocated so little paid care that the daughter is trapped into a full-time domestic role; and the other fifty with an unwilling old lady cared for under a contract with Alzheimer Associates, who have bought and renovated the old workhouse. Under these particular liberal principles all these arrangements come out as 'voluntary' because they are either moral or contractual, and hence the sum total of all these individual 'agreements' comes out as chosen, free and fair.

Suppose that central government policy, instead of trying to individualise and privatise care, allows the local authority to renovate the old workhouse, and it in turn allows this to become a resource centre for the one hundred Joans and their mothers. Suppose they pool their invalid care allowances, the daughters take turns to look after groups of mothers, and with the help of staff, organise activities for themselves and the old ladies, covering for each other during working hours, and for leisure, sport and political participation.

This scenario sounds a great deal more 'voluntary' than the previous one, but it is not easily captured in the form of individual moral duties and contracts. It implies co-operation, sharing and collective action, and a role for the state which fosters these through making common interests more visible, and public facilities more accessible. It is for this alternative view of the moral basis of social relations that I argue in later chapters.

References

1. For a useful discussion of this aspect of social work, and its ethical implications, see Michael Horne, *Values in Social Work* (Wildwood House/Community Care, 1987), especially chs 9 and 10.
2. See, for example, Felix P. Biestek, *The Casework Relationship* (Allen and Unwin, 1961); Zofia Butrym, *The Nature of Social Work* (Macmillan, 1976); Charles S. Levy, *Social Work Ethics* (Human Science Press, 1976); F. E. McDermott (ed.), *Self-determination in Social Work* (Routledge and Kegal Paul, 1975); Noel Timms, *Social Work Values: An enquiry* (Routledge and Kegan Paul, 1983).
3. See R. S. Downie and Elizabeth Telfer, *Respect for Persons* (Allen and Unwin, 1969); Ruth Wilkes, *Social Work and Undervalued Groups* (Tavistock, 1981).
4. See Raymond Plant, *Social and Moral Theory in Casework* (Routledge and Kegan Paul, 1970).
5. See especially Biestek, *op. cit.*
6. For example, Dorothy Emmet, *Ethics and the Social Worker* (Association of Psychiatric Social Workers, 1962); S. I. Benn and R. S. Peters, *Social Principles and the Democratic State* (Allen and Unwin, 1959).
7. Aristotle, *Politics*, especially bk III.
8. For example, St Augustine, *The City of God*; St Thomas Aquinas, *Summa Philosophica*; more ambiguously and satirically, Sir Thomas More, *Utopia*.
9. Karl Marx, *Grandrisse: Foundations of the critique of political economy* (written 1857–8; Penguin edition, 1973).
10. Charles E. Larmore, *Patterns of Moral Complexity* (Cambridge University Press, 1987), especially chs 2 and 3.
11. Albert Weale, *Political Theory and Social Policy* (Macmillan, 1983), especially pp. 24–9; Bill Jordan, *Rethinking Welfare* (Blackwell, 1987), ch. 2.
12. Larmore, *op. cit.*, ch. 3.
13. John Stuart Mill, 'On Liberty' (1859), in *Utilitarianism, Liberty, Representative Government* (Dent, 1912).
14. Samuel Bowles and Herbert Gintis, *Democracy and Capitalism: Property, community and the contradictions of modern social thought* (Routledge and Kegan Paul, 1986).
15. For different versions of this position see Robert Nozick, *Anarchy, State and Utopia* (Blackwell, 1974); and F. A. Hayek, *The Constitution of Liberty* (Routledge and Kegan Paul, 1960).

16. Bowles and Gintis, *op. cit.*
17. John Rawls, *A Theory of Justice* (Clarendon Press, 1972).
18. Ronald Dworkin, 'What is equality? Part II: equality of resources', *Philosophy and Public Affairs*, vol. 10, no. 4 (1981) pp. 283–344.
19. In other words, distributed so as to produce the maximum product consistent with the poorest group getting at least their original share – see Rawls, *op. cit.*
20. This is a modified version of the list chosen by Dworkin in 'What is equality? Part I: equality of welfare', *Philosophy and Public Affairs*, vol. 10, no. 3 (1981) pp. 185–224. In his list, too, the projects and needs are highly individualistic.
21. Antony Black, *State, Community and Human Desire: A group-centred account of human values* (Harvester Wheatsheaf, 1988).
22. Jordan, *op. cit.*, chs 2–4; R. F. Curtis, 'Household and family in theory on inequality', *American Sociological Review*, vol. 51, pp. 168–80.
23. Bill Jordan, *The Common Good: Citizenship, morality and self-interest* (Blackwell, 1989), especially chs 5, 8 and 9.
24. Larmore, *op. cit.*, ch. 1.
25. Immanuel Kant, *Critique of Pure Reason* (1781).
26. Plant, *op. cit.*, ch. 1.
27. Alasdair MacIntyre, *After Virtue: A study in moral theory* (Duckworth, 1981).
28. Larmore, *op. cit.*, ch. 2; Horne, *op. cit.*, chs 10 and 11.
29. Amy Gutmann, 'Communitarian critics of liberalism', *Philosophy and Public Affairs*, vol. 14, no. 3 (1985), especially p. 320.
30. Aristotle, *Politics* (translated by Ernest Barker), (Oxford University Press, 1948), bk III, ch. XII, 5.1 and ch. VI, 5.3.
31. Michael Freeden, 'Liberal-communitarianism and basic income', paper given at the Conference on the Ethical Foundations for Basic Income, Louvain-la-Neuve, Belgium, 31 August–2 September 1989.
32. See, for instance, David Marquand, *The Unprincipled Society* (Fontana, 1988); Paddy Ashdown, *Citizens' Britain: A radical agenda for the 1990s* (Fourth Estate, 1989).
33. Ronald Dworkin, *Taking Rights Seriously* (Duckworth, 1977), p. 90.
34. *Ibid.*, p. 174.
35. White Paper, *Caring for People: Community care in the next decade and beyond*, Cm. 849 (HMSO, 1989).
36. *Ibid.*, para. 1.11, p. 5.
37. *Ibid.*
38. *Ibid.*, 3.4.11, p. 24.

3

OUTCOMES, ASSETS AND CITIZENSHIP

So far we have looked at our examples of ethical problems solely from the point of view of the individual clients and their social workers. In as much as we have given attention to wider social factors, we have done so only by constructing a series of imaginary societies, built up out of the personal projects and instrumental preferences of such individuals. These have all been examples of the 'thought experiments' which typify liberal moral and political philosophy: they start from schematic, abstract persons and go on to create notional 'societies' which are supposed to provide insight into the essential characteristics of moral concepts or to test ethical arguments.

This way of going about things is open to rather serious doubts. Although (as we have seen) these mental exercises can sometimes show how particular social institutions or even whole structures could develop spontaneously through the rational choices of individuals, or how specific concepts (such as moral standards) are closely tied to certain forms of relationship, they are open to criticism about the extent to which they help us understand and evaluate the real world. So there is a strong case for starting all over again – for looking at all these issues afresh from the point of view of society as a social system, and relations as developing out of that system, rather than being constructed through individual choices in a never-never land.

After all, none of us lives on a desert island. We form our projects and preferences, and make our commitments to others, within an existing structure of social relations, which shapes our perceptions, constrains our choices and moulds our interests. We are not born as individuals, but as members of families, communities, classes and nations, with identifiable economic roles and interests, acting these out within a given structure of

52

historically generated institutions. So there is a strong case for seeking a kind of analysis which helps us understand the social system in which individuals are embedded before we try to analyse their specific options and strategies for living a better life. It may even be that ethical choices can only be properly analysed in the context of group relations and institutional constraints – that the only path to moral progress for individuals lies through joint action, politically motivated, aimed at changing society's structures, and liberating humanity from the moral as well as the material fetters of a corrupt order.

To do this, we shift our perspective from the close-up one of the previous chapter to a rather loftier standpoint from which we can gain an overview of society, its development and dynamics. Our aim is to analyse the structural factors which determine individuals' welfare, their life-chances and their opportunities for self-development, so as to develop a more realistic way of understanding the context of their moral choices. Hence individuals are to be considered more as cogs in the wheels of the social system, and less as autonomous planners of their own projects; more as bearers of roles and interests than as agents who make things happen.[1] Also, people's relationships are to be considered more for their structure than their content, and more for their quantitative outcome than for their emotional quality. It will be seen that this mode of analysis has its weaknesses, from an ethical standpoint, as well as its strengths.

Ethical outcomes

If we look at society as a system of relations (co-operative or exploitative, free or coerced) rather than as the sum of individual choices, then we shall be more concerned with the characteristics and the outcomes of these relations than with the decisions of individual actors. Instead of focusing on the subject's reasons, motives and beliefs we shall pay more attention to the objective characteristics of the context of social action, and its material outcomes.[2] It is this concern with the conditions and consequences of choices, and with overall aggregate social welfare, that links together a large number of otherwise dissimilar theories, from utilitarianism through various kinds of socialism to Marxism.

It is not my purpose to consider these theories in any detail, but only to point out some features of their methods of analysis which may help us better to understand the issues raised by the examples in the first chapter. They lead us to look at the situations facing Michael, Donna, Brian, Louise, Samantha, Joan and George as ones which confront many others of their class, race or gender, and as understandable only through an approach which takes these concepts into account.

Societies are social systems for generating goods and services relevant to the welfare of their members. Utilitarianism starts from the idea that we must take into account the total sum of welfare in any society, and seek ways of maximising it from the potential resources available, while optimising its distribution.[3] This is the famous principle of the 'greatest happiness of the greatest number', which has many possible interpretations and many difficulties. But its central insight is the notion that each individual's welfare relates to that of all others in society; and that the state, as the central authority of society, has a responsibility to organise and structure society so as to maximise production and optimise the distribution of welfare. Hence attention shifts from the individual to the state (or the statesman, as Bentham, the original utilitarian, would have said[4]) as having a moral duty to construct institutions which give all citizens the best possible lives.

The original utilitarians were also political economists – followers of Adam Smith and his colleagues in believing that a free market would be the best way of generating the largest possible national income, and channelling it to the whole population in the fairest possible proportions. But they were also social engineers in the sense that they tried to construct very complex institutions for solving the problems that markets could not overcome, such as social deviance, destitution, public health, education and order. In Britain it was they who most imaginatively proposed and most energetically pursued the interventionist measures through which the Victorian state eventually set up an infrastructure of roads, sewers, postal services, schools, hospitals, workhouses, prisons and asylums.[5] They believed that society could be improved, and the characters of individual citizens uplifted, by public measures aimed at changing the social environment, restructuring incentives and penalties, and constraining harmful actions. So although they were liberals in the economic sphere, their social and moral philosophy led to an active state role; they can therefore be seen as the ancestors of both Fabian and municipal socialism, and hence ultimately of the welfare state.[6] Mainstream British socialism adopted ideas from other traditions, grafting onto utilitarianism the notion of public ownership of productive enterprises, the goal of which would be a fundamental shift of resources to the working class, and particularly wages which reflected the true value of its labour in the productive process.

Marx's thought was a far more complex and subtle development of British political economy, in combination with French and German socialist theory. Marx was concerned to analyse both economic exploitation – the way in which some people were able to extract benefit from the labour of others – and alienation – the process by which the worker's labour became a commodity in the productive process. His theory of exploitation was designed to show how capitalism entailed an opaque process of turning the surplus product of labour power into profits. Although he critically analysed the ideological mystifications by which bourgeois economists justified this process, he did not regard capitalism as inherently unjust; rather, he argued that at a certain point of development its institutions would become an artificial fetter on the expansion of productive forces, and hence on opportunities for human self-development.[7] At this point a revolutionary transformation of society, brought about by working-class action, would usher in socialism, as the means to maximise both material and moral potentialities. Hence the socialist state would be the means of achieving the ethically optimum society at this point of economic evolution.[8]

But this was not to be the final stage of progress. Full communism would come only when the social needs of all were met by the unalienated work of all. In other words, society would eventually become a system of voluntary co-operation, with no wage labour and no state. True moral autonomy for individuals would be expressed not in an infinite diversity of conceptions of the good life but in spontaneous co-ordination of each citizen's efforts and energies for the good of all. The communist society would be a harmonious anarchy not because of a socially enlightened government but because its members would have internalised its needs and goals as their own.[9]

So Marx's special contribution to the analysis of social systems was his account of how productive relations gave rise to class interests, which in turn formed an essential element in the emergence of all social institutions, from the political organs of the state to the co-operative societies of the proletariat. He insisted that individuals' choices and chances could be understood only within a framework of class relations, and the conflicts and constraints that characterised the mode of production. Hence it was only through a consciousness of their interests as workers, and through action directed at bringing about socialism, that individuals could further their moral development, by ending capitalist forms of exploitation and substituting the more extensive resources and opportunities of a socialist order.

Even if we reject out of hand the economic reductivism and determinism of Marx's theories, and his predictions about social evolution, several aspects of his analysis seem indispensable. We need to be able to locate the dilemmas facing people like the clients in our examples in a set of institutions in which some people have a different range of choices available to them from others. This differentiation between the terms on which individuals' or groups' choices are made seems to take two forms. On the one hand, there are relationships in which some people, through their ownership or control of certain resources, can induce others to act in ways which further their own interests, when those others would not have chosen to act in these ways if they had not been restricted to those resource-related options.[10] I have deliberately phrased this account of what might be regarded as 'exploitation' in a far more general way than Marx or his followers did because we may well want to use this insight to include relations where the advantage gained by one person over another does not take the form of a labour service performed by the latter on the former's behalf.

For example, we may want to be able to say that unemployed people are exploited in relation to people with regular jobs.[11]

Second, there are relationships in which the capacity to limit choices is derived from one person's authority over the other rather than by ownership or control of resources. One person or group simply sets the rules under which the other's life is led.[12] We may not agree with Marx that such power is always ultimately based on economic relations, and we will certainly want to distinguish the ability to enforce compliance ('domination') from the ability to gain material advantage. But both exploitation and domination in their different ways enable a person or group to limit the choices available to others through, respectively, the possession of resources and power.

For instance, in the Smortham example in Chapter 1, David Jackson – as a husband, senior social worker and head of a team working with disadvantaged clients – could readily be seen as the holder of assets which give him unjustifiable advantages. Being male, white, in a regular full-time job, owning a house, and subscribing to a pension, all give him personal and property rights which are enjoyed neither by the women in that scenario (or are enjoyed only as the subordinate partners of men) nor by the majority of clients, many of whom are denied them mainly because they are black.

It is also fairly obvious that these concepts apply to the case examples in the first chapter. People like the clients in those stories conduct their lives within very constrained opportunities. If Michael owned his own house, had a regular job and earned a decent wage, it is unlikely that he would be on probation. If Donna could get income support and a flat, or even if she could find sympathetic foster parents, she would not have to submit to her parents' control. If Louise were married to a rich man, she could afford to employ a nanny instead of asking for her children to come into care; but if Samantha were a man, with access to the status and salary of a professional position, then she would have a range of options for personal development outside her domestic role. Brian, despite being in the prime of life, has not even reached the position of earning a subsistence income and is dependent for material and psychological support on bureaucrats and professionals who can control his life. Joan's unpaid role as carer strictly limits her autonomy, excluding her from economic participation and eroding all her other social roles. George must plead with a doctor even to be allowed to die as he chooses, because he depends on public services as an alternative to residential care.

In so far as clients can be said to be exploited or dominated in their relations with others, the social worker's ethical dilemmas have an additional dimension. Clients are not making their choices as the autonomous moral agents of liberal theory; they are making them within an institutional framework of relationships in which they face a choice of evils. Just as for the classic proletarian in Marx's theory, capitalism offers Hobson's choice of labour or starve, so perhaps under modern social arrangements clients like these do not have the opportunities available to others in society, but instead are trapped in poverty, dependence or subordination. They can command neither the resources nor the authority to broaden their choices because of their status in the social system.

Furthermore, the social worker is not neutral in this situation. Society is concerned about these clients' behaviour and has given the social worker the authority to intervene. Ultimately it has given her the power to take compulsory action to bring about certain outcomes or prevent others. And it has provided her with resources which may be crucial to the quality of their lives and the options available to them. So, if these clients are in some sense exploited or dominated as members of their class, race or gender, then the social worker is potentially an active accessory to that exploitation and domination. She has to consider the possibility that she is reinforcing precisely those constraints, exclusions and coercions which entrap and disempower clients like these. So she has to evaluate the moral implications of her role, her authority and her command over resources.

Interests and choices

If these ideas are to be used in a way which clarifies the dilemmas in the examples, we need to be able to recognise the forms of exploitation and domination which exist in our society. We require a specific analysis of how some people's choices are limited in relation to those of others, and of the ethical implications of these constraints.

We can start by looking at the notion of someone's interests. Within the liberal individualist tradition, to say that it is in a person's interests to do something is to suggest that doing it will put them in a better position to get what they want – whether this is to achieve a specific project, attain a particular preference, or improve their overall welfare (e.g. by being healthier).[13] People are assumed to be the best judges of their own interests in most circumstances, and their choices of where to work, what to buy, whom to elect, and whom to marry, etc., are taken to be the expression of their pursuit of their interests. In most economic, political and social trans-actions, individuals are regarded as behaving in self-interested ways, though in families and among friends they may sacrifice their interests for the good of others when this is required.

But this account fails to capture the insight that was being explored in the previous section. It especially misses the dimension of social relations in which some people's scope for choosing is far narrower than others', and the latter have direct material advantage or coercive power over the former. We want to be able to say something which reflects the conflict of interests between those who can exploit their material assets advantageously, or can dominate through their positions of authority, and those exploited or dominated.[14] These ideas cannot be readily explained through the liberal individualist analysis; indeed, they seem to be obscured by it. In the liberal tradition, each individual seems to have the same scope to follow his or her projects and preferences as any other, as long as they all live in a free market democracy. But it is easy to see that this may not be an adequate account of the social structure.

Imagine a society in which a small group of people own all the sources of water supply, and have used this to exact from the rest of the population a large tax, sufficient to allow them to live in luxury, and to construct a desirable way of life. Imagine also that some of this group hold the positions of authority in society, or at least the power to determine who should hold them and on what terms. This would clearly be a society in which this small group was both exploiting and dominating the majority, placing constraints on the latter's lives while at the same time expanding their own range of choices, and excluding the majority from access either to the asset through which they extract their advantage or to the power to change the rules of the game. We can recognise in this imaginary society many features of South Africa, where white people form a group rather like the water-source owners, with both economic and political ascendancy. But we can also recognise that these two are logically distinct, because in Zimbabwe, for example, white people still hold the vast majority of wealth, but black people have political power.

The broader notions being put forward in this chapter allow us to see that in this imaginary society the majority have an interest in changing the overall situation under which their choices are so constrained. We can capture this idea of a 'meta-interest' in changing the distribution of resources and the rules of society by saying that the majority have an interest in abolishing the advantages, in terms of income and power, that the minority possess. Whether this is achieved through direct redistribution of the relevant asset or through nationalising it, by revolution or by democratic process, the key question is whether some people's possession of an asset gives them such advantages, and hence whether it is in others' interests to reorganise society in such a way that these advantages disappear.[15]

Marx saw capitalists as a group like the water-source owners, whose ownership of this asset gave them just such advantages in the developed societies of his day. He saw the working class as having an interest in overthrowing capitalism by the only way he conceived as possible. Capitalists would not voluntarily surrender their ability to exploit workers, since this alone gave them profits. Nor would they voluntarily concede true democracy, since the working class would use it to seize power and to end capitalist exploitation. Instead, the capitalist class would hold onto power by a combination of electoral ruses, small concessions to influential groups, dividing the working class, and ideological justifications of its processes ('hegemony').[16]

Many people still regard this conflict between class interests as fundamental in capitalist societies, and any attempt to extend the Marxian insight into other areas of social relations as potentially mystifying and confusing. Others regard the idea of interests as allowing us to see the equally important conflicts between groups over assets other than capital. For example, maleness is an asset which gives its holders enormous advantages of income and power in most societies. Men own more, earn more, consume more and relax more than women; they also have far more power, and in the domestic sphere especially, their roles allow them to subordinate women and lead to an unequal division of unpaid work tasks. Hence, argue feminists, women have an interest as women in overthrowing patriarchy, and this interest overrides their position in relation to the means of production. Similarly, in North American and western European societies as well as in South Africa and Australasia, white people have similar advantages in terms of income and power over black people, and use systematic discrimination so effectively to deny them access to these resources and positions of authority, that anti-racist writers have argued that whiteness constitutes an asset whose advantages should be abolished, and that black people (irrespective of their actual position in society) have a meta-interest in achieving this change.

Another whole dimension of advantage and disadvantage in modern western societies concerns the labour market. It is now a well-recognised feature of employment in all but the Nordic economies that a dwindling number of well-paid and secure jobs are increasingly differentiated (in terms of pay, hours, conditions, fringe benefits, etc.) from a growing number of low-paid, part-time, short-term or variable forms of employment.[17] The latter provide neither subsistence-level earnings nor the security and protection against contingencies that are enjoyed by the former; and of course there is a large proportion of the population which has no employment at all. We can distinguish between a majority of citizens who live in households with at least one job-holding member (usually a white male), and hence with other members with incentives to take part-time employment; and a minority who live in households with no such member, and whose income is therefore determined by state benefits.[18] In Britain, for example, households containing no-one with a decently-paid, full-time job usually depend on means-tested income support, and hence no member has an incentive to take insecure, low-paid or part-time work since not only are the resulting loss of benefits, travelling expenses and child care costs likely to be greater than the earnings after taxation, but also extra earnings are subject to effective marginal tax rates of around 90 per cent.[19]

Under these circumstances society can be seen as comprising two further conflicting interest groups – job-rich households, with several earners, and hence access to owner-occupied housing, occupational or private pensions, and the stock market, as well as higher incomes and market choices; and job-poor households, restricted to incomes determined by the state through benefit rates, to local authority housing and services, and denied access to status-giving goods. This division of interests according to holdings of 'job-assets'[20] has been described as one between a market-orientated majority, with a stake in the 'property-owning democracy', and an 'underclass' or 'claiming class' which depends on state benefits and services.[21] The former has a clear interest in continuing to exclude the latter from a share of assets and power, while the latter has an interest in overthrowing this exclusive order and redistributing these advantages.

My purpose here is not to argue for or against any of these concepts of class or interest conflict but to point out how ideas of this kind are relevant for our examples. Whether we see all these clients as having the same interests as members of a working class, or as being representatives of a number of disadvantaged fragments (women, black people, claimants), all of whom might share interests in challenging the ascendancy of white, male, job-holders, the crucial insight available from this analysis is of a meta-interest which transcends individual preferences and projects by showing the constraints imposed by economic and political structures on individual choices. How can this insight benefit the clients themselves?

Interests and ethics

One of the most useful things about this view of interests is that it allows us to identify what certain people have in common as disadvantaged or subordinate members of society, to criticise their structural position from the standpoint of fairness, and to resist the stigma and constraint imposed on them. Once we see that these groups are systematically denied their share of assets (or excluded altogether from an asset) and hence suffer disadvantages in terms of income and power, then we can recognise ways in which they can get together to combat the negative consequences of their status. Instead of women, for example, being treated as irrational, child-like, fit only for an unpaid domestic role, weak, or submissive, they can support each other in recognising these stereotypes as the products of male exploitation and domination, and as convenient rationalisations of women's exclusion from the advantages associated with maleness. Instead of black people being regarded as impulsive, primitive, noisy, physical, aggressive or lazy, they can join together to construct a positive image for their skin colour, and a realistic evaluation of their capacities, seeing white racism as the source of their exclusion from material resources and political power. Thus the consciousness generated by perception of interests allows both a criticism of existing social systems and a recognition of common interests in co-operation and mutual support.

The analysis is also valuable in pointing to the necessary direction for change. In identifying the sources of exploitation and domination, it indicates which assets need to be redistributed, or to have their advantageous consequences abolished. Hence, in combination with liberal criteria of justice, or as an alternative theory of justice, they suggest strong moral grounds for criticising a particular social order, and the ways in which it might be made more ethically defensible.

Thinking of our original examples, it is obvious that these approaches would usefully complement the individualism of the liberal tradition, or even replace it altogether. Instead of seeing the clients' predicaments as relating only to their individual projects and commitments, or their rights and duties in relations with other individuals, it allows us to see them as having certain common interests with others – black people, workers, claimants or women – who are similarly disadvantaged, and to draw strength, support and a more positive identity from recognising this, and from joining with

groups whose purpose is to promote these interests. This is the
starting point of radical social work, whether it is derived from
Marxist, feminist or anti-racist analyses.[22]

The difficulties occur when we come to try to link these
understandings and actions with a specifically ethical framework for decision-making, either by clients or by social
workers. As with liberal justice, the idea of interests gives us a
criterion for examining the whole social system. If there are
conflicts of interests such that some people are systematically
disadvantaged in terms of income or power, we have a *prima
facie* case of injustice, and an argument for using some means –
the most obvious one being state power – for changing the
rules, reallocating resources, and redistributing power. But we
do not have any clear ethical guidelines from this particular
philosophical tradition on how to go about the process of
change. Whereas liberalism is strong on individual moral
autonomy and the rights of each person to seek his or her own
good, utilitarianism, socialism and Marxism are not so clear on
these issues. In so far as the state has a better overview of
society than has any individual, it sometimes takes the role of
moral agent or entrepreneur, identifying the needs and
interests of citizens, and engineering it for the greatest good of
the greatest number. This puts a high value on control of the
state apparatus as the means of achieving the good of the
individuals who make up society. It implies that an élite or
vanguard may claim superior insight on enlightenment in the
interests of the masses, or that the pursuit of power by any
means in the cause of a new social order may be justified. It
puts a low value on individuals' perceptions of their own good,
their specific projects and commitments, especially when these
go against the proposed interests of the class, gender or race.

Clearly this raises special difficulties for the social worker.
In cases such as those we are considering, she may well want to
suggest to clients that they consider their problems in a wider
context, that they recognise their links with others through
shared disadvantages, that they reject the scornful stereotypes
of privileged insiders, and so on. But she must also offer them
some immediate counsel with their problems in relation to
daily living, and perhaps some resources to assist them to
move in one direction or another.[23] In all this she must surely

give some weight to the meanings they attach to their roles and relationships, the values they pursue in their lives, and their own goals as members of families, groups or neighbourhoods. If these conflict with their interests as members of disadvantaged coalitions, how is this conflict to be resolved?

What we mean by an ethical perspective on social relations is one that tells us something about the means of achieving good outcomes as well as what those good outcomes are like. In other words, it tells us about right ways of behaving as well as good ends of behaviour. The approaches considered in this chapter are much stronger on good outcomes as the ends of social processes than on right ways of getting to them. Utilitarianism, for example, faces notorious problems over why we should take seriously the processes by which decisions over rewards and punishments are made. For example, if we know that it is important, for the sake of preventing high rates of serious crime, that someone should be seen to be punished for an offence, why should we be scrupulous about who is convicted? After all, if we can save several lives by risking punishing an innocent person rather than punishing no one, why be so fussy about proof of guilt? The greatest happiness of the greatest number requires us to be decisive and ruthless. Yet intuitively we rebel against this conclusion and assert the individual's right not to be sacrificed for the good of society. Similarly, the revolutionary path of socialism runs through many capitalists' property rights and some politicians' authority. How much violence is justified in the pursuit of socialist justice and liberation and which bourgeois rights, if any, should be rejected? Recent events in eastern Europe show that modern socialist revolutionaries feel some embarrassment about the excesses of their predecessors, and now propose methods of moving forward to greater social justice which restore many of the individual rights which were regarded as worthless during the original revolution.

Democratic socialists argue that they can and do reconcile respect for individual rights and personal values with the redistributive and egalitarian goals of social justice. Yet this has not been a process which has always been conspicuously successful. The social services themselves have often been criticised as involving more social engineering than democratic participation. They are concerned as much with social control and discipline as with counselling.[24] The goals of social policy are seldom explicitly debated with the electorate but are more often set in deals between powerful groups or by experts in policy analysis. The delivery of services is usually accomplished by bureaucrats or professionals, according to their criteria, to essentially passive consumers.[25] Neither the community as a whole nor those who receive public services are actively involved in decisions about how welfare should be shared or the form in which it should be given. In other words, decision-making over broad issues of social provision owes much more to political overviews of the general distribution of welfare in society than to considerations of democratic participation or the subjective meanings which beneficiaries attach to receiving it. Hence it is perhaps no coincidence that social democratic versions of the welfare state have been attacked both by libertarians of both the right,[26] who insist on individuals' rights to pursue their own good in a free market, and the left,[27] who criticise the paternalistic manner in which services are given and accuse the social services of actually reinforcing the disadvantaged and dependent status of their clientele.

Ethical democracy

The accusation of paternalism and social engineering raises another issue about ethics in social work. The problem of specifiably moral means of achieving social work goals is only one aspect of a more general problem about ethical theories which see outcomes as the relevant moral tests. As we have already recognised, social work is in part the expression of society's concerns about certain forms of action and relationships. This implies that social workers are expressing a public morality in their work, a morality that reflects wider social norms, goals and taboos. It is a matter not just of acting according to individual conscience but also of expressing some sort of collective conscience on society's behalf.

This has two very clear implications. On the one hand, social workers – especially those in the public services – have to be able to justify their actions publicly. They are accountable to their employers, ultimately elected politicians, for everything they do and all the resources they dispense. This does not imply that they simply do their political masters' bidding, or that the moral responsibility for their actions rests with others, and not with them. But it does imply that they should be able and willing to give an account of what they do and why they do it. So, for example, radical and revolutionary social workers cannot expect to be answerable only to their peers or their clients; they are also answerable to the democratic process. Even if they regard the exclusion, exploitation and powerlessness of their clientele as iniquitous, they cannot ethically justify unilateral or subversive action. They must ultimately declare themselves, even if it means risking their job in the process.

Empirical research about work practice suggests that social workers do condone isolated, occasional or trivial acts of 'banditry' – breaking rules, flouting policies, making un-authorised or disguised payments, giving misleading infor-mation or withholding relevant facts, colluding with clients against large organisations or their own department, and so on.[28] This can quite easily be justified in an *ad hoc* way as necessary for the survival of worker and client alike. But systematic, regular and frequent breaches of this kind would surely signal something much more radically wrong, which demanded a public debate. One of the moral dilemmas which confronts social workers all the time is when to 'blow the whistle' on other agencies or their own, or sometimes on clients, over important issues of exploitation or abuse of power. If the rules are so stacked against clients that they are having to be bent all the time to achieve any sustainable relations, then the rules demand to be changed, and it can scarcely be morally justifiable to postpone this issue indefinitely.

The second implication concerns the need to be open with clients. There is an ever-present temptation for social workers to do things for or to their clients, over their heads, without proper consultation or consent. That temptation is particularly obvious in the cases of Brian and George in our examples. The social worker would save herself a great deal of trouble by avoiding discussing the issues with them and making arrangements in which they are not directly involved. She could arrange for Brian to stay at the hostel or to be discharged ('for his own good' in either case) avoiding the uncomfortable business of talking about his longer-term plans, and particularly of his attachment to herself. She could arrange for George to stay in hospital, go into residential care, or get extra home help, without discussing with him the implications of any of these decisions in terms of his desire to die at home. In each of these examples she could consider the moral dilemmas entirely in terms of her own responsibilities as a public servant, and in terms of outcomes of public concern, rather than in terms of a publicly explicable morality. If there is indeed an ethical basis for social work, then it should be understandable to clients as well as to politicians. She owes it to those most directly affected by her decisions to justify these to them as well.

This does not mean that she just consults her conscience, or departmental policies, or her senior colleagues, and then tells the clients what she is bound to do. It means that she also listens to what they want, what they value, to whom they feel obliged, and with what groups they identify, and tries to reconcile her public concerns as a social worker with their personal projects, commitments and standards. This requires a process of negotiation, using a language which expresses shared meanings and values, about what is right and what is good. In other words, democracy implies both that social workers are answerable to elected authority and that they are answerable to their clients as fellow citizens. This is investigated in the next chapter.

Citizenship

We are still in need of a firm ethical foundation for social relations – one that will both justify fair allocations of roles and resources to all and bind individuals to their commitments to each other in a reasonable way. We need some basis, for example, for the moral reasoning introduced in the negotiations between David Jackson and his wife, colleagues and clients in Smortham, that will allow them to conduct these within a clear framework of principles about what is due to each of them.

In this section I argue that this ethical foundation must lie in the idea of membership of a social unit, which shares certain indivisible goods, from which no-one can be excluded, and hence shares in a certain quality of life.[29] Because members are automatically included in the benefits of these 'public' goods, they have a common interest in prizing, promoting and improving their amenities, standards and culture. This implies a social morality, in which people share in mutual benefits, so they act in such a way as to pursue the good of others as well as themselves – the common good.

In simple societies (such as hunter–gatherer communities) the relevant social unit for membership was small enough for everyone to know each other. Because people had very few personal possessions, the advantages of co-operation and sharing, in hunting, building shelters, settling disputes and repelling attacks, were obvious. Each person's duty, and their due, was defined in terms of the burdens and benefits of a life style in which virtually all goods were common to all members.[30]

With the advent of agriculture, markets and states, property and power greatly complicated this communal harmony of interests. As individuals and groups were able to gain competitive economic advantage over others, and as duties – such as defence and the enforcement of order – ceased to be an equal responsibility on all and became the special roles of some, so the interests of individuals and classes came into conflict; exploitation and domination became possible. Wealth and power created injustice and undermined the shared and co-operative basis of small communities.[31]

Yet it was recognised by early moral and political philosophers that the members of such polities still had common interests in a quality of life which owed little to wealth or power. They used the word *citizenship* to denote the form of membership which bound people within the same state together, and defined their duties and dues. Aristotle, for instance, described a political community as like a household or an association, and citizens as sharing and bonded together like friends, or people who were all in the same small boat. He thought that the goal of a political community was to achieve the common good of its members, but that those members must be active in the process of creating their quality of life, must rule themselves, and must use power only to promote common interests.[32]

This way of thinking about citizenship persisted well into the modern age – for example, in the writings of Machiavelli and Rousseau.[33] But in the eighteenth century the liberal approach largely displaced it with the principles that have been analysed in the two foregoing chapters. Their distinctive feature was to split what were previously regarded as the unitary duties and dues of citizenship into the personal and property *rights* of individuals on the one hand, and the *powers* of the state to provide public goods (like defence and order) and protect the public interest. The two spheres were rather precariously linked by social institutions like the law (connecting civil and economic rights with the state's authority), democracy (supplying citizens with some political rights to control state power), and the welfare state (making claims on state agencies in the name of social rights). As we have seen, the egalitarian project of liberalism, as much as its promotion of individual freedom, has come to focus on dividing up goods into packages of rights and resources, and distributing them to citizens.

Yet the ultimate moral basis for this process of sharing out has always continued to be what people share in as members of the same community. This has been a recurrent theme in political thought – the seventeenth-century Diggers' concept of the common land as shared by all,[34] Marx's vision of full communism, and Sir Richard Acland's ideal of common wealth in this century.[35] If it were possible to divide everything up so that nothing was shared by all (for instance, by privatising the air, the sea, the mountains and the wildernesses as well as water and electricity, and making everyone pay for an exclusive piece of them) then we would finally have destroyed the ethical foundation of social relations, and the possibility of reasoning about morality or politics other than in a purely instrumental and contractual way.

Clearly citizenship is not the only way to think about membership and sharing. The modern environmental movement has drawn our attention to the common interests we all share, as inhabitants of the planet, in certain indivisible yet finite resources. The hole in the ozone layer and the greenhouse effect remind us that there is a universal common good of humanity, and even of the natural world, which transcends states, and is shared in by all who breathe. President Gorbachev has recently argued that in the nuclear age peace is part of that wider common good, since all nations would suffer almost equally in the event of a nuclear war.[36] Clearly also there are transnational communities of common interest, for example based on religion; and there are millions of local geographical communities and associations of all sizes. While these all make the notion of citizenship more problematic by cutting across common interests between members of states or by creating exclusive common interests of their own, they also serve to keep alive the values of mutuality, co-operation and sharing on which citizenship ultimately depends.

Modern citizenship, then – at least in the advanced western economies – necessarily contains elements of both the sharing out of rights and resources in order to give each individual his or her due measure of autonomy, and sharing in the quality of life promoted by the common culture, environment, political institutions and public amenities of the society. The most alarming feature of neo-liberalism (the property-owning democracy) is its neglect of the second element – its failure to recognise the vital necessity of common interests in inclusive forms of social relations as the moral basis of any viable political community. This in turn leads its advocates (such as Mrs Thatcher) to over-value those economic rights (property ownership, access to private markets in welfare) which allow individuals to gain advantages over their fellow citizens, and to under-value political and social rights (democratic participation, access to inclusive public services such as the NHS) which allow citizens to share in decision-making and to achieve basic equality of status.

We might think of the kind of society that is being created in Britain by taking the example of a public park. In a community where citizens have a civic culture which takes pride in spaces where they can meet, can share in recreational and political gatherings, can admire and cherish their local flora and the beauty of their local environment, parks are focal points and are regarded as important amenities. This was indeed part of the British tradition, and is still the case in many European countries, in New Zealand, in Zimbabwe, and no doubt in other parts of the world. But in a community which values only exclusive, private property and exclusive social relations, a park becomes part of the under-valued public environment. For some individuals it is a place to dump rubbish; for others, to pick flowers or dig up shrubs; for others still, to pick fights, get drunk, or do damage. Ultimately a public space which is treated like this becomes so neglected, vandalised and haunted by predators that it is thoroughly dangerous and is avoided by most of the respectable community. This indeed has been the fate of many parks in the United States, and is becoming that of others in Britain.

To address the problems of injustice and exclusion that neo-liberal policies create, we must therefore take account both of the requirement to revalue the public sphere (shared facilities, civic amenities, public transport, the common environment, our political culture), and the distribution of rights and resources among individuals and groups in society. Only a revaluation of what is public and communal will restore the significance of sharing and co-operation between citizens. Only a reassertion of political and social rights will allow excluded groups – poor people, women, black people, those with handicaps – to participate in every sphere of life on terms which reflect the status of full citizenship.

There is plenty of scope for disagreement about the best means of achieving these changes. There are still many people in western Europe who believe that the social democratic institutions of the post-war welfare state can, with suitable additions of anti-sexist and anti-racist policies, provide an adequate framework of rights for inclusive and co-operative social relations. After all, Sweden has managed to update its political and social institutions in line with economic change, to preserve full employment, promote women's rights, protect vulnerable citizens yet allow participation by people with handicaps, prevent poverty, and so on. Others believe that more radical changes will be needed, especially in those countries which (like Britain) have created excluded under-classes and which have endemic racial discrimination. I would argue that only an extension of democratic participation, along with the creation of new social rights (such as an unconditional basic income for each adult citizen) will allow terms of citizenship consistent with social justice for all.

The important point is that a combination of economic change and neo-liberal policies has altered the rules of social relations in such a way as to undermine social democratic forms of citizenship; it would take another change of the rules to restore them, even to the imperfect (notably in relation to sexism and racism) version which existed in the post-war period. Market-minded governments have (in the name of the new moral orthodoxy) used their power to increase the advantages of white, male job-holders, and to give a stake in an unjust social order to those who share a household with such citizens. They have also used their power to erode the rights of all those without access to jobs and property, and to coerce them into yet more disadvantaged roles. The moral justification for the use of power – once democratically attained – for changing these rules in favour of the disadvantaged, to give them adequate rights of citizenship, must be derived from their membership of a community in which all share a common interest in co-operation, harmonious social relations and a good quality of life.

Social workers and citizens

It should be clear from the above discussion that resolving the current issues of citizenship in societies like Britain is well beyond the scope of social workers. Although they are often in the best possible position to bear witness to injustice, and hence to give eloquent support to any challenge to the rules governing social relations, their roles do not directly address the structural sources of injustice. Recent British history indicates how central government can alter the terms of membership of a modern society through legislation on important areas of the economy and its own services, and how it can limit the influence of local government agencies. Whatever social workers have been able to do to alleviate the consequences for their clients has been fairly minor in the face of these major changes in the balance of income and power between sections of the community.

This presents a paradox. I have argued in the previous section that the ethical foundation for social justice must lie in shared membership of a community with common interests in a good quality of life. This must therefore be the moral basis of social work – that clients are fellow citizens and are due the respect that all citizens owe each other.[37] Yet most clients do not have the rights of full citizenship in a 'property-owning democracy'. Like excluded minorities in many states, or the excluded majority in South Africa and several Latin American countries, they are denied access to the choices and the goods available to the advantaged. So the very basis of the respect that is due to them is denied to clients – and worse still, social workers are often required to connive in this denial of full citizenship, by colluding with exclusion or coercion which would never be practised on members of advantaged groups.

We can see all these issues in recent debates about the rights of people with handicaps and unpaid carers. Campaigns for 'normalisation' have had some success in persuading professionals and some local and health authorities that having a physical or mental handicap should not be regarded as a bar to inclusion in ordinary social relations – in community, household, employment, recreation and culture – and that these citizens and their carers were being denied access to all these spheres, not by the handicap itself so much as by the majority's prejudiced assumptions, thoughtless practices and restrictive or inappropriate provision of services. New policies have been demanded in the name of full citizenship and participation. Yet, even where these have evoked a positive response from health and local authorities, there are rather serious limits on their success. Receiving a normal education, gaining entry to libraries and sports clubs, even getting training for employment, are all progressive measures; but if the housing market denies people with handicaps affordable accommodation, if the labour market can offer only poverty wages, and if the benefit system traps them in dependent roles (in hostels or at their parents' home) then they have only got as far as entering the underclass, not achieving full citizenship. For carers (most of whom are women), the payment of a small allowance (the invalid care allowance) on condition they give up their jobs and provide 35 hours or more a week in unpaid care, actually serves to trap them in what is often a highly stressful as well as isolated role, and to deny them access to the wider community.

It is rules like these that social workers can most effectively challenge in campaigns and actions because organisations of people with handicaps and of carers, although they may have some public sympathy, are generally regarded as knowing less well about their own needs than professionals do, and their leaders are often patronised or tokenised in their dealings with those in powerful positions. But in wider issues of social justice, such as those concerning poverty, homelessness and the disadvantaged status of women and black people, social workers are only likely to have influence for major political change as part of far wider movements of these groups and through gaining the support of large-scale political and economic forces.

Yet it is those wider issues which most impinge on everyday social work in major agencies and on the lives of social workers themselves. For example, in Smortham it is the situation that most of his team's clients are black and excluded from jobs and property, that all his team are women and in marginal forms of employment, and that his wife not only suffers this disadvantage, but also has major responsibility for unpaid domestic tasks, that requires David Jackson to take stock of his relationships and question their moral basis. Yet according to the dominant political orthodoxy there is nothing wrong with this situation; the various characters in the Smortham scenario are simply acting out their social roles according to the rules laid down by the 'property-owning democracy'. To challenge these rules, David and his colleagues must appeal to some different standard – some idea of the rights of citizenship that should be enjoyed by black people, by women, and by poor people in this country.

This appeal therefore goes beyond the present terms of citizenship and refers to something else – sometimes called 'human rights' – which lies outside current social relations in Britain. We are familiar with such appeals from the writings of eastern European dissidents and detainees in South Africa, as well as from the victims of injustice and discrimination in other parts of the world. 'Human rights' are not rights in the strict sense of recognised claims or immunities within existing formal relationships; they are claims against the present distributions of roles and resources, and for fairer terms of membership. In this sense they are much more problematic and contestable since their detailed implementation and integration with other rights is not yet worked out or established. For this reason it must always be more difficult to set up any informal system of social relations (David's partnership with Sarah, the team's new arrangements, new ways of working in the community) according to these standards than to stick to well-tried patterns which operate within currently-sanctioned rules.

Yet there must be circumstances in which people – as citizens and as social workers – are morally required to try to do just this. These circumstances must include the consciousness (derived from their own experiences, from group discussions, from training, and so on) of the ethical repugnance of racism and sexism; the awareness of discrimination and injustice in their own personal behaviour, their social work practice, and in the policies of their agency; the pressure from groups asserting their claims to rights, and demanding change; the evidence that ordinary people are conscious that the current rules are unfair (for example, a recent opinion poll revealed that 71 per cent of a sample of British respondents endorsed the statement that 'there is one rule for the rich and one for the poor'[38]).

To launch upon changes in one's relationships from this ethical starting point is philosophically as well as practically perilous. Male readers may already have shuddered slightly at the risks to which David Jackson was exposing himself in embarking on his course of action by consulting with Sarah; experienced social workers will have heaved a sigh as the Smortham team set off towards democracy, participation and community involvement. In the absence of clear-cut rights and responsibilities none has a safe fallback position, except the attempt to return to the roles they have already rejected as unjust. From a philosophical standpoint, the human rights to which they appeal, and whose standards they are flying, seem to lack firm foundations and solid defences. They are likely to find themselves bobbing about on a flimsy raft of optimism in a turbulent sea of conflict, with 'negotiation' and 'debate' as their only means of steering their vessel.[39]

Yet what is their alternative? To remain stiffly obedient to the roles in which they have been cast and the rules of neo-liberal society? To desert their posts, move right away from the deprived area of Smortham, and concentrate on philosophical rectitude? To join a revolutionary political group and use their energies on subversive activities? None of these seems obviously more ethically appropriate to their present situation, given their actual abilities, skills and potential contributions to the lives of their fellow citizens.

There may, of course, be yet another option. One such is explored in Chapter 4. But I would argue that any that claims a moral basis must take account both of the citizenship of all the other members of that community, not in the narrow sense of their current rights but in the broader sense of those rights they require for full inclusion in society, and of those opportunities for sharing in the common good which are necessary for humam flourishing.

Conclusions

Clients are not isolated individuals, nor are their problems theirs alone. Their ethical dilemmas arise in their social roles, which in turn are part of a wider system of social relations. These give them certain interests in common with others in similar roles, which arc relevant to the examples we have examined.

A situation where clients share an interest in overthrowing a system in which they are exploited or dominated, as a result of exclusion from certain assets has important implications for social work. It implies that society's apparent concern about their destitution, deviance or distress may mask an interest by some group, or even by a majority, in perpetuating this exclusion and disadvantage. The terms in which concern is expressed – the desire to give treatment, assistance or training – may mystify a process of stigmatisation in which clients learn to accept a spoiled identity, a subordinate status or a passive attitude of compliance. Social work is in danger of becoming the instrument of exclusion and injustice if it is not awake to conflicts of interests between classes, genders and races.

These insights can also inform a style of practice which allows clients to support each other, to perceive themselves more positively, to organise for social action, and to challenge social structures. There are plenty of examples of such organised action bringing about important changes, and some of it actually transforming societies. Social workers have sometimes been able to support and assist these processes. At other times they have (often to their subsequent shame) tried to resist them.

These analyses seem, however, to need to be linked in another way with the ethical problems that were our starting point. They require explication in terms of individual needs and personal meanings so that apparent conflicts between a client's individual good and the good of an interest group can be resolved. They also need to be expressed in terms which allow them to be justified both to elected representatives and to clients themselves if they are to be a basis of social work decisions. These issues are tackled in Chapters 5, 6 and 7.

Lastly, the moral basis of social relations and social work practice has been traced to membership of human communities with common interests in a good quality of life together. In modern states, social workers should respect their clients' rights as fellow citizens and try to uphold their sharing in the common good. But the unjust rules of many societies, including present-day Britain, preclude reliance on current terms of citizenship. Social work cannot isolate itself from injustice, as is argued in the next chapter.

References

1. In *Capital*, vol. 1 (1867) Marx wrote, 'Individuals are dealt with here only in so far as they are personifications of economic categories, the bearers of particular class relations and interests' (Penguin edition, 1976), p. 92.
2. Michael Horne, *Values in Social Work* (Wildwood House/ Community Care, 1987), ch. 3.
3. See, for example, John Bowring (ed.), *The Works of Jeremy Bentham*, 2 vols (Tate, 1843); John Stuart Mill, 'Utilitarianism',

in *Utilitarianism, Liberty, Representative Government* (Dent, 1912).

4. For example, 'Essay on the Influence of Time and Place in Matters of Legislation', ch. V, p. 193.

5. S. E. Finer, *The Life and Times of Edwin Chadwick* (Methuen, 1952).

6. Bill Jordan, *The State: Authority and autonomy* (Blackwell, 1985).

7. John E. Roemer, *A General Theory of Exploitation and Class* (Harvard University Press, 1982), p. 266.

8. Karl Marx, 'Critique of the Gotha Programme', in D. Fernbach (ed.), *The First International and After: Political writings*, vol. 3 (Penguin, 1974).

9. Karl Marx, *Grundrisse: Foundations of the critique of political economy* (written 1857–8; Penguin edition, 1973).

10. Roemer, *op. cit.*; Erik O. Wright, *Classes* (New Left Books, 1985).

11. Philippe Van Parijs, 'A revolution in class theory', *Politics and Society*, vol. 15, no. 4 (1986/7), pp. 453–82.

12. Steven Lukes, *Power: A radical view* (Macmillan, 1974).

13. Brian Barry, *Political Argument* (Routledge and Kegan Paul, 1965), pp. 174–84.

14. Bill Jordan, *The Common Good: Citizenship, morality and self-interest* (Blackwell, 1989), chs 6 and 7.

15. *Ibid.*

16. Antonio Gramsci, *Selections from the Prison Notebooks of Antonio Gramsci* (written 1929–35), edited by Q. Hoare and G. Nowell-Smith (Lawrence and Wishart, 1971).

17. Guy Standing, 'Meshing labour flexibility with security: an answer to British unemployment?' *International Labour Review*, vol. 125 (1986), pp. 87–107.

18. Jordan, *The Common Good*, ch. 6.

19. Brandon Rhys-Williams, *Stepping Stones to Independence: National insurance after Beveridge*, edited by Hermione Parker (Aberdeen University Press, 1989).

20. Van Parijs, *op. cit.*

21. Jordan, *The Common Good*, ch. 6; Ralf Dahrendorf, 'The underclass and the future of Britain', Annual Lecture at St George's Chapel, Windsor Castle, April 1987.

22. Fiona Williams, *Social Policy: A critical introduction* (Allen and Unwin, 1988).

23. David Howe, *An Introduction to Social Work Theory* (Wildwood House, 1987), chs 13 and 14.

24. Michel Foucault, *Discipline and Punish* (Peregrine, 1979); Michael Ignatieff, *A Just Measure of Pain* (Macmillan, 1978); Erving Goffman, *Asylums* (Penguin, 1968).

25. Roger Hadley and Stephen Hatch, *Social Welfare and the Failure of the State: Centralised social services and participatory alternatives* (Allen and Unwin, 1981).

26. For example, F. A. Hayek, Milton Friedman, Robert Nozick.
27. For example, Ivan Illich, Herbert Marcuse, R. D. Laing, David Cooper.
28. Geoffrey Pearson, 'The politics of uncertainty: a study in the socialization of the social worker', in H. Jones (ed.), *Towards a New Social Work* (Routledge and Kegan Paul, 1975).
29. Jordan, *The Common Good*, ch. 5.
30. Michael Taylor, *Anarchy and Co-operation* (Wiley, 1976), ch. 3; and *Community, Anarchy and Liberty* (Cambridge University Press, 1982), pp. 65–94; Marshall Sahlins, *Stone Age Economics* (Tavistock, 1974).
31. E. R. Service, *Origins of the State and Civilization: The process of cultural evolution* (Norton, 1975); A. B. Smookler, *The Parable of the Tribes: The problem of power in social evolution* (University of California Press, 1984).
32. Aristotle, *Politics* (translated by Ernest Barker), Oxford University Press, 1948), bk I, ch. I, s. 1; ch. II, s. 14; bk III, ch. IV, s. 4; ch. XII, s. 1; ch. I, ss. 6 and 12; ch. XII, s. 8; ch. VI, ss. 3, 9 and 11.
33. Niccolo Machiavelli, *Discourses on the First Decade of Titus Livius* (1520), Jean-Jacques Rousseau, *The Social Contract* (1762) and *Discourse on Political Economy* (1755).
34. Gerrard Winstanley, *The Law of Freedom, and other Writings*, (1649) (edited by Christopher Hill) (Penguin, 1973).
35. Richard Acland, *What it will be like in the New Britain* (Gollancz, 1942).
36. Mikhail Gorbachev, speech to the United Nations, *The Guardian*, 8 December 1988.
37. British Association of Social Workers, *Clients are Fellow Citizens* (BASW, 1980); Bill Jordan, 'Is the client a fellow citizen?', *Social Work Today*, 2 October 1975.
38. ICM national poll, *The Guardian*, 18 September 1989.
39. Martin Hollis, personal communication.

4

RIGHTS, POWERS AND RULES

The previous chapter concludes by arguing for a kind of social work that challenges the rules of current social relations, by trying to treat colleagues and clients as fellow citizens. This may involve going beyond existing roles, requiring an appeal to human rights derived from what is due to members of a community sharing in a valued quality of life.

This is a very controversial and contested viewpoint. Many writers and practitioners insist that such an endeavour is far too ambitious and quite unrealistic. They suggest that social work should confine itself to a territory of social relations defined by the law and official policies, and should work within the dominant (i.e. politically ascendant) values of the society in which it is located.

This would not necessarily mean wholesale changes in the ethical basis of social work with each change of government. Both liberal and social democratic values and practices have strongly influenced the development of social policy, and social work ethics might be understood as a kind of compromise between these two schools of thought, which tries to take something from each, and use their insights to struggle with difficult issues like the ones raised in our examples.

What would this compromise look like? First, it would contain elements of the liberal principles of moral autonomy and self-responsibility, based on personal and property rights, and corresponding duties. We might find these reflected in the familiar litany of social work values – respect for persons, self-determination, individualisation, non-judgementalism, confidentiality, and so on. But second, it would include responsibility for promoting certain outcomes seen as socially desirable – such as allowing handicapped people to live as normal a life as possible – and avoid other outcomes seen as undesirable – such as child abuse, physical injury to old people, or the anguish of untreated madness.

On the surface there are no great problems in trying to fuse together these two approaches, so long as we define clearly the territory of social relations in which we are planning to operate. If we can assume that other state agencies are successfully balancing the two sets of principles, so that (for example) health services, housing policy and income maintenance systems are allowing scope for individual choice within a framework of acceptable equality and access, then social work should be able to justify a field of its own in which to work out a similar balance. In the liberal tradition, the idea of the neutrality of the state towards different conceptions of the good life should provide a solid basis for respecting clients' autonomy and choice. In the utilitarian and socialist traditions, there are strong indications about how to reach objective definitions of welfare outcomes and unacceptable distributions; hence it should be possible to specify what people need, what they should get, and what evils should be combatted, if necessary through compulsion. In other words, the second tradition should define the justifiable powers and duties of social workers, while the first should define the essential rights and responsibilities of clients.

But this solution is rather too neat. It tries to draw a circle around the relationship between clients and social workers, and to define clients' rights and social workers' duties without reference to wider social relations. When injustice, inequality and exploitation are most evident in a society, the temptation to isolate the client–worker relationship in this way is strongest. It is the theoretical equivalent of seeing all one's clients in one's office, and never in their homes or communities – a defence against recognising the factors in clients' lives that seem beyond the reach of our helping powers, and the social distance that separates our lives as citizens of the same society.

Consider Michael, the black youth who is on probation. The probation officer knows that Michael is on the fringes of a group of young black people who angrily reject the criminal justice system, who regard the police and courts as racist, and who include himself as part of that corrupt and oppressive system. When Michael fails to turn up for interviews or to notify his changes of address, it is far easier to understand his actions purely in terms of the probation order which defines their respective rights and duties than to see Michael's behaviour in that wider context, and try to address those beliefs and values. Even though his probation officer has a pretty good idea where Michael is to be found, it is far more economical (in terms of his own already stretched helping resources and professional confidence) to start proceedings for breach of his order than to try to meet Michael on his own ground, among his friends who challenge the whole basis of official authority.

This too convenient solution has become more widely canvassed as Britain has drifted into deeper social divisiveness, and as the coercive and restrictive tasks in social work have assumed more prominent priority. Social workers and probation officers are certainly not alone in adopting it. In every branch of the beleaguered welfare state – the health service, housing, social security, the employment services, the Training Commission – officials are in the position of only being able to offer disadvantaged people much less than they need to live a decent life and of requiring them to abide by rules which are designed to push them into choices they would not willingly make. Uncomfortably aware that this is so, that their own agencies cannot do enough to give their clientele a fair deal, they adopt an approach which evades issues of fairness as much as possible.

The evasive approach emphasises legal and procedural correctness – doing the job by the book. This disguises from the workers their clients' lack of opportunity or incentive for real change, their lack of real options. It gives them pseudo-choices – between a YTS course they do not need or a part-time job that does not pay enough to live on – within a framework of highly conditional assistance. It emphasises well-defined rules and decision-making powers. In this way it reduces much of the discomfort that comes from emotional proximity and mutual influence. It stresses the separate spheres in which workers and clients exercise their rights and duties, and the non-negotiability of regulations.

The effect of all this is to reduce the moral content of social work to a minimum, and to emphasise instead the legal and procedural elements in practice. Robert Harris has recently argued,

> Social workers are agents of law and policy, and it is hence knowledge of law and policy and the ability to work effectively and creatively with them that lie at the heart of the enterprise ... [Social work] has to do with the balancing of individual rights and social or legal duties. This position implies that there is hard information which social workers must know in some detail, and that they exercise their judgements in relation to difficult cases in the light of that knowledge.[1]

No-one would dispute the need for expertise in these fields; what is disputed is the insistence that this must take precedence over all other considerations. For instance, Harris criticises Olive Stevenson's claim that the 'pivot' of social work is 'the ethical duty of care to the client', commenting that 'caring functions ... are in fact by-products of some of these central tasks'.[2] In arguing that moral issues in social work stem from wider social relations, I am also arguing that these cannot be excluded by focusing narrowly on the roles of social worker and client, and treating legal or procedural rights and powers as definitive.

The problems and contradictions of the position taken by Harris and others are highlighted by what is probably the most contentious issue in present-day social work, child protection.

The problem of child abuse

At first sight, the problem of child abuse seems to fit this framework very well. On the one hand, social workers have the role of investigating allegations of cruelty, exploitation or neglect of children, and intervening to protect them. Recent thinking and the reports of the inquiries into child abuse scandals in Britain (Maria Colwell,[3] Jasmine Beckford,[4] Tyra Henry,[5] Kimberley Carlile,[6] etc.) have pointed towards clear criteria of abuse, procedures for gathering and checking information, co-ordination between agencies with relevant knowledge, and the use of research findings as pointers to risk.

The result has been a body of law, codes of practice, training packages and liaison groups, all of which help social workers to marshal evidence, reach decisions, intervene purposefully and plan outcomes. Instead of muddle and vagueness, social workers are urged to seek clarity about their powers and duties, to communicate this to their clients, and to reinforce it through their agency's supervisory processes and court juris-diction. In these ways the risks and uncertainties of the role can be minimised, if not eliminated.

On the other hand, as was well illustrated in the Cleveland situation,[7] there are occasions when parents assert that social workers and doctors have made grave errors, that they have been falsely accused of abuse, that their children have been wrongfully removed, and that official power has been mis-directed. The framework in which these grievances are expressed is usually one of rights. It is asserted that parents have, or should have, rights to privacy, rights to fulfil their parental role (including legitimate power over their children over certain issues), and rights against interference and arbitrary removal of children. In both the popular (media) and professional debates, the aim of defining such rights more clearly (and constructing institutions to protect them) is seen as an important priority, and a balance to the definition of social workers' responsibilities. Organisations such as the Family Rights Group champion this approach to the defence of parental autonomy and family integrity.

I shall argue that this approach cannot resolve the dilemmas of child protection, for the following reasons.

1. RIGHTS AS EXCLUSION ZONES

When people talk of 'parental rights' in this context they are trying to define a no-go area for officials. They are wanting to put a perimeter fence around something (the family's territory/property, or the performance of parental roles) so as to exclude social workers and others from any access, as critics, super-visors or protectors of children.

Yet, clearly, certain actions by parents or problems of children must automatically trigger a mechanism for switching off the electric fence, or whatever marks the exclusion zone.

The triggers must include violence to children, sexual abuse and health-endangering neglect. But they should also include the fact that a child is deeply unhappy, or seriously disturbed, or delinquent, or suffering from an illness which the parents do not recognise or refuse to have treated; and they may also include educational or developmental factors through which the child is not reaching his or her potential. Some of these will be situations in which parents are knowingly acting against their children's interests and needs; others may just be the unwitting actions of distracted, distressed or ill-informed parents.

So we are talking about several different kinds of trigger for switching off the exclusion mechanism. This suggests that perhaps the idea of rights as ring fences does not really capture the nature of parenting nor the role of social service agencies. Parenting is not the exclusive activity of two people (or one person), carried out on their own territory. It is often shared between a number of kin, or a group of friends, or an employer and an employee (nurse or nanny); it involves a number of others – health visitors, playgroup leaders, nursery assistants, teachers, club leaders, and so on. These are not interfering usurpers of parental rights, but others who have a complementary role in the tasks of bringing up children.

Ideally, the social services co-ordinated by social workers should be part of this network. For many parents of handicapped children they are. When parents need advice, aids and adaptations, daily breaks, assistance at busy times, respite care, or day care during holidays, these services are exactly the same, in function and in value, as the help given by kin and neighbours to parents of able-bodied children, or by nannies to the children of the rich. For hard-pressed single parents, or parents without helpful relatives, a period in foster or residential care during an illness, a bereavement or a confinement may be much the same supportive service as a period staying with a grandparent or neighbour is for a well-resourced family.

In this sense, the raising of children (parenting, socialisation, education, care) is a project shared between a number of members of a family, a neighbourhood and a community. This is not surprising, since children are being prepared for membership of all these social units – they are learning to be friends, neighbours and citizens as well as sons, daughters and parents in their turn. Parents do have certain special responsibilities in this process, but these are not well captured by the idea of exclusive rights. On the contrary, one of the responsibilities of being a parent is to share the project of bringing up children with all those others who can contribute to their socialisation as members of society, and not to block them from the influences and opportunities of this wider community. A good parent is not someone who is able to meet all their children's needs, but someone who is good at enabling their children to get the benefits of participating in an ever-widening circle of membership organisations (playgroups, schools, clubs, national associations). This has at last been recognised as applying also to parents of handicapped children, in that parents who were forced (through official neglect, stigma and lack of inclusive policies and practices in most organisations) to provide for all that their children needed within the household became over-protective and over-involved with their offspring, and found it hard to let them take opportunities for wider contacts when these were eventually offered.

None of this is meant to suggest that sharing between parents, kin and others is easy; it is notoriously difficult. Grandparents can be an enormous help and support, or a source of pressure and inconsistency. Although partnership between parents and teachers is now recognised as crucial for children's educational progress, in the past they have tended to define their responsibilities exclusively rather than co-operatively. For many years hospital doctors excluded parents from children's wards, though nowadays they are included and seen as making an important contribution to their offspring's care and recovery. But perhaps most difficult of all has been the aftermath of divorce, when parents have had to divide up their responsibilities in such a way as to do justice to their children's claims on both of them, yet also somehow continue to share them after separating their lives. Although the history of divorce has been one of conflicts over exclusive rights and duties, modern development has mainly been in the direction of a continued parental partnership after divorce, based on negotiated agreements and shared responsibilities. Although many divorcing parents still find this hard to achieve, there is widespread endorsement of the ideal of co-operation and sharing rather than confict over competing exclusive rights.[8]

Welfare services for children (school meals, medical inspections, ante-natal clinics) were among the first social services to be developed, and although the state's role always included powers to remove children from parents who were not meeting required standards, the purpose of all these agencies was primarily to strengthen the network of care surrounding the family. The image of an exclusion zone therefore does no justice to the role of social services in supporting good parenting, and the positive potential of child care provision, as a valued part of the state's contribution to family resources. It can, of course, be argued that these services, which are valued by parents, are accepted voluntarily – so it is the parents themselves who switch off the electric fence and allow social workers and others in. But the metaphor is still misleading, because it implies that acceptance of each service requires a decision by the parent. In practice, the partnership between mother and midwife, parent and health visitor, and parent and primary school teacher seldom involves a debate about whether to accept a service – though there might be cases where parents insist on delivering their own baby, refuse post-natal care or withdraw their child from schooling, and conversely cases where doctors or education authorities consider compulsory action to ensure a safe delivery or an adequate education.

Another way of looking at the relationship, and one that was recommended in an interdepartmental report on child care law[9] and a subsequent White Paper,[10] is to start from this notion of services as supportive and voluntarily received. Parents should be encouraged to see services as assisting in their children's upbringing rather than compensating for their own inadequacies; and this should include reception into care, just as periods living with relatives or friends are normal features of any family's supportive network. Parents should be able to request these periods of respite (as those of handicapped children can already do) and would be closely consulted about placement and other arrangements, and included in all decision-making. The phrase 'shared care', used in these reports, captured the different spirit and thinking behind these recommendations. The aim was to make care more available on a voluntary basis, reversing the trend under which compulsory routes into care were becoming more prevalent. Court adjudication would be used only where voluntary agreements could not be reached. So the expectation becomes that of a partnership, based on co-operation, as the norm, but which provides for situations of conflict by defining ways of resolving that conflict. Rights as exclusion zones do neither of these things. They suggest that the task is to keep officials out, or to receive their help entirely on the parents' own terms; and they do not point towards a solution to conflicts between the parents' views of their children's good and social workers'.

2. POWERS TO PRODUCE DESIRABLE OUTCOMES

Social workers' legal powers tend to be defined in terms of promoting good outcomes or preventing bad ones. They are empowered to further people's welfare and to take action to prevent harm. In the case of child abuse, their duty is to remove children to a place of safety in an emergency and to seek legal arrangements to ensure that the child is properly cared for in the longer term.

Attention in the child abuse scandals has understandably focused on examples of social workers' failure to act decisively when a child was in danger. In all the notorious cases, there was something that one or more social worker should have done on one or more occasions that would have saved the child's life. There is no denying that such fateful moments occur. But they do not occur as isolated, identifiable incidents. In the cases of Maria Colwell, Jasmine Beckford and Tyra Henry, the children had been in care, and had been allowed to return to parents, as part of long-term attempts to bring about the best possible arrangements for their upbringing. In other words, the issue was not whether to intervene, or whether to remove the child from parents, but how – following such an intervention – to bring about a desirable outcome: the healthy, safe and well-adjusted development of that child.

There are two popular misconceptions about social workers' powers in child abuse cases. One is that decisions present themselves as discrete events which demand a simple remove/

leave answer. In practice, as these cases illustrate, tragic mistakes more often occur because social workers do not see that there is a decision to be made, because they are blinkered by certain assumptions that have determined their long-term strategy for the child. For example, with Maria Colwell, the assumption was that she could and should make the break with her aunt and settle with her mother and stepfather. With Jasmine Beckford, it was assumed that her parents would be good enough to provide for her if their housing, income and employment needs were met; and with Tyra Henry that she was safe so long as her grandmother was somewhere in the picture. There was also an assumption in all these cases that the social worker knew what was going on, and that arrangements which had been negotiated with one or both parents at an earlier date still stood. All these assumptions, and some others, turned out to be false; but it was these, not a specific wrong decision, that constituted the fatal mistakes.

The second popular misconception is that if the right decisions are made, a good outcome will follow. Every social worker knows this is fallacious and is strongly influenced by this knowledge. Suppose that she knows that a parent has severe and irremediable shortcomings in relation to a particular child, and that the child is unlikely to do well, and may suffer greatly, if he or she is allowed to remain at home. It seems obvious that this implies that the child should be removed, even if the parent objects strongly. But suppose the social worker also knows that the child will greatly resent such a compulsory intervention, and that facilities for an alternative placement are woefully lacking. She is bound to be influenced by her knowledge of the difficulty of bringing about a desired outcome in recommending a decision. There seems little point in initiating care proceedings to protect a child from an unquantifiable and unpredictable amount of suffering (which may be mitigated by a number of chance factors, like friends, a new step-parent or a change in family fortunes) when the other options are so unpromising.

In the child abuse scandal inquiries, attention has focused on decision-making at the expense of probable future outcomes. But inevitably a bad situation over placements, resulting in a constant stream of foster-home breakdowns, rejections,

abscondings, short-term arrangements, and eventual incarcer-
ation for children who have come into care for their own
protection undermines social workers' belief in the positive
value of removing children from families. If the reason that
social workers have these powers is seen not merely in terms of
preventing specific evils (such as injury or death) but also as
trying to promote certain desired outcomes, such as normal
development and good adjustment, then the subsequent his-
tories of children in care are very relevant. And legal powers
do not in themselves give any guarantees of such success; nor
do 'right' decisions by courts.

3. A CULTURE OF ANTAGONISM

The juxtaposition of parental rights and social workers' powers
implies an adversarial situation. On the one hand, the family
sets up its exclusion zone with its boundary fence of rights
against interference, and the assumption is that its objective is
to keep out social workers and their like. We have already seen
that this may be unrealistic, since social workers have access
to, or control of, many services which parents value. Let us
assume, though, that parents do indeed want to exclude social
workers in their statutory hats. On the other hand, the
workers have powers and duties relating to undesirable and
desirable outcomes which require them to intervene in certain
situations for the sake of protecting the child. They must do
this, even if they know that their ability to do good is rather
limited – which is often the case.

How then can this adversarial stance resolve itself for the
child's benefit? The implied starting point is some evidence –
an allegation, complaint or suspicion – that the child is
suffering abuse. The social worker is to investigate and reach a
decision about whether this is true. But what then? Does it
follow automatically from the fact that a child has been hurt or
harmed in some way on a particular occasion that he or she
will be better off away from these parents? Apparently not:
research suggests that most investigations which conclude
that there is cause for concern do not end in removal, but in the
child being put on the Child Protection (formerly At Risk)
Register.[11] So the purpose of the investigation must go beyond

the issue of whether or not harm has been done, to that of
whether removal is appropriate, with something other than a
straight deduction of the second conclusion from the answer
to the first question – in other words, something other than
the facts about the abuse to the child must influence this
decision.

In practice, the key factor in whether children are admitted
to care in Britain is whether the parents are co-operative.[12] By
this is meant whether they acknowledge the evidence of harm
to the child, take responsibility for their part in causing it, and
agree to measures to avoid its reoccurring, including a
programme for monitoring and, if necessary changing their
parenting behaviour. If they are co-operative, even quite
serious incidents of abuse may well not lead to an admission to
care, and certainly not to a compulsory admission. Para-
doxically, if children are already on the Child Protection
Register they are less likely to be admitted when a decision
about care arises than if they are not on the register.[13]

So the outcome of the encounter between allegedly abusive
parents and investigating social workers is crucially affected
by whether their relations are adversarial or co-operative. This
is hardly surprising: social workers are unable to ensure good
outcomes for children just by making the 'right' decision
because of all the variables that are beyond their control – the
child's response to being removed from parents, suitable
placements, availability of counselling, and so on. As in
everything else that social workers do, whether or not the
desired outcome is achieved depends on a process of interaction
between a large number of factors, only some of which can be
influenced, and on the meanings and emotional significances of
people and events to the participants. So the social worker has
to try to take account of the likely course of events from the end
of the investigation to a stage in the future (ultimately when
the child is 18 years old) when her department's responsibility
will end. In other words, the social worker has to make a
complex judgement about the outcome, in terms of the child's
welfare and development, of a process which includes the
possibility of co-operation between the parents and her department, the use of supportive or therapeutic resources, or even of
a temporary, voluntary admission to care. She also has to try to

calculate the medium-term consequences of compulsory removal of the child, in terms of disruption, upset to education and other relationships, and the hostility of the parents towards the department and its sources of help.

It seems implausible that the framework of rights as exclusion zones and powers of complusion is the most useful one for analysing the rights and wrongs of this decision and the process which follows. There is no room, in this framework, for understanding how co-operation can come about, or conflict be abated. The tests of parental rights are all factual – did they or did they not commit harmful actions? And the test of social workers' powers are a mixture of similar factual evidence and hypothesis about intrinsically unpredictable future outcomes. If the parents dispute the social worker's interpretation of the evidence for her presence on their doorstep, there seems to be little for them to say to each other except, 'I'll see you in court'.

In the next part of the book I argue that any adequate ethical theory for social work must allow for the possibility of a dialogue between worker and client about ambiguous evidence, shared responsibility and uncertain outcomes, in which the aim is to reach an agreement for at least partial co-operation towards common goals. While legal rights and duties will be the bottom line in such encounters, understanding of the moral implications for the participants must go well beyond these to be of any use to either side.

Unfortunately child abuse work has been beset by muddled thinking on these issues; talk of rights and powers has contributed to mutual antagonism in an atmosphere of moral panic, such as the one over parental violence which followed the Maria Colwell inquiry, and the one over child sexual abuse which followed Cleveland. Research suggests that antagonism and conflict still prevail in this area of practice,[14] and a number of studies recommend policies and practices which would reduce this, or provide ways of resolving it. In particular the government was urged to change the law, and departments their practice guidelines, so as to make voluntary receptions into care more readily agreed, and less a last resort; to locate child protection more clearly in a field of family support; and to maintain constructive links with parents wherever possible. The rights that parents need under this approach are ones that give them influence over decisions and opportunities to refer disputes for arbitration.

4. CONTRACTS AND FAIRNESS

Another important strand in social work theory and practice in recent years has been the attempt to spell out more clearly the rights and responsibilities of both client and worker towards each other, often by means of a short written agreement, in which both undertake to carry out certain tasks, or to act or refrain from acting in certain ways. These contracts, which are widely used in cases of alleged or proved child abuse, aim to clarify mutual obligations and objectives, and define the limits of social workers' concerns, powers and resources.[15] More ambitiously, they can be seen as part of a range of measures to provide 'informal justice' for deprived people in areas of the state's provision where previously rights were ill-defined, and tribunals inaccessible for the poor.[16]

There is nothing in these developments which inherently links them with the legal, procedural and impersonal trends in social work which are being criticised in this chapter. On the contrary, contracts can be a way of spelling out terms for voluntary co-operation and agreed purposes; they can define a shared project between client and social worker, or between parents and a social services department. Even more importantly, contracts can give expression to what might be considered the most important element in any such agreement – a negotiation over fairness, resulting in an outcome which both sides recognise to be fair. In particular, the social worker can offer resources, support, counselling and respite, which will allow the parent a reasonable chance of changing a situation which is agreed to be unsatisfactory, or behaviour which is recognised as bad for the child. If the content of a contract is a genuine bargain or consensus of this kind, it could surely be regarded as the best possible ethical basis for work in child abuse cases, or any other kind of social work.

Furthermore, there is some evidence that deprived people living in extremely risky, dangerous, unpredictable and crisis-ridden social environments value well-defined statements of their entitlements to security and protection.[17] After all, they have usually experienced the hazards of sudden redundancy, punitive, slow, inefficient or arbitrary social security cover, bureaucratic responses from various agencies on which they depend, and often also personal violence or property theft from members of their own community. It is not surprising that they use the mechanisms of such informal justice systems to defend themselves from various risks and threats, and prefer to have clearly stated terms for relationships rather than to negotiate from what they see as vulnerable positions in which they have no real autonomy.

However, none of this justifies the use that some departments have made of 'contracts' in child abuse cases. Far from being negotiated agreements based on fairness, some of these are clearly unilateral, imposed plans, drawn up by officials according to their own professional standards, and presented to the clients in a deliberately intimidating way, in the manner of binding legal agreements. The following is an extract from a 'sample child care planning letter' from one local authority,[18] drawn up in the early 1980s, to be sent to all parents of children who came into care.

Sample child care career planning letter where rehabilitation is proposed

Dear Mr and Mrs Jones

re: your children Tom and Jerry

You may have been (or will have been) advised by your social worker, Mrs Green, that when children are received into care of the local authority for whatever reason, and whatever legislation, it is my department's policy to make a formal plan for their future at the earliest appropriate time. The purpose of this letter is to advise you that a plan has now been made for your children and to give you full details of that plan. In making it the following facts were considered.

(State here such matters as)

  (a) The reasons the children were received or taken into care.
  (b) The individual contributions the addressees made towards care being necessary.
  (c) The influence that the addressees' conduct/behaviour has had on the children since the commencement of the care episode (e.g. access, co-operation with SSD, mode of life, etc.).
  (d) The effect that care has had on the children (e.g. behaviour, misery, distress, bed-wetting, evident love and need for parents, etc.).
  (e) The evident need of the children to be able to enjoy contact with their other relatives (e.g. grandparents, aunts).
  (f) That despite (this and that) you do have (this and that) to offer your children.
  (g) You do therefore appear to constitute a viable family unit to which the children can return.

Subject to clearly defined conditions which are detailed later in this letter, the plan my department has made for Tom and Jerry is as follows:

  (a) An attempt will be made successfully to return them to your care.
  (b) The period over which rehabilitation will be attempted is six months.
  (c) If the children have not been successfully rehabilitated at the end of six months, alternative arrangements will be made for permanent substitute care which may include legally to free them for adoption.

The conditions you are required to meet if successful rehabilitation is to take place are as follows:

(State here such matters as)

  (a) You will not subject your children to further physical violence.
  (b) You will never again leave them unattended either by yourselves or a responsible person, day or night.
  (c) You will clean your home to a level accepted by your social worker and will not continue to live in squalor.
  (d) Your children will be adequately nourished.
  (e) They will be properly clothed.

(f) They will have clean, dry, warm bedding at all times.

(g) They will have toys to play with.

(h) Your home will be kept adequately warm.

(i) You will have regular contact with the children during the rehabilitation period, with a minimum of one contact per week (details to be agreed with your social worker).

(j) The initiative for contacting the children will rest with you.

(k) You will co-operate with your social worker and my department at all times.

(l) You will accept the services of a Family Home Help.

During the course of the rehabilitation period, the behaviour and reaction of Tom and Jerry will be closely monitored and if at any time the proposed plan is seen to be having an adverse effect on them, which is inconsistent with their long-term best interests, the plan will be terminated forthwith. To assist you in meeting the above-mentioned conditions I am prepared to offer you the following support from my department.

(State here such matters as)

(a) The free service of a Family Home Help.

(b) Railway warrants to enable you to collect and return your children to and from your home.

(c) Provide written confirmation to DHSS of each time you have the children home.

This letter will be delivered personally and explained to you by your social worker, Mrs Green, who will continue to work with you and the children in the future. A copy of the letter has been sent to your solicitor and the children's solicitor for their information.

Yours sincerely

Area Organiser of Social Services

Such clarifications of mutual responsibilties are clearly not agreements in any meaningful sense; they represent an abuse of the power that departments gain by holding a child (even one admitted voluntarily to care). A similar use of contracts *before* an admission, as a way of mobilising a threat or enforcing compliance, or even as evidence to use in courts to gain an order, was noted in David Nelken's research on contracts in social work.

> As one worker put it: 'I suppose I see them mainly as to do with working with resistant people because if people aren't resistant you don't need a written agreement.' Or in the words of another, contracts were to be used 'when all the cajoling and nice approach has no effect'. From this it is a short step to contracts as a weapon to protect social workers in cases where conflict is anticipated. Contracts, explained one social worker, are appropriate 'when we're the last resort for them but we haven't really got anything to offer'. Candidly, she admitted, 'It's almost a way of rationalizing the denying the service to people . . . the feeling that this isn't working but we need proof, we need evidence.'[19]

In child protection cases, 'contracts to fail' allow the department either to prove that parents can pass a test against the odds, or to prove in court that they could not reach the required standards:

> As one NSPCC officer agreed: '. . . Yes, there are times, in most cases, where you ask for more than you can expect.' He went on to describe a particular case as follows: 'They as parents have a responsibility to the child, to act responsibly, and in this case clearly we realised that it was going to be extraordinarily hard for them to fulfil these conditions. Actually it would have required a major change in the way they conduct their lives simply to go along with the most basic of these conditions.'[20]

These quotations acknowledge that the contracts they describe are not fair in the sense defined at the start of this section. They do not supply resources or support that they expect to be sufficient to allow the client to change, yet they require that change as a condition for refraining from removing a child. Of course, it may well be that the removal of the child was itself justified, on balance, taking account of developmental needs and past events. But the point here is that contracts, which pose as procedural means of clarifying rights and duties for the sake of fairness, actually serve exactly the opposite purpose in such examples. They deliberately cloak with the garments of agreement, co-operation and fairness the use of compulsory power. If that power's use is justified, it should not need such a disguise.

5. DANGEROUSNESS

Another trend in British social work, especially in the field of child abuse, is the idea of assessing dangerousness, and discriminating between dangerous and non-dangerous clients. According to Tony Bottoms, there is a widespread belief that certain individuals have 'a propensity to cause serious physical injury or lasting psychological harm', and that a small, identifiable group of individuals are violence-prone and potential perpetrators of violent crime.[21] Social work practice is therefore concerned with the assessment and prediction of dangerousness, especially in child protection cases.[22] The task is to identify parents who belong in this group and protect children from them, while offering support and monitoring progress in cases where the assessment is doubtful and ambiguous. The Jasmine Beckford Report in particular emphasises this approach: 'The proportion of "high risk" cases out of all proved cases of persistent child abuse may be small, and the task of identifying them may not be easy. But the attempt to isolate such cases from the majority of child abuse cases must always be made.'[23] A DHSS circular makes a similar point in relation to training: the knowledge and skill required for protective services are 'related to child care law, the concept of child protection and the assessment of danger, and alternative forms of intervention'.[24]

These developments put a strong emphasis on assessment as the most important task of social workers in these situations, and on the idea that what is to be assessed are the characteristics of the abusive parents. The implication is that knowledge about dangerousness is available to social workers which allows them to reach a reasonably reliable estimate of this, if not at first then over a period of contact in which various services are being provided and monitoring carried out.

Clearly, in child protection work the ability to recognise dangerous situations is crucial; much more questionable is the idea that this can be done by identifying groups of dangerous people. There is nothing in the scientific and professional literature to suggest that we have the knowledge to make such identifications, or even that such a discrete group exists.[25] Such evidence as exists points much more towards an inter-actionist approach, where child abuse usually occurs among a great many other disturbed behaviours in highly stressful situations and relationships, and where the response of social workers and other officials is one of the influences on outcomes.

This last point suggests that assessment and monitoring can never be divided from 'treatment' or 'intervention'. The social worker's actions are always going to be perceived by the parents in an ethical as well as an expert framework; they are going to be judged by criteria of humanity and fairness and not just as if they were the performers of exploratory operations. Work that takes no account of these expectations, and of the feelings of frustration and anger which a distant, impersonal approach can provoke, may well influence the parents' beha-viour in a negative way. In a study by Celia Brown of twenty-five parents who had been investigated for child abuse, the major criticisms of social workers were of poor communications, lack of openness and honesty, failure to value parents' strengths and to treat them as equals, and failure to involve them in decisions. For some parents the social workers' visits made them fearful and anxious, and their self-esteem was reduced.[26]

The gravity of the issues in serious abuse cases might still override these considerations if it could be shown that research gave accurate predictions of the likelihood of certain indi-viduals or situations proving dangerous to children. In practice, the most recent survey of the evidence from studies estimates that, 'whatever method of screening is used, prediction rates rise no higher than two wrong judgements for every right judgement'.[27] Hence the case for ethical management of uncertainty remains.

6. THE RIGHTS OF THE CHILD

Lastly, the struggle between parental right to exclude social

workers, and official powers to intervene, entirely overlooks
the possibility that children may have needs and interests of
their own.[28] Until recently, British legislation made no
provision for consulting children about compulsory intervention aimed at protecting them, though there was provision
for them to be consulted later (when they were in care) about
decisions affecting them. It was assumed that good parents
would know what was good for their children, and good social
workers would know what was good for bad parents' children.
The model on which the legislation was based was of an infant,
or a helpless, inarticulate child, unable to express preferences,
let alone a view of long-term interests. This persisted even
after the scandals indicated that social workers in tragic cases
could and should have acted differently if they had listened to
the child, or observed it more carefully. But research reinforced
this message much more strongly, by pointing out that the
subjects of most child protection interventions are not infants
or inarticulate. In Jean Packman's study, 46 per cent of those
admitted through emergency orders were teenagers.[29] Indeed,
in one area studied it was not unknown for the subjects of Place
of Safety Orders to be led away to their haven of refuge in
handcuffs.

These findings give the lie to the idea that child protection
is an arena that can be safely left to a struggle between
parents' perceptions of the children's good and social workers'
rival views. Children themselves should be consulted, even
though this complicates matters considerably. They already
are, of course, in cases where the court appoints a *guardian ad
litem*, and over placement decisions. And in future social
workers will have legal duties to consult them over decisions to
remove them, and young people of 16 and 17 years who are
homeless will be able to seek 'accommodation' (i.e. care) on
their own behalf.[30]

These rights are certainly not of the exclusion zone type;
they might best be described as 'negotiation rights' – the rights
to be consulted, to have a say in decisions, and to be treated as
having some moral competence and autonomy. This seems
much more in line with the view of moral dialogue that was
put forward at the end of the previous section.

Morality as the following of rules

It might be objected against the arguments put forward so far in this chapter that they are all drawn from the extreme case of child abuse, and hence misleadingly start from an assumption that the client's rights are to protect him or her against compulsory and unwarranted intervention, while the social worker's powers are to give her access to dangerous situations. Perhaps a better case can be made for the model outlined at the beginning of the chapter if we adopt a more complex idea of clients' rights than the one used up to now. Instead of exclusion zones, they might be seen as a set of concentric rings around the individual or household, which are permeable under certain circumstances by certain people. So, for example, rights of control over and privacy of parts of one's body would be permeable by doctors (with consent if one was conscious, without if one was an unconscious patient in an emergency). Another set of rights would consist of claims against other people. These might also be depicted as rings spreading outwards, denoting what we could draw on from certain others in certain circumstances. This would allow us to recognise the positive role of social workers in providing services like domiciliary assistance, day care and aids. It would also allow us to see social workers' powers and duties as the counterpart of these rights, expressing the state's positive concerns to promote good outcomes, and to prevent bad ones.

This solution is particularly attractive if we believe that morality consists in following rules, and that the moral content of our relationships can be captured in rules about how we should behave towards each other.[31] But as we have already seen, this view has many problems. No-one would want to deny that rules and rule-following are an essential feature of any human community. But there are at least two obvious difficulties about trying to describe moral behaviour purely in terms of rule-following. The first is that many rules – for example, the rules of etiquette, or of games – have no distinctively moral content; so how do we distinguish between ethical and merely instrumental rules of conduct, and what gives moral rules that binding force that is claimed for them, that they apply to all and not merely to those who happen to belong to a certain social circle (as in the case of etiquette), or to those who choose to take part in a particular game? The second is that situations do not present themselves in ordinary life with labels which signal that they fall within certain rules. While it is fairly easy to recognise a case of my duty to keep a promise or repay a debt (though not necessarily *when* exactly I should do these things), it is far harder for me to know whether I am called upon to offer advice, overlook a lapse or challenge racism, when a friend makes a tactless and unamusing joke. Our rules are too general and schematic to be easily applied to the detail, complexity and contradictory reality of ordinary living. They require some other form of reasoning to be useful to us, and another form of communication to influence others.[32]

Without these two elements – a distinctively moral basis for rules and a process of reasoning over their application which can be communicated convincingly by one person to another – social work as rule-following degenerates into legalism.[33] Clients come to see their rights as technical defences against interference or as instrumental claims against the state for specific services. Social workers come to see their duties as grounds for action or inaction which take no account of the clients' experiences, projects or commitments, but only of their legal rights. This drains their encounter of all moral content, and of most of its creative and helpful potential. It reduces it to a purely formal exchange, the outcome of which is highly predictable, and (if not so readily calculated) best settled by a tribunal, held under legal procedures.

There is a good deal of evidence that British social work has moved in this direction. This is not altogether surprising. It was a product of the post-war political settlement, when optimistic assumptions were made about the social services as guarantors of inclusive citizenship. Full employment and more generous social rights would give all citizens a stake in the reconstituted post-war society, and create common interests in democracy and prosperity. Hence social workers would be recognised as helpful and enabling 'social servants', rather than seen as malign intruders or niggardly bureaucrats. But by the late 1960s and early 1970s these assumptions were challenged. The welfare state had not achieved the degree of equality and social justice that had been expected, and excluded groups were readily identifiable. Women and ethnic minorities had never been treated as full citizens. The social services were involved in compulsion and punishment of deviants, and social workers were often recognisably paternalistic in their assumptions about methods and purposes of intervention. Lastly, the child care scandals revealed stark conflicts of interest between parents and children which had not been adequately addressed by post-war policy and practice. In the face of all these shortcomings, legalism has provided a convenient defensive response.

This has been evident in the reports of the inquiries into the child care tragedies, which have emphasised changes in the law and departmental procedures. But as well as seeking to strengthen and clarify social workers' legal powers, the Beckford Report actually recommended a new understanding of social work as an official activity. 'We are strongly of the view that social work can in fact be defined *only* in terms of the functions required of it by their employing agency operating within a statutory framework.'[34] Later the report reinforced this notion of a legal charter for social work: 'We are conscious that social workers do not always take readily, or kindly to legal interventions in the practice of social work . . . but the law provides the basic framework in which social workers must operate.'[35] This notion of increased monitoring by courts and tribunals' of social work practice was echoed in the Carlile and Henry Reports, and in recent publications by the Central Council for Education and Training in Social Work.

However, this new tendency to seek the justification and the methodology of social work in law and regulations is implicitly contradicted by the Cleveland Report. Here, although no opinion could be expressed about the propriety of interventions in particular cases, the report recognised that the child protection system had broken down, not because of the excessive timidity or woolliness of social workers, but because of excessive reliance on compulsory measures to remove children, without any real attempt to reason or communicate with parents. In other words, statutory interventions, whether or not they were justified on legal grounds, needed to be located in a moral and human framework of compassion, care and empathy. This was really the obverse of the message of the Beckford Report. When the Cleveland Report stated that 'a child is a person, not an object of concern',[36] it was asserting the responsibility of social workers and doctors to deal with the alleged victims and their parents in a way which paid respect to their feelings, loyalties and values, as well as their legal rights. This was the opposite of the message of legalism.

Once we recognise the limitations of rule-following as a basis for morality, we also see why social workers who are concerned only with formal and procedural fairness in their dealings with their clients are falling short of the moral requirement of their roles. It is not enough to acknowledge people's rights to privacy, non-coercion and confidentiality, or to give them their legal entitlement of services. Part of what it is to be a social worker is the attempt to negotiate about moral issues, to reason over commitments and relationships, to offer not only time and support while the implications of these are explored but also scope for personal development and change. Even when the role demands firm intervention, or simply the giving of practical assistance, it requires these to be done in a way which acknowledges the ethical basis of these for both sides in the transaction.

This is particularly difficult in the context of under-resourced social services encountering hard-pressed and under-privileged clients.[37] In a society such as present-day Britain, social workers are perpetually dealing with the consequences of inequality and exclusion, and with issues over which their clients have been denied an adequate service by other state agencies. So the attempt to provide a welcoming, open, empathetic, sensitive approach must contend with the most adverse circumstances, when both workers and clients are faced with constraints of time, energy and resources, and the frustrations of being denied access to what they need. It is understandable that both adopt a defensive posture in which they meet only as roles, sticking to the rules implicit in these, and refusing to explore the other significances of their encounter.

However, once this step is taken, the positive potential of social work is largely lost – especially in a context of social distance between worker and client, when the agency can readily reinforce rather than combat exclusion. Given the statutory powers of social workers, a legalistic interpretation of their roles in a context of social injustice amounts to turning the screw on the client. So the moral choice for social workers is not one between justifiable legality or coercive excess; it is between oppressive legalism or the creative possibilities of an open moral dialogue.

This does not apply just to cases such as child abuse. The everyday story of social work contains a stream of people who cannot get their social security benefits, who are threatened with homelessness, who have been discharged from hospital with nowhere to go, who have been abandoned in debt by a spouse, and so on. Every office has its standard procedures for dealing with this flood of human misery, aimed at keeping it flowing onwards without drowning its staff or washing away all its resources.[38] The ability to retain humanity, respect and courtesy, along with a passionate concern for the plight of fellow citizens whose basic rights are in jeopardy, is the hallmark of an ethical social worker.

Conclusions

There is a strong temptation to try to resolve the difficulties and shortcomings of the two views of ethics – the liberal-individualist and the social-collectivist – which were discussed in the previous chapters by linking the two together. But we have seen that juxtaposing the concepts of clients' rights and social workers' powers is unhelpful because most of the positive potential of social work falls down the gap between them, leaving an unbridgeable gulf of mutual antagonism (at worst) or formal indifference (at best).

The alternative is to abandon the liberal idea of individuals as free-standing, self-sufficient atoms, ringed around with exclusionary rights, in favour of a notion of social relations involving overlapping projects, shared commitments, co-operative relations and common interests. If social services are located in such relations, then they are not only the expression of the state's concern to promote certain goals or ensure certain outcomes, but also part of the fabric of the life that people construct for themselves, involving collaboration, sharing and mutual support. In other words, the ethical content of relations between social workers and clients becomes less formal and official and more informal and voluntary.

Clearly, this gives us a different starting point, but does not on its own provide all the answers. The example of child abuse illustrates this point. It is important to see social work for child protection in a context of child care services, most of which are given on a basis of agreement, partnership and support. But there are situations where interests do conflict, and where parents abuse their power over children, or social workers abuse their official power. Law, policy and good practice should recognise that both parents and social workers require the moral autonomy to be able to insist on fairness, and a framework in which they can settle disputes about the needs of children; children too require a chance to have their say, and to be heard in arbitration over conflicts.

The child abuse scandals were not examples of clashes between parental rights and social work powers so much as examples of failure to reach realistic agreements about the care of children. In most cases the social workers thought they had such agreements, but had in fact failed to negotiate a proper understanding of the shared responsibilities for the child's welfare and safety. A more thorough and realistic assessment, based on a franker exchange of feelings and facts, would have revealed that their plans had no sound basis. The social workers' moral failure was not so much that they omitted to exercise their statutory powers as that they failed to explore the ethical implications of a superficial and unrealistic agreement with the other parties.

In the example of Louise in Chapter 1, the social worker calls because of alleged neglect of her children, to make a statutory investigation. It quickly emerges that this is not a conflict between her parental rights over her children and the social worker's legal powers. The problem is Louise's genuine perplexity about how to do the best for her children, and the social worker's dilemma about how best to supplement and strengthen her fragile moral and material resources.

When the example of Louise was given to a group of experienced social workers to discuss and role play, they ended up arguing about whether it should properly be analysed in terms of her rights as a single parent (to employment, child-minding services, etc.) or her responsibilities for her children. Neither side engaged in a dialogue with Louise about her aspirations, or her values; there was little attempt to get into partnership or share responsibility with her. Each group presented her with a package for the children's needs, unilaterally decided by the department which would allow it to assess and monitor her and the children more carefully. The participants who took the roles of Louise and her children were far from happy about this.

The orthodox reconciliation between a rights-based account of social relations and an outcomes-orientated account of state social policies leaves little space for negotiation, sharing and co-operation. In a society containing a very large number of people like Louise, who are poor and hard-pressed by their parental burdens, an army of social workers will spend a great deal of time rationing, regulating, monitoring and scrutinising them at an arm's length, and intervening decisively to take their children away on some occasions. This does not seem to be a satisfactory ethical basis for a child protection service.

Nor does this approach help the social worker faced with runaway Donna and her parents at the police station. Unless she can find evidence that they are abusing Donna in some way, she cannot establish that the teenager has a right to leave home, or that she has a power to admit her to a foster or residential home. Her only slim hope is to discover some common ground with the parents, or between them and Donna, under which responsibilities for surviving the conflicts of the next few years can be shared, and terms for tenuous co-operation drawn up. If this fails, there can be no real progress, merely legalistic, antagonistic disengagement, until the next time Donna absconds.

Child care and child protection work involves conflicts of interests which cannot always be harmoniously resolved; but the legalistic approach discussed in this chapter cannot even show in principle how agreements and negotiated strategies might be reached, or why they might be preferable to official intervention, monitoring and regulation. In the next chapter a framework is developed in which the ethical basis of co-operative relations can be better understood.

References

1. Robert Harris, *Suffer the Children: The family, the state and the social worker* (Hull University Press, 1989), pp. 9, 15.
2. *Ibid.*, p. 8.
3. Secretary of State for Social Services, *Report of the Committee of Inquiry into the Care and Supervision provided in relation to Maria Colwell* (HMSO, 1974). Maria Colwell was fostered by her aunt for five years, but at the age of 6 years 8 months was returned to her mother and step-father, under the supervision of the local authority. She died on 7 January 1973, aged 7, and her step-father was convicted of manslaughter and imprisoned for eight years. A public inquiry was held from May 1973 to September 1974.
4. *A Child in Trust: Report of the Panel of Inquiry into the circumstances surrounding the death of Jasmine Beckford* (London Borough of Brent, 1985). Jasmine Beckford (born 2 December 1979) was made the subject of a care order by Willesden Juvenile Court on 9 September 1981, after her sister had been assaulted by their father. In March 1982, she and her sister were returned from a foster home to their parents, Morris Beckford and Beverley Lorrington. On 5 July 1984 she was killed – her father was subsequently convicted of manslaughter and her mother of wilful neglect.
5. *Whose Child? The report of the panel appointed to inquire into the death of Tyra Henry* (London Borough of Lambeth, 1987). Tyra Henry, whose brother Tyrone had been severely injured at home, was made the subject of a care order shortly after her birth in November 1982. Lambeth Borough Council placed her with her maternal grandmother and mother, but on 29 August 1984 she was killed by her father Andrew Neil with whom her mother had been living without the knowledge of the department. He is now serving a sentence of life imprisonment.
6. *A Child in Mind: Protection of children in a responsible society. Report of the Commission of Inquiry into the circumstances surrounding the death of Kimberley Carlile* (London Borough of Greenwich, 1987). Kimberley Carlile (born 3 November 1981) was admitted to care by Wirral Social Services at her mother's request, along with her brother and sister, in May 1984. In October 1985 her mother discharged the children from care and took them to London, where she and a baby born in November 1984 were living with Nigel Hall. Attempts by Greenwich Social Services Department to assess and monitor the children were unsuccessful, and Kimberley died on 8 June 1986. Nigel Hall was convicted of murder and Pauline Carlile of grievous bodily harm.
7. Secretary of State for Social Services, *Report of the Inquiry into Child Abuse in Cleveland, 1987* (HMSO, 1988). In June 1987, local newspapers in Cleveland published accounts by parents who

complained that their children had been removed from their care
by the local authority on the basis of disputed diagnoses of sexual
abuse by two local paediatricians. It emerged, in the wake of
coverage by national media, and the campaign of a local MP, that
between 100 and 200 children had been removed on Place of
Safety Orders in less than two months. A judicial inquiry, chaired
by a High Court Judge, Mrs Justice Butler Sloss, was set up in
July 1987, and reported in July 1988.

8. J. S. Wallerstein and J. B. Kelly, *Surviving the Breakup: How
   children and parents cope with divorce* (Grant McIntyre, 1980);
   Mervyn Murch, *Justice and Welfare in Divorce* (Sweet and
   Maxwell, 1980); Lisa Parkinson, *Conciliation in Separation and
   Divorce* (Croom Helm, 1986).
9. DHSS, *Review of Child Care Law: Report to ministers of an
   interdepartmental working party* (HMSO, 1985).
10. DHSS, *The Law on Child Care and Family Services*, Cm. 62
    (HMSO, 1987).
11. Jean Packman and John Randall, 'Decisions about children at
    risk', in Patrick Sills (ed.), *Child Abuse: Challenges for policy and
    practice* (Community Care/London Boroughs Training Committee,
    1989).
12. Robert Dingwall, John Eekelar and Topsy Murray, *The Protection
    of Children* (Blackwell, 1983).
13. Packman and Randall, *op. cit.*
14. See, for example, Jean Packman, *Who Needs Care? Social-work
    decisions about children* (Blackwell, 1986), p. 184.
15. J. Corden and M. Preston-Shoot, *Contracts in Social Work*
    (Gower, 1987).
16. David Nelken, 'Social work contracts and social control', in Roger
    Matthews (ed.), *Informal Justice?* (Sage, 1988).
17. S. Merry and S. Sibley, 'What do plaintiffs want? Re-examining
    the concept of dispute', *The Justice System Journal*, vol. 9 (1984),
    pp. 150–77; S. Merry, 'Defining "success" in the neighbourhood
    justice movement', in R. Tomasic (ed.), *Neighbourhood Justice:
    An assessment of an emerging idea* (Longman, 1982).
18. This is a genuine document from an English local authority. Bill
    Jordan, 'Client Participation in Decision Making', address to
    British Association of Social Workers' Annual Conference, Bath,
    1982.
19. Nelken, *op. cit.*, p. 116.
20. *Ibid.*, p. 117.
21. A. E. Bottoms, 'Reflections on the renaissance of dangerousness',
    Howard Journal, vol. 16 (1977), pp. 70–96.
22. Nigel Parton and Neil Small, 'Violence, social work and the
    emergence of dangerousness', in Phil Lee and Mary Langan (eds),
    Social Work in Recession: A radical contribution (Unwin Hyman,
    1989).
23. Beckford Report, *A Child in Trust*, p. 288.

24. DHSS, *Child Abuse – Working Together: A draft guide to arrangements for inter-agency co-operation for the protection of children* (1986), p. 33.
25. Nigel Parton, 'The current state of child abuse research: what we "know" and how we might proceed', in Barbara Kahan (ed.), *Child Care Research, Policy and Practice* (Hodder and Stoughton, 1990), ch. 4.
26. Celia Brown, *'Child abuse parents speaking: parents' impressions of social workers and the social work process'*, School of Advanced Urban Studies, Bristol, Working paper 63 (1986).
27. Parton, *op. cit.*
28. M. D. A. Freeman, *The Rights and Wrongs of Children* (Pointer, 1983).
29. Packman, *op. cit.*, p. 53.
30. *Children Act, 1989*, section 20(3).
31. Judith Shklar, *Legalism* (Cambridge University Press, 1964).
32. Charles E. Larmore, *Patterns of Moral Complexity* (Cambridge University Press, 1987), ch. 1.
33. Nigel Parton and Norma Martin, 'Public inquiries, legalism and child care in Britain', *International Journal of Law and the Family*, vol. 3, no. 1 (1989), pp. 21–39.
34. Beckford Report, p. 12.
35. *Ibid.*, p. 152.
36. *Cleveland Report*, p. 246.
37. Carole Satyamurti, *Occupational Survival: The case of the local authority social worker* (Blackwell, 1980).
38. George Gammack, 'Social work as uncommon sense', *British Journal of Social Work*, vol. 12, no. 1 (1982), pp. 3–22.

5

SHARING AND CO-OPERATION

So far I have put forward, and challenged, three ways of looking at the moral issues raised by the examples given in the first chapter. While they all have something useful to say about the dilemmas facing the clients and the social workers in those situations, none seems to provide a coherent guide to the right way of resolving the problems, or the best solutions for the parties. Of course, it may be far too ambitious to expect this of any moral analysis – we should not treat it as if it were a crossword puzzle. But we could expect a convincing ethical theory to provide us with a method of moral reasoning which would indicate how the parties in the examples might try to move forward from the stalemate in which they have been placed.

Let us go back to the only example offered so far of someone actually trying to tackle a set of moral problems – the story of David Jackson, the senior social worker with two young children, a mortgage, a part-time working wife, a team of women social workers employed on various disadvantageous terms by Smortham Council, and a clientele of alienated, multi-racial inner-city residents. The example was introduced originally to show that the ethical issues raised in personal relationships (like the fact that his wife's career prospects were suffering because she was doing most of the unpaid household work), in relationships with colleagues (like the fact that he, a white male, was the only team member with a secure, pensionable, full-time job) and in relationships with clients (like the fact that his team spent a lot of time in court, presenting critical reports about members of poor black families, leading to various kinds of compulsory orders) were not separate, but linked together; and to show that he could tackle all of them simultaneously by a series of decisions

112

involving the others in his family, his team and in his agency's work.

It is time now to examine the principles and processes that underpin this example. Why might we regard it as morally right for David Jackson to share the unpaid child care and housework with Sarah, to share his job with Sonia Ridgeway, and to include his clients in decisions about local priorities and projects? And why might we see these outcomes as improvements on the original situation simply because they resulted from discussions held with Sarah, his team, his agency and with clients and others in his community?

Put in its simplest terms, we could say that the answer to both these questions lies in the shared nature of the Jacksons' marriage, the team's work, and the community's life in that district of Smortham. Households, social work teams and inner-city communities, however beleaguered they may be, are all in some way shared projects, in the sense that all involve relationships (chosen or circumstantial) arising out of or giving rise to common activities, resources and problems.[1] Because sharing is therefore an inevitable, integral part of membership of these groups and communities, all of them demand ways of allocating roles and responsibilities, distributing benefits (status, power, income) and burdens (stigma, compliance, work), and devising rules (for routines and emergencies). They also all involve joint decision-making of some kind – formal or informal – about the goals of the group and how they are to pursue them.

Any convincing moral analysis of the situations faced by the people in this story must tell us something about the principles according to which they share in these projects, and the processes by which they make these decisions. The stalemate at the start of the story is recognisable because it is only a slightly exaggerated version of many marriages, many social work teams and many deprived communities. The relationships between the characters, their roles and responsibilities towards each other, and the ways in which power and resources are distributed are fairly typical of those between husbands and wives, seniors and team members, and social workers and clients in present-day Britain. As we saw in Chapter 3, these are the products of wider social relations between classes, between men and women, and between white and black people. But although the formal content of their relationships can be explained largely in terms of those wider forces, their moral implications cannot be relegated to a separate political sphere. In so far as they share in these common projects (family, team, community) they have scope for rearranging their relationships, and hence for changing the terms of membership of their associations. This in turn allows them to redefine the goals and means of their shared projects.

All this sounds extremely ambitious and idealistic. Can we really expect white males like David Jackson to negotiate away large portions of their jobs, salaries and decision-making authority in favour of their wives and their female and black colleagues, receiving only household chores in return? Can we expect social workers who have taken years to qualify and gain professional expertise to allow lay people and clients to tell them how to do their jobs? Why should they share their precarious power with unauthorised others, and in what sense do the people of Smortham form a community, as opposed to a potentially disruptive rabble, badly in need of the controlling influence of properly qualified and supervised officials?

In this Chapter I argue that the reason that all these changes sound so unrealistic is that we lack an adequate way of analysing shared projects, common interests and the quality of our life in communities. We are familiar with an account of the original situation in terms of the individual rights and responsibilities of the parties, and the interests which stem from these. We are also able to recognise a rather more sophisticated analysis in terms of the political and economic forces which influence the distribution of these individual rights and interests, and of the formal changes that might alter them. What is missing is a way of showing how the people in the story could change their own situation by reasoning about how they may be doing wrong to themselves and each other, and how they might improve their lives together. I suggest later that the kind of moral reasoning to be outlined is characteristic of what we call a 'good relationship' and 'good social work'.

Shared projects: the household

It is easiest to recognise the characteristics of a shared project in David Jackson's relationship with his wife Sarah. Marrying as students on their respective courses at Smortham Polytechnic, they moved from a rented flat in the city centre to a small suburban housing development in a residential area soon after qualifying and starting work in the social services and housing departments of the two adjacent boroughs. Their two children were born three and five years later, and they moved to their present, larger semi-detached house last year. Their joint incomes just cover the mortgage repayments, which rose sharply last December.

Their decision to share their lives by pooling their resources, living together and having children was one which explicitly or implicitly required them to plan the work they would do, outside and inside the home, and how this could be most efficiently and fairly divided between them. Since they first came together as students on training courses for their chosen professions, it was always understood between them that both would have jobs when they left the college – in any case, they needed the income to buy their first house. Having decided to have their first child when Sarah was 30, she was able to return to her previous job after maternity leave, thanks to the availability of a suitable child-minder near by. But with the birth of their second, Sarah wanted to spend part of the week with the children and opted to take a part-time post in the same department. It is only now, with their eldest about to start school, that this arrangement is coming into question.

Unless couples like David and Sarah derive the details of their roles uncritically from their parents or their college friends, the sharing of their lives must involve them in discussions and decisions about these issues. They are constrained by the biological facts of child-bearing and the way that jobs and pay are structured in Smortham Borough Council. But apart from this, they must somehow sort out their own criteria for choosing who works, for what hours and in which roles. These have to cope with the changing needs of the adults and children in the household as time goes by (and

perhaps eventually with the needs of David's parents, who live
in Smortham and are growing rather frail).

So their life together is a shared project both in the sense
that it involves using common resources and in the sense that
it requires them to make choices that take account of each
other's needs and aspirations. Because they spend their leisure
together, and are jointly responsible for their children, they
share an interest in improving the quality of their life as a
family – the degree of their intimacy and the sensitivity of
their mutual understanding, as well as their ability to
communicate clearly and solve common problems, and to
sustain their separate roles in the wider community.

We cannot understand the processes of co-operation that go
to make up family life unless we recognise that shared projects
give rise to common interests in a good quality of life, such that
one partner's good cannot be seen in isolation from the other's.
A qualitative evaluation of the family's life together requires
us to look at how the members meet each other's needs as well
as their own, how they reach decisions about roles and
resources, and how they plan for the future. In all these
processes, what is at stake is the good of the family rather than
the good of its constituent individuals, because their common
interests in improving their quality of life are mutual, and it is
only by co-operation and joint decision-making that they can
make progress towards agreed goals.

Of course, this does not mean that David and Sarah do not
have individual interests that at times conflict. Almost any
domestic situation can be represented as a conflict of interests
between the partners – from who should get up to attend to the
crying baby to where to take the family's annual holiday. In all
these choices, what David would want to happen purely for his
sake and what Sarah would want to happen purely for hers
would be quite different, and in a certain proportion of such
situations this kind of reasoning will strongly influence each of
them. The point about a shared project is that another kind of
reasoning is recognisably more appropriate for the maintenance
or improvement of the quality of relationships in the household. This is the reasoning that requires each of them to take
account of what the other is feeling about the situation either
by asking or anticipating, and then to act in such a way as to

ensure that similar co-operation is achieved over future decisions. In other words, although David may pretend to be asleep on one or two occasions when the baby starts to cry in the night, he should sooner or later start to think about the consequences of this on his relationship with Sarah over all the other decisions they have to make as a partnership, including where they will go on holiday this year. The co-operative and mutually sensitive quality of their relationship depends on the maintenance of non-individualistic, non-competitive reasoning over a significant number of decisions.

Any shared project involves constant shifting between these two perspectives. Unless we know what we want for ourselves, we will be unable to take independent actions, to join other groups, or to influence their decisions. So we need to be able to be conscious and assertive of our own individual preferences. On the other hand, unless we can understand what others need for their own sakes, and how to co-operate in joint projects, we will have little to contribute to relationships and will quickly find ourselves living a solitary life. As individuals we alternate between thinking and behaviour which is based on our own needs and preferences, and thinking and behaviour which takes account of others. One can often detect people shifting focus in the course of a sentence or an action, and a good deal of television situation comedy revolves around the tensions between these two kinds of thought and behaviour.

These two ways of reasoning and choosing are catered for by the two different systems – contracting and sharing – outlined in Chapter 2. Contracting (which is a wider term under which I include market exchange) is a system for co-ordinating individual preferences. It is a quick and efficient way of allowing people to relate their wants to their resources without having to take any detailed account of other people's needs, using the shorthand of prices as a way of reading facts about a very large number of others' preferences. Paying for goods and services allows us to gather things for our purposes without having to think about who else might need them, and to require others to act as we wish without consulting them over how they would like us to act. All this contrasts strongly with the flexible, personal but time-consuming processes involved in sharing, where the consolations of intimacy and communication are balanced by the effort of empathy and consideration.

The real difficulty occurs, of course, when the roles and resources bestowed on individuals by the society-wide system of contracting give them economic interests which are at odds with their system of sharing. In the case of domestic relations between men and women, the history of gender-differentiated employment has meant that attempts to share paid and unpaid work equally between partners have to overcome unequal pay and conditions, prejudice and rigid institutional structures. Even though David and Sarah are both professionally qualified, the labour market for their skills is such that it is far easier for him to get a regular full-time job and promotion (with all the implicit advantages in terms of income and power) than it is for her. Accordingly, it will be economically advantageous for them as a couple to maximise his earning potential, even if this gradually erodes her career prospects. Eventually the household's stake in his job (his pension rights as well as his current salary) will run strongly counter to any attempts to equalise their work roles.

This raises two problems. First, why should an equal division of paid and unpaid work between them be regarded as desirable? By what criteria is this particular allocation of roles better than others? Second, what if Sarah actually prefers to stay at home with the children? And does it matter whether she prefers this on the grounds that she likes child care, or because she thinks it is women's duty to do unpaid work, or because she thinks this is the best long-term strategy for maximising their household income?

Roles and fairness

At this stage of our exploration of the ethical foundations of social relationships we are looking for a link between the terms of membership of society as a whole and the terms of a shared project. Without some such link, David and Sarah will be negotiating in a vacuum, with no baseline of what is due to each of them as an individual from which to consider how they can best share their lives together.

In Chapter 3, I concluded that the terms of membership of

modern advanced western societies must include provision for the equal autonomy of all adult citizens, giving them access to all the major spheres of social co-operation, and hence to the goods valued by those societies. This takes the form of individual rights – civil, economic, political and social – which allow all citizens to exercise choice and to participate on the same terms, as equal members of the community. These rights supply a floor to the more flexible and informal relations that are characteristic of partnerships such as David and Sarah's. They bring these rights with them into their relationship.

The major problem, which was also identified at the end of Chapter 3 is that existing societies do not provide terms of membership which are just. Women have belatedly acquired most of the civil and political rights enjoyed by men, but not their economic and social rights. Few women have employment security or any of the entitlements that go with a decent full-time job; and few have rights to income security, since most insurance-based state benefits are linked to such jobs. Only in Scandinavia does women's access to employment and social rights give them an economic status approaching that of men.

This means that the current terms of citizenship in Britain do not give David and Sarah a moral baseline for their relationship. If they want to find an ethically justifiable basis for it, they must look to something like the 'human rights' approach introduced in that chapter. Only by imaginatively creating a model of a good society, in which women have equal rights and opportunities, can they provide themselves with the kind of framework of what is due to each of them as individuals against which to test out the moral soundness of their shared arrangements. In practice, of course, this is extremely difficult, since few couples make explicit to each other their views about the citizenship of men and women; yet it is hard to see how this can be dispensed with in an ethical analysis. Without it, David and Sarah will have nothing to fall back on except the current rules – the law and the policies of various employers and social agencies – and hence would soon fall into a kind of legalism, such as was explored in Chapter 4.

But as soon as we acknowledge that the picture of a better society they are going to create is an imaginary one, then all sorts of other difficulties are revealed. Will they imagine the same kind of better society as other couples do, and does it matter if they do not? If their roles and responsibilities are not to be determined by the formal rules of the existing social order, why should they take any particular pattern? Why not adopt their own patterns quite idiosyncratically, and change them from one day to the next?

The answer to this last question must lie in the idea that David and Sarah are seeking a moral basis for their relationship – roles which can be justified according to ethical standards. To do this, they need to know what rights individual men and women would have in a just society so that they can check whether their roles are consistent with those rights. Of course, they may be mistaken about what they regard as morally justifiable citizenship; but what matters is that they can reason with each other, and with other couples, about such terms as justice and equality, and refer to standards which can apply to individuals and partnerships other than themselves.

The first issue for them to consider, before looking at the details of their roles, is whether their partnership is a freely chosen one for both of them. Given that young people, and especially young women, often form relationships to escape from dependency and subordination in their families, or for sheer economic survival, they cannot assume that both entered the partnership from a basis of equal autonomy. One or both of them may have been so oppressed that they lacked a feasible alternative. Next, they need some standard by which to judge whether their relationship is fair in the sense that it is based on willing co-operation between them rather than on the imposition of the needs and purposes of one on the other. Again, since one may have entered the relationship with great advantages over the other, and they have not necessarily both had the same opportunities of leaving it, equal autonomy cannot be assumed.

By referring back to the 'human rights' view of citizenship, David and Sarah can ask themselves whether their original agreement to share their lives was freely made and whether it is sustained through willing co-operation – would it have started if both had equal autonomy, and would it take its present form, or exist at all, if both were free and equal citizens? (A negative answer to the first question need not, of course, necessarily imply a negative one to the second – the basis of their relationship may have changed.) These questions require them to think both about their relative statuses as individual choosers (their individual rights and resources), and about the way in which they co-operate and share. The two are closely linked, since justice in relationships depends both on its original terms and on how it is sustained over time. If David and Sarah started as more-or-less autonomous equals, and have become very unequal in their asset-holdings, then this says something important about what has been happening to them – for example, about the consequences for Sarah of having two young children.

However, there are also some puzzles about the links between these two elements, which arise from the fact that personal relationships are very different from formal ones. Suppose, for instance, that David is deeply in love with Sarah, but that she does not really care for him. This could lead to a very unequal relationship in the sense that David might agree to let Sarah make all the important decisions, and might be quite willing to go out to work all day, and then fetch and carry for her every evening and all weekend. Would this be fair?

In most examples of freely-agreed, willing co-operation between a group of equals, the relevant standards of fairness are that all have an equal say in decisions about the good of their shared project, and that the burdens and benefits of what they do together are equalised as far as possible.[2] These are the criteria that would apply, for instance, to a group of friends who decided to share a house during a college course – that no-one, or no minority, was excluded from joint decision-making, and none gained more of the advantages, and avoided more of the penalties (such as chores) than others. On the face of it, this would not be the case at all if David's adoration of Sarah was not reciprocated; she would be the unchallenged boss, and he the compliant slave. But what if he counts dancing attendance on her every whim as a benefit, and actually enjoys being exploited and dominated by her? Does that make the pattern of their relations justifiable?

Once again, we can seek an answer by referring back to the definition of justice in citizenship. In any unjust society, there are many individuals who embrace the roles allocated to those who are treated as subordinate or superfluous. Plenty of women are seemingly content with a life of obedient dependence on men; lots of claimants of income support say they are grateful and satisfied. This is not, in itself, strong evidence that powerlessness and poverty are morally acceptable, any more than the fact that others enjoy being rich and powerful would be. The relevant question is whether we could find some arguments for saying that these relations are just. As was seen in Chapter 2, one argument is that people *choose* their relationships; according to this view, what matters above all else is that individuals act according to their preferences, both in personal relationships and in formal transactions. So on this account David and Sarah's relationship is very like a contract to exchange services, and David's willingness to forgo all influence on decisions and do all the chores is evidence that this is the price he is willing to pay for being around Sarah by day, and in her bed at night. Since this is what they choose to do, it must be fair.

But this will not do. As we saw in Chapter 3, it is absurd to abstract choices from their context, and the framework of rules in which they are made. David's choice of dutiful devotion (and Sarah's of regal relaxation) would only be feasible in a framework of relations in which it was possible to exchange 'love' for 'financial security', or 'protection' for 'dependence'. The same rules would also allow David to exercise his individual choice (preference) to forgo all his influence on joint choices in the partnership (i.e. to have no preferences in joint decisions). By treating relationships as instrumental, con-tractual exchanges between bargain-hunting individuals and ignoring inequalities of power, this analysis keeps them within these rules, and denies the possibility of choices which refer to the good of both, and of their partnership. I am arguing for a view of fairness which insists on both partners being autono-mous and equal, in the sense of their holding certain human rights and being able to make choices about the good of their shared project which refer beyond their individual preferences for themselves. Once we conceive of David and Sarah in this way, the standards of fairness that apply to their relationship imply that they form their partnership as equal citizens (who cannot alienate these rights) and co-operate by sharing in joint decision-making about their lives together.

This certainly does not resolve all the puzzles set by personal relationships. What, for example, is to count as a benefit or a burden in partnerships where deep affection makes the most arduous duties into pleasures? And what about the rather more common example of disillusion which changes what were the benefits of sharing into burdens, for one partner or both? I do not pretend to be able to tackle these here. Instead, we return to the questions about Sarah's role and child care which were set at the end of the previous section.

Relevant differences

The foregoing section explains why an equal division of paid and unpaid work between the partners might be regarded as the fairest pattern of marital roles, and bases this on the ideal of David and Sarah meeting as equal citizens and members of a just society. But it has also been argued that the advantage of a shared project like their partnership is its flexibility, and the possibility of reaching negotiated agreements about how to live together, and create a good quality of life. So David and Sarah cannot be bound by a rigid rule of equality – in the sense of precise parity of hours of paid and unpaid work – or no such flexibility would be gained.

The second question, then, concerns the possibility that Sarah wants to stay at home and look after the children. She may have a number of reasons for wanting to do this, but the point is that in any discussion between David and herself the reasoning towards her adopting this role would be required to justify it in terms of the long-term equalisation of burdens and benefits, and hence in terms of fairness.

In any form of co-operation the parties may well have different skills and needs, as reflected by their divisions of labour and distributions of benefits.[3] Equality does not imply that each does exactly the same work or gets exactly the same benefits; it allows for contributions according to abilities and distributions according to needs. Within households the system of co-operation can be adaptable to take account of short- or long-term changes in abilities and needs. For example, children can gradually be included in family decision-making and work roles. In reasoning about who would do what in the household and outside it, only relevant differences between household members should count as good reasons for differentiation.[4] Being a child, being handicapped or being ill are clearly relevant for most roles and tasks. Being a woman was at one time seen as a relevant difference; women's roles were clearly differentiated from men's, to the point that married women did little paid work and men did little housework or child care. Although most of this differentiation was unjustified in terms of women's abilities, it stemmed from the facts that men enjoyed greater power and wealth, that women were in a subordinate and disadvantaged position, and that their rights as citizens were impoverished. As equal citizens with equal rights, women's opportunities to show that their abilities are similar would be much improved, and their roles might correspondingly become much more similar to men's. So, if Sarah wants to have a purely domestic role, her arguments for doing so must rely on reasoning from something other than the fact that she is a woman.

At the end of the previous section, three possible reasons were given that Sarah might use. She could say that she likes child care, that she thinks it is her duty to do the unpaid household work, or that her doing it will serve the long-term interests of David's career. Each of these is now looked at in turn.

Sarah's preference for the unpaid domestic role can be seen as like any other bid by one of the partners for a short-term change with beneficial long-term consequences for their shared project. It could be David who suggested that he took this role, or either of them bidding for a sabbatical from paid work in order to gain higher qualifications through study. In terms of the proposed analysis, this could be a good reason for suggesting the change, if Sarah and David could agree that their partnership would benefit in the long run from it, and if meanwhile they could adjust their roles in other ways so that the result was fair, according to the equalisation principle. Of course, if either of them likes child care much more than paid work, or vice versa, then that kind of work enters the equation as a benefit, not a burden. If Sarah likes child care at home and David likes social work in the department, then this is a perfectly good reason for giving up her job, provided that it is consistent with the long-term good of the family in every other way – especially since unpaid work can be seen as just as socially valuable as paid work. But it would not be a good reason if Sarah was simply proposing that she should opt out of paid work, leaving David to be responsible for the mortgage and all the other household expenses. This would be a unilateral breach of co-operation and fairness.

Sarah's insistence that it is her duty to do the unpaid work would be a puzzling statement according to my analysis. If being a woman is not to count as a relevant difference in their partnership, then Sarah must give some other reason why she regards this role as her duty. There is nothing in the previous terms of their relationship to indicate an agreement that she should give up paid work at this stage for the good of the household. Perhaps Sarah has undergone a conversion to a fundamentalist religious faith which prescribes such a role for women. Her conversion might involve a new attitude towards women's abilities – that, according to religious teaching, they are better at child care than men – or (in a much more challenging way) a new attitude towards women's rights – that women's citizenship is different from men's, that they should be subordinate to men in all relationships, and should do unpaid rather than paid work.

The former claim will be difficult to dispute if Sarah simply asserts it on some form of divine authority; here again, David may be faced with a unilateral attempt to change the terms of their partnership, which it will be hard for him to accept unless he is convinced by her assertions. The latter claim will pose an even tougher problem since it involves a rejection of the original basis of their partnership in favour of a system of relations which they previously agreed to be fundamentally unjust. Sarah seems here to be adopting a concept of justice which is quite different from the one which informed their relationship at its beginning, so it is hard to see how they can agree unless he is converted to the same faith. Sarah is seeking a whole new ethical foundation for their relationship – one based on a religious rather than a human rights view of what is due to her as a woman.

As a shared project, their partnership creates its own good from their co-operation. David may decide that the good of his family is more important than any other, and hence that he should try to share Sarah's new beliefs for the sake of domestic harmony. He is then faced with how to implement these newly-embraced ethical principles in his relationships with his women colleagues at work. The price of domestic harmony is paid in terms of moral integration.

The proposal that Sarah should stay at home full-time to support David in furthering his career is in some ways the most difficult to analyse. It is here that moral reasoning, in terms of the quality of their relationship, is most likely to conflict with economic reasoning, in terms of maximising their household resources. Sarah could probably present quite a strong case for the economic advantages of giving up her rather poorly-paid part-time job if, as a result, David had a better chance of concentrating on gaining promotion and moving up the ladder into the highly-paid echelons of senior management. She could strengthen this case by arguing that the time she spent at home could partly be devoted to improving the house – an unskilled activity which might well, during a year of house price inflation, yield a more substantial pay-off than her part-time employment. All this could amount to a strong case for the change as a way of improving the long-term economic prospects of the household.

On the other hand, David could counter that the qualitative effects on their relationship could be very adverse. A home-based Sarah could feel isolated, trapped and depressed, and might have real difficulties in getting back into a suitable job if she wanted one later. Forced to work harder and compete more strenuously for promotion, he could become exclusively pre-occupied with his career at the expensive of family, friendships and other interests. They would have less and less in common, and the process of maintaining a balance of fairness and co-operation would become more difficult as their roles became more segregated and their interests diverged. Even though they might gain more material resources, the quality of their partnership would probably suffer.

Such a conflict between the economic and qualitative interests of their partnership is characteristic of relations between men and women in households in modern Britain. Because of the dual labour market, with much better opportunities of secure, well-paid jobs for men, the attempt to sustain equality and co-operation in relationships is bedevilled by the temptation to maximise income through increasing differentiation of roles. The ideology of household self-sufficiency, which emphasises economic independence as its chief value, encourages couples to overlook equality and sharing for the sake of quantitative gain.

This means that couples that try to maintain an equal, democratic partnership on fair terms do so at some economic cost, and have to go against the grain of wider social relations. It means that their common interests in their shared project are constantly undermined by the incentives of the economy. In a just society, this would not be the case. But even the unfair structure of roles and incentives in employment is not entirely beyond the scope of action by individuals.

Shared projects: the team

If the social work team led by David Jackson is to be regarded as a shared project, it is certainly rather different from a household. Its members are employed under contract by Smortham Borough Council; their pay and conditions are negotiated through agreements with the local government trade unions; their roles and responsibilities are defined mainly by the law and the social services department's policies; they are answerable through David as their senior and the department's senior management team to an elected committee; and they had only a very limited part in choosing each other as colleagues (an informal team interview, the conclusions from which were relayed by David to the formal interview panel, of which he was a member). Lastly, three of them are employed on temporary contracts (two covering maternity leave and the other long-term sick leave, due to stress), while the others are part-timers.

Yet in other ways they do work co-operatively and democratically. At team meetings, every member is invited to express his or her views, and every effort is made to reach consensus on policy issues or to negotiate compromise deals where disagreements remain. There is an attempt to share the work fairly between team members, taking account of expertise, experience and the demands of their existing caseloads. The social workers offer each other a good deal of informal support both over personal and professional issues. David Jackson's supervision is relaxed and enabling; and he is more likely to offer encouragement and useful suggestions about resources than to criticise or remind people about agency procedures. Although he has his own office, he is more likely to be found in the team room, discussing a crisis, or helping a social worker to check a legal detail.

Thus there is something of a contrast between the formal and the informal organisation of the team. At a formal level it is rather hierarchically structured, with the members employed on different terms, and subject to fairly well-defined legal, administrative and managerial regulation. At an informal level, relations are far more flexible, democratic and co-operative, as in a group of friends who are undertaking some form of activity together. There are some sound reasons for both aspects of the team's structure. As officials of the local authority, with considerable power over the lives of their fellow citizens, and some community resources at their disposal, they must be answerable to the public, through their elected representatives. The formal organisation of the team allows them to be employed and paid to do some very politically sensitive tasks. On the other hand, they are doing stressful work, handling difficult personal feelings, tolerating conflict and uncertainty, and coping with a variety of unpredictable demands. All this suggests a structure of mutual support in which individual team members can both absorb crises and emergencies, and provide the flexibility to cover for each other under the pressure of fluctuating workloads. Co-operation is essential for them to sustain a good quality of social work.

However, some aspects of the formal structure of David Jackson's team have nothing to do with the sound reasons for accountability and cut across the informal processes of co-operation, potentially reducing their scope. There is no good reason why the only man in the team should have a full-time, secure job, and all the women have temporary or part-time employment. Nor, given the ethnic composition of the area, is there any good reason why there should be only one black social worker in the team, and she in a junior, part-time post. These features of the team's organisation mean that the justifiable increment to his pay allowed to David Jackson to compensate for his additional responsibilities as senior is reinforced by unjustifiable differentials in income, authority and security between himself and other members of his team, where the fact that he is a white male seems to have unduly influenced his chances of gaining these advantages. Furthermore, the efficient functioning of the team is jeopardised by the virtual 'casualisation' of the social work posts, with a high turnover of staff, high stress levels and low morale among team members.

Thus the team is in some respects part of a large department with a semi-bureaucratic structure, and in some respects a co-operative working group. The bureaucratic aspects of its organisation are discussed in the next chapter. As a co-operative group, although the team's functions are quite different from those of the Jackson family, the moral standards that apply to their relationships with each other are largely the same. Their implicit choice to support and enable each other in their work, and to consult each other about decisions affecting their team, adopts a set of working relations which rely on negotiation, debate and persuasion (rather than power and compulsion) to reach agreements (rather than imposed rulings); and flexible, permeable, complementary roles (rather than fixed and rigid ones). In other words, the way the group's working relations are regulated and sustained is by discussion, support, give-and-take, trust and reciprocity, rather than by rules and procedures. This is clearly a form of co-operation, relying on a moral rather than a bureaucratic dynamism, even though it is located within a larger structure of formal, rational–legal relationships.

If we recognise the team's informal structure as co-operative, then this implies that the members' relations are governed by standards of democracy (equal power in decision-making) and fairness (equalisation of burdens and benefits). Observing their behaviour with each other this seems to be roughly what is going on. They share out the new referrals at allocation in a way that deliberately takes account of each other's stress and work loads; they swop duties at short notice to take account of each other's crises; they console or congratulate each other over especially difficult pieces of work, and freely consult and advise each other over law, policy and resources. They seem to work as if what matters is the good of the team, rather than their own individual advantage within it.

This being so, David Jackson's position seems anomalous. In addition to the formal decision-making powers and additional pay he has as a result of his position in the management structure, his highly differentiated security, status and fringe benefits as the only full-time post-holder mark him out as quite different from the rest of the group. In so far as they can reasonably attribute these advantages to the fact that he is a white male, the women (and especially the black woman) have good grounds for resenting these differentials, and for seeing them as destructive of trust, goodwill and co-operation. Why should they equalise their work-effort, flexibility and support with his, since the benefits he enjoys from his job are so much more substantial than theirs? Everything about his formal terms of employment weighs against the rest of the team regarding his position as consistent with the democratic and co-operative standards which apply to their working relations. As much as in his partnership with Sarah, such inequalities threaten the co-operative group because they are breaches of fairness.

It is on the basis of this reasoning that, having negotiated with Sarah that he seeks to convert his present job into a part-time one, he now approaches the team about how this might be tackled. He draws attention to the staffing difficulties that the team has faced this year, and to his own embarrassment and personal discomfort over the discrepancy between his terms of employment and theirs. He says that he feels that they have all contributed admirably to the maintenance of morale and a good standard of work in their beleaguered district, but that the long-term future of the team's co-operation requires some structural changes in its composition. He confides that, for domestic reasons, he is going to try to work part-time for the next five years, and proposes a discussion about the possible implications of this for the team.

At first the other members are rather nonplussed. Does

David intend to resign as their senior? If not, what are the implications of having a part-time team leader? How, if at all, will this help their situation? Will it not actually accelerate the process of casualisation and fragmentation of the already inadequate staffing establishment? Surely the first priority must be to secure a regular number of permanent posts, and staff to occupy them who will stay and build up the team's stability? David agrees that this is indeed their long-term goal, but the personnel department has told him that it will be several months before any new post can be established, and the team members on maternity and sick leave have not yet indicated whether or when they are likely to return to work. In the meantime, the question must be whether the opportunity for him to work part-time can be used to improve the team's co-operation and mutual support in any way, or whether it is merely disruptive and a further threat to long-term stability. It is in the context of this discussion that the team comes up with the novel idea of David sharing his job with Sonia Ridgeway, reasoning that this would be a way of retaining his valued skills as an enabling supervisor and a knowledgeable manager, while introducing a new dynamism and new ideas into the leadership of the team, and recognising the high-quality contribution she already makes.

The rationale behind these changes is that, given that David is willing to give up part of his job, and that there is no immediate prospect of the other posts being filled by permanent full-time occupants, there is nothing to be lost, and possibly something to be gained in terms of the good of the team. As a group they do not want to lose David, and they respect his reasons for wanting to change the terms of his employment. They recognise that the main factors sustaining their working relationships are the goodwill and reciprocity between team members, and that Sonia's promotion is more likely to increase than to damage these democratic and co-operative aspects of their relations. Sonia herself is pleased to have the opportunity of gaining this extra responsibility and experience without changing the hours of a working arrangement which suits her family responsibilities and the demands of her other interests (she is also an elected councillor in a nearby borough).

Two rejoinders

This analysis is open to two kinds of objection which are roughly in line with the rival systems of moral thought outlined in Chapters 2 and 3. Both would accuse David Jackson and his colleagues of ethical 'ad-hockery' – of adopting principles and drawing conclusions from them in a dangerously personal and context-bound way, without proper consideration of the wider implications.

The first rejoinder is about the limits and divisions of the workers' responsibilities. On its account, Smortham's Social Services Department is a complex institutional system of relations in which all the roles interlock. Each official's responsibilities can only be understood in terms of this whole system, since the borough's legal duties for social welfare, and its policies in relation to its community, are carried out through this network of posts, none of which is free-standing. Roles like senior social worker and social worker are thus definable only in terms of the system or network, and are to be understood as accountable through managers to a director and a committee, with duties that are specified accordingly.

All this affects the analysis of fairness. It means that what is due to David from his team cannot be understood in terms of his status as a man, or as white, or even as a senior social worker; it must be understood in terms of the roles of officials in this system of relations. If within this network seniors have the right and responsibility to supervise, allocate and account for their social workers' tasks, then he is entitled to his salary, and the security of his post, just as he is required to perform those functions. What fairness means is that each person occupying a role in the system gets what is due to that role. To tinker with one part of the system is unfair, because it could mean that people in similar roles do not get similar rewards and responsibilities.

This style of reasoning seems to illustrate all the weaknesses of the system outlined in Chapter 2. In the first place, we cannot just assume that David got his job by processes which were fair; even if the procedures were followed, it may well be that as a white male he had unfair advantages over other applicants and non-applicants. So all the team may have good ethical grounds for trying to change the procedures for appointing people like David to their posts. Second, they may well want to challenge the system of treating full-time posts as a kind of property, owned by people like David, and part-time post-holders as having almost no employment rights and security. The first rejoinder offers little scope for such challenges to roles and rules as can be made through trade union or other collective pressure.

Yet the actions described above are not of this kind. The third and most important point is that there is always, in every shared project (from a household to a large organisation) tension between fairness as procedural (what is due to people in their current roles and under existing rules) and fairness in co-operation[5] (what is due to them as members of a co-operative working group). Roles and rules are constantly in transition (people negotiate new arrangements, official re-organisations take place, a new committee is elected). Procedural fairness tries to provide clear definitions of what is due to a particular role at a point in time; fairness in co-operation tries to go beyond the rules, and look for principles of justice which provide ethical foundations for relationships.

The first rejoinder is salutary in reminding us that the team cannot just make up its own rules, as if it operated in isolation from the rest of the department. What it can do, and is surely morally required to do, is to look for ways, within the framework of the department's rules, of making its relations as consistent as possible with the rights of citizenship (as defined in previous sections). If they believe that women and black people should have the same citizenship as men and white people, then they should look for ways of combating the implicit racism and sexism in the team's structure. The way the team chooses to do this in the example is consistent with Smortham Social Services Department's current system of roles and responsibilities, but ameliorates the previously unjust distribution of advantages.

The second rejoinder is that this team's problems are much more to do with Smortham Borough Council's political priorities than they are to do with the ability of team members to co-operate democratically. It is because Smortham councillors ran up considerable debts through 'creative accounting' in their housing budget that they now cannot afford to fund the posts now vacant, and that they are demonstrably short of social workers, especially in this area. It is because of central government's restrictive stranglehold on local government funding, though, that Smortham, as a deprived borough, has been forced to resort to desperate measures to defend jobs and services. Only a broader political analysis of these factors can allow David and his team to understand their difficulties and to play their part in local and national responses to what are essentially issues about the ownership and control of resources and the exercise of power.

Without challenging the basis of this analysis, I would respond that it overlooks the way in which structural inequalities between classes, genders and ethnic groups affect the relationships between individuals in groups like this team. David and his colleagues have not overlooked these dimensions of the problem, and they are committed to the wider struggle to get a proper establishment of social workers for their team. Their choice of these actions does not imply a rejection of the fight for justice, but a commitment to it. Subscribing verbally to the ideals of justice is cheap; even going to union and political meetings occasionally is not very costly in terms of time and effort. They are trying to live out these principles in the day-to-day details of their team work. If justice means anything, it means that we take seriously the claims of those we work with for a fair deal from us. The duty of solidarity with our fellow-workers is not just a matter of going on strike when they do; it is also a matter of co-operating to achieve fairness in our working relations.

The kind of job-sharing arrangements reached by David, Sonia and the rest of the team are not claimed as general solutions to staff shortages and low morale in social services departments. But they are claimed to be a creative response, illustrating the principles of equality, fairness and co-operation, and a specific instance of anti-sexism and anti-racism within the severe constraints of a particular situation. In this way they apply general moral principles from the wider political sphere to the details of daily working life.

Conclusions

A specific example has been used to develop an account of how a certain kind of moral reasoning might be applied to small-scale relations between members of a household and members of a social work team. It has been argued that individuals in these social units have common interests in the good of each other and of their group, and need to be able to analyse situations and make decisions so as to take account of the common good. The ways of reasoning and choosing which can sustain in the quality of shared projects are democratic and co-operative processes, leading to egalitarian relations, which are monitored according to standards of justice.

This exercise is far from straightforward because their society is unjust. In the examples discussed, the inequalities of income and power between men and women, white and black people, required them to look beyond the terms of their immediate relationships to their membership of society. Before they could negotiate about how to share their work and improve the quality of their lives, they had to establish a baseline in terms of their individual rights. As no justifiable baseline exists in British society, they had to appeal to a notion of 'human rights' – citizenship under a just order – to establish what was their due as individuals.

Ideally, the link between membership of society (citizenship) and membership of shared projects could be straightforward, because the first would provide equality of rights and resources and access to the public goods of the community (a share in the good life), while the latter would allow individuals to co-operate democratically for their mutual benefit. In an unjust society, the unfair advantages of some citizens over others reinforce and are reinforced by the domination and exploitation that occur in shared projects, such as households, unless the terms on which individuals encounter each other are challenged, and an alternative moral basis established by agreement. But inevitably such agreements are fragile, and have to withstand pressures, both from the fact that so much of daily life has to be conducted under the existing rules and relationships and from the tempting instrumental advantages associated with the ways of thinking and acting promoted by those rules.

This chapter has explored only some of the snags and objections to the way of thinking that was proposed. There may well be many others, both theoretical and practical. What if Sarah started off with a much poorer education than David, or much fewer abilities? What if the team looked as if it would get fewer resources and lose credibility in the department by having a split senior post? These questions are worth considering, but would not (I suspect) undermine the analysis of the moral reasoning through which the pattern of their relationships is negotiated between them.

So far we have dealt only with small groups in which discussions about the common good can readily be held, and in which relations are face-to-face and personal. It is now time to tackle the much more difficult issues of large groups and communities, to see whether the same principles can be applied.

References

1. Bill Jordan, *The Common Good: Citizenship, morality and self-interest* (Blackwell, 1989), ch. 5.
2. Richard Norman, *Free and Equal: A philosophical examination of political values* (Oxford University Press, 1987), pp. 69–73. See also Bill Jordan, *Rethinking Welfare* (Blackwell, 1987), chs 1–3.
3. Norman, *op. cit.*, pp. 76–85.
4. Bernard Williams, 'The idea of equality', in Peter Laslett and W. G. Runciman (eds), *Philosophy, Politics and Society: Second Series* (Oxford University Press, 1962).
5. John Rawls, *A Theory of Justice* (Oxford University Press, 1972), p. 15.

6

COMMUNITY AND DEMOCRACY

It is now time to consider social work's relationship with its clientele in the context of shared projects. In what sense, if any, can social workers and their clients be said to share in common purposes, have common interests in a good quality of relationship, or partake of the same common good? Are there any ethical bonds linking them, in ties of mutuality or reciprocity, allowing a language of moral reasoning about their responsibilities towards each other to be developed as a dialogue between members, committed to standards of equality, cooperation and fairness?

It has been argued in Chapters 2 to 4 that an analysis of these relations in terms of abstract individual rights and authoritative state duties is inadequate. The language of rights traps ethical reasoning inside the heads of each person who is supposed to be guided by the search for his or her own good, and some rules about how to behave to others. The language of state responsibilities is concerned with social outcomes which take little account of people's personal projects and commitments or the meanings they attach to their relationships. In combination they produce a legalistic, impersonal encounter, a dialogue of the deaf between a clientele concerned only with defining its autonomy, and a profession exercising its official authority within departmental procedural guidelines.

In the introductory story about David Jackson and his colleagues, as soon as Sonia Ridgeway became part-time team leader she argued for changes in the way the team worked, including a much more open approach to members of the local community, and an attempt to involve client groups more actively as members or users of the department's facilities and resources, rather than as passive recipients of services. Instead of waiting for referrals, and treating each one as an isolated 'case', the team members were encouraged to adopt a higher profile in their district, and to be seen as actively finding out about local needs and people's perceptions of how they might be met. Instead of seeing themselves as having sole responsibility for assessing individuals and allocating them rations of resources, Sonia Ridgeway urged the team to see some of their homes, day centres, hostels and nurseries as facilities to be shared by local people – providing amenities for neighbourhood groups of various kinds, and opportunities to generate mutual support, rather than being reserved exclusively for those identified as needy according to official criteria. She encouraged field social workers, day care and residential staff to regard their groups of clients more as clubs or membership organisations, with a voice and a stake in their resources, and less as helpless victims or disruptive deviants.

None of these notions is especially innovatory or unusual. Such ideas and practices have been argued for in the Barclay Report[1] and a wide range of other social work literature, and adopted by teams all over the country. The principle of including service-users as participants and members in decisions about the running of their facilities has featured strongly in the literature, especially about people with handicaps and about mental health,[2] and is now widely accepted as best practice. Starting from attempts to include and consult with informal carers and other relatives many residential and day facilities now adopt a far more open approach – for example, allowing would-be users to approach them directly, or encouraging local residents to drop in for advice about family problems.[3] In some areas, residential and day care staff have been in the vanguard of these practices, which allow a much wider population to see social services resources as 'theirs', and regular users to have more influence on the running of the department's facilities.

The terms associated with these developments are ones like 'community social work', 'participation', 'partnership' and 'normalisation'. They are open to a variety of interpretations, from the very cautious (as in the majority version of the Barclay Report and most official publications[4]) to the radical (for example, Peter Beresford and Suzie Croft's writings on

community social work,[5] and the publications of some campaigning groups on the rights of people with handicaps[6]). What
links them is the notion that service-users should be included,
as far as possible, as fellow citizens in the lives and decision-
making processes of their local communities, and that social
services departments and other agencies should not serve to
exclude, stigmatise or disempower them, but to enable them to
be full citizens. They differ mainly in their assessment of how
far this is possible. In particular, the cautious interpretations
put a good deal of emphasis on the need to identify and contain
dangerous or disturbed clients, and to use control and compulsion in their cases, to protect others and defuse the threat to
orderly and peaceful relationships. Their ethic of inclusion and
participation is therefore much more guarded and conditional
than that of the radicals.

In the probation service, this caution and categorisation has
been even more marked. Although participatory approaches
are often found in day centres and hostels, the trend is towards
a more conditional liberty for clients, and a more challenging
style of supervision, with groupwork as a way of 'confronting
offending behaviour' rather than promoting communal integration. The government's proposed measures of punishment
in the community go a good deal further in this direction, with
a strong emphasis on assessing the threat posed by offenders,
and devising methods of punishment and surveillance that are
less restrictive than imprisonment, but take away some of the
rights and freedoms enjoyed by law-abiding citizens.[7]

In one respect, Sonia Ridgeway's proposed changes raise
important issues. As a black social worker, she is very aware of
the way in which her department is perceived by black
residents of Smortham. Efforts to establish community social
work and partipation by clients will have to overcome the
perception by black people that the agency is based on the
discriminatory use of white power against them. The fact that
the local authority employs so few black people in senior
positions is one part of the evidence of institutional racism; the
fact that black people receive so few of the resources that are in
demand from social services, and so much of the coercion that
is carried out by the department is another. While her
appointment is a small challenge to these covert policies, she is

determined to extend this into the spheres which affect black clients.

Here both theory and practice recognise some more difficult issues. Anti-racists demand positive action to combat discrimination and exclusion, and a recognition of the special needs and strengths of black individuals, families and communities.[8] Some critics doubt whether these can be reconciled with principles of justice;[9] others doubt whether the term 'black' really connotes a group with common interests.[10] These questions require us to examine the nature of relations between groups of residents of Smortham as well as between clients and social workers. They take us beyond the use of the word 'community' as a soothing noise, and into issues about how groups settle conflicts of interests in larger-scale societies. In this chapter, I propose to tackle these questions first, so as to provide a theoretical context in which to place social workers' relations with their clients. This is because the ethical principles relevant to these relationships should not be seen as deriving primarily from social workers' professional responsibilities, but from the qualitative relations between the people of Smortham – broadly speaking, from their political relations. I shall argue that the relevant principles have more to do with democracy than with professionalism.

Defining responsibilities

The description of Sonia's initiatives will already have raised some people's hackles. It may sound as if she and the team have embarked on a radical political programme of decentralisation and direct democracy without the sanction of the council's elected committee. If so – many will want to argue – her crusade is exceeding her limited responsibilities as a part-time senior social worker, and disrupting the balance of accountability and control, as well as the established processes of representative democracy.

Let it be stressed that this is not what the story is about. Sonia does believe in decentralisation of decision-making and in increased political participation. In her other life, as a politician in the next borough, she is working towards changes in the structure of local government departments which have these goals. But in this post she is quite willing to work within the definition of her responsibilities set by the present Labour council – a rather cautious bunch by comparison with their predecessors of the early 1980s. They have adopted policies of moderate decentralisation – local budgets devolved to districts, localised district plans, local decision-making about the use of resources – and approved the publication of a series of departmental papers on participation and user control in their services. In addition, the council's anti-racism policies and women's committee's statement on carers' rights, though scarcely implemented, still stand as official guidelines. So she is working well within the limits of her role and professional responsibility in the initiatives she is encouraging.

The story would be different, of course, if Smortham were being ruled by a strongly centralising council of any political colour – one which insisted on controlling the process of planning, the use of resources and the details of policy-implementation from the town hall, and regarded district teams as carrying out its bidding. But Smortham has been depicted as a moderately decentralising authority because this is probably more representative of the present situation in this country, and poses some important ethical issues for social workers.

It is well-recognised that the devolution of decision-making from town and county halls to district offices, and from district offices to community centres and tenants associations, has had some cynical motives. When local authorities were rich in resources and their powers were growing there were few such moves; as soon as budgets shrank and cuts were to be made, localities and consumers were brought into the process of deciding how to ration themselves. Participation became the watchword precisely when people were to participate in their own deprivation – in saying no to themselves.

As a professional group, social workers have not been in the forefront of moves towards decentralisation of decision-making. They have often resisted them, pointing out that they disguised shortages of much-needed resources, particularly for groups with special needs. When the reorganisations have taken place, patch teams established, and locality planning begun, reactions among teams have been very mixed. Some have responded with enthusiasm and commitment; others have seemed frozen in their previous ways, trapped by heavy caseloads of statutory work, and unable to use the new opportunities offered to them. Among the latter, fieldworkers have often been especially negative and suspicious, seeming to prefer the exclusive control over their work provided by traditional casework methods, and to avoid responding to wider community issues and debates. Where this has happened, day care and residential workers have sometimes taken on the role of vanguard in the new initiatives, opening up their facilities for wider use, and reaching out into their community to offer services to people who would not otherwise have received help.

So the challenge for the Smortham team is to see what room for manoeuvre they have within the constraints of their situation. There are few new resources on offer, and desperate shortages of existing ones – not least of staff time. Yet the council is encouraging teams (within limits) to seek new resources by new methods, involving the community in planning and developing its services. This poses plenty of ethical problems, as we discover in this chapter. But it should not be seen as depicting a crusade by social workers in search of extended political influence or covert subversion, but rather the project of over-burdened and rather jaded officials trying to find morally acceptable ways of doing their jobs.

In an unjust society, social workers – like policemen and emergency service workers – have too many and too demanding responsibilities; they are not looking for more. The temptation is constantly to fall back into legalism, into the style of practice and ways of thinking described in Chapter 4, in which they stick to strictly-defined responsibilities, well-rehearsed procedures, and limited relationships as a way of dealing with complexity and overload. The proactive approach taken by Sonia and her colleagues is an attempt to look beyond these practices and to seek a moral justification for what they do in their membership of a community with interests in good services for all.

Social choice

The community in this team's area of Smortham is a diverse
multi-racial one. In addition to the large Afro-Caribbean
population, there is a smaller Asian one, which in turn
contains both Muslim and Hindu religious congregations.
Religion plays an important part in the communal life of all
these groups and gives them different values and needs as well
as contributing to their identity. For example, although there
was no demonstration in Smortham over the Salman Rushdie
affair, Muslims from Smortham travelled to other cities to take
part in marches and express outrage during the height of that
controversy.

The white population of the area is by no means uniform
either. There is a substantial Irish Catholic community, and
other groups of Polish and Armenian origins with strong
cultural identities. Although the area contains three large
council estates, there are also concentrations of older houses in
multi-occupation and some inter-war and modern residential
developments, with higher-income residents. Plurality
and diversity rather than uniformity are thus the major
characteristics of the team's 'patch'.

If our focus is on shared projects as living or working
arrangements or cultural associations involving common
purposes, interests and processes of decision-making, then it is
clear that the area is not one community but several. If each
household is a shared project of a kind, so too is each church,
temple and mosque, each voluntary organisation, sporting
club, tenants' association, neighbourhood group, and so on.
Political and administrative boundaries, such as the one
marking out the team's territory, cut across these communities
of interest, with their shared values and practices. They
impose a spurious unity on groups who identify with their
members in other districts (or even in other countries) more
strongly than they do with fellow-residents of the area marked
on the office map as 'Team 4'.

This being so, how can the team hope to base its practice
principles and methods on the 'needs of the community', since
the needs and preferences of all these groups are at best

different, and at worst in conflict with each other? Are we not again back in the same set of problems that inspired the liberal solution of Chapter 2? If there is not one agreed set of practices which go to make up the good life, then each group must be given the opportunity and the right to seek its own good in its own way, like the individuals in liberal theory. The important ethical questions concern the resources to be allocated to each group, and the rules defining their scope for autonomy and protecting each from interference or coercion by the others.

Yet, as we have already seen, this kind of analysis misses many of the most important aspects of life in the area. Even though people form exclusive associations based on property, religion, taste, skill or recreational proclivity, they also share many aspects of their lives simply by living in the same area. They walk the same streets, breathe the same air, play in the same parks and fields, and use the same facilities, from shops and cinemas to museums, swimming pools and concert halls to rubbish dumps and sewers. Hence the quality of their lives depends on the quality of their communal resources and relations as citizens of this area of Smortham, as well as on their membership of exclusive groups, churches and clubs. They have as much a common interest in improving these as in developing the same aspects of their household and associations.

It has already been argued that the idea of a shared project implies co-operation and a process of decision-making. Clearly these are much more difficult to establish satisfactorily in a large and diverse community than in a small group whose members can meet face to face to discuss and negotiate. But the fact that the people living in this area of Smortham share in all these aspects of life together demands that they make certain choices about how they share them – collective life requires some process of collective decision-making or social choice. One has only to think of a community in which these processes have broken down, like Beirut, to recognise how important it is for life itself that an orderly and accepted way of making these decisions should operate.

Clearly the subjects under discussion are what are usually called political processes and decisions – those by which the community, under its own authority, organises itself and distributes its resources. In most people's minds, politics is about the use of power, and political decisions are the outcomes of a competitive struggle for power – in the case of a democracy, a competition between rival groups for votes.[11] This makes politics very different from ethics, because politics is structured around competitive advantage whereas ethics is about mutual responsibility. According to this way of thinking, this chapter is already straying from the main themes of the book.

But the power we are talking about is not a commodity, it is a relationship, in which one group of people are able to influence or limit the choices or behaviours of another.[12] In this sense, the authority of a central or local government is no different from that of the committee of a sports club or a village hall. It is the authority we vest in this group to make decisions on our behalf, for which – if the system is to any significant degree democratic – they are ultimately answerable to us. So a 'competition for power' is a necessary element in any representative system of social choice, which allows some people (in theory any member of the whole group) to make decisions which are binding on the others who have elected them. But this does not imply that the power-relations established by such a system are concerned with competitive advantage and not with the common good, as some authors have argued.[13] I shall contend that a democratic form of government is fully consistent with decision-making according to moral criteria, and with every citizen's moral responsibility for political decisions. In other words, I shall argue against a distinction between politics and ethics.

The first major objection that must be countered is the argument that any moral analysis of choice implies a subject with moral autonomy – an individual who has the ability to make his or her own choice between various courses of action, according to his or her own ethical criteria. Political decisions deny moral autonomy to individuals, because they involve the imposition of some people's choices on others – for example, they could force a conscientious minority to accept the majority's decision to make education compulsory. So political processes constantly lead to decisions from which individuals must disassociate themselves as moral subjects, decisions that allow actions that they would forbid, or vice versa. This leads to laws which, for all their legal force, many regard as not morally binding.

But social units of all kinds have to reach decisions on a similar range of issues to those that face individuals as moral choices; and then they have to apply the principles they decide upon (such as rules of fairness) to their members, just as individuals apply their moral principles to themselves. This objection, if valid, would rob any form of collective decision of morally binding force. To return to David Jackson and his team, it would imply that the discussion about whether or not he was to share his senior's post was a purely political one, with no ethical content, because one team-member might object in principle to job-sharing. It would mean that only individual decisions, affecting their own direct relations with others, could be regarded as moral, and hence would deny moral significance even to joint family decisions.

There are, to be sure, real issues about minorities, and especially minorities with strong moral views which run against those of the majority. But it is precisely because collective decisions should be morally as well as legally binding that these issues should be taken seriously. This is why mechanisms for social choice may have to include ones aimed specifically at protecting minority interests or values.

In relation to those aspects of life that they share as residents of this area of Smortham, the members of this community have a common interest in a good quality of life together. The same standards of fairness apply to their co-operation over these issues as to the members of the social work team, or to those of the Jackson family. And although the mechanisms and procedures will have to be different because of the numbers involved, the same principles apply to decision-making – that all should have an equal voice in choices about the common good. Where social choices are to be made, the moral order is created not by the isolated decisions of individuals but by the democratic self-rule of the group or community.[14]

Democracy

If we accept that all forms of sharing in human relations

require co-operation (and hence choices) in which the participants take account of each other's needs, then democratic standards must apply to all forms of association, from the smallest groups to the largest nation states. But democracy is not to be understood as a formal procedure which consists in each person having a vote, and counting the votes in a certain way. Any way of reaching decisions which allows people to influence social choices that affect their lives establishes a degree of democracy, and any measure that increases this influence makes the group or community more democratic. Cunningham suggests three criteria for judging whether social unit A is more democratic than social unit B:

1. Proportionately more people in A have control over their common social environment than do people in B; and/or
2. People in A have control over proportionately more aspects of their social environment than do people in B; and/or
3. The aspects of their life over which people in A have control are more important from the point of view of democracy than those over which people in B have control.[15]

Having control over one's shared environment means making happen what one wants to happen. But if all are interested only in getting their own way – in the sense of achieving their first choice irrespective of the consequences for everyone else – then no decision can be reached. To refer back to the example of David and Sarah Jackson's baby crying in the night, if both stick to their guns and insist that the other must see to him, then nothing will get done. So they must reach a decision which is acceptable to each (such as taking turns), even though this is neither's first preference if they think only of their own needs. A good reason for accepting this compromise is their wish to go on exerting equal control over other choices. In the same way, larger-scale democratic processes aim to reach decisions which are acceptable to all, in the sense that they will not jeopardise participation in social choice at the level the participants already enjoy. In a perfectly democratic social unit, everyone would always take part in using whatever means of control over decisions allowed him or her to make the shared social environment acceptable to each.[16] In other

words, each member would care enough about the other's
needs to make sure that every social choice was based on
agreement.

Agreements can take several forms. Where people meet as
bearers of different interests, they may negotiate and bargain
to reach agreement. Where they meet as citizens who recognise
a common interest in the good of the community, they may
reach consensus over co-operation. Most democratic processes
in most social units contain elements of both kinds of search for
agreement – as we have already recognised in the discussions
within the Jackson household and the team. The important
point is that people should not negotiate in such a way as to
prevent them reaching consensus, or go on debating the
common good so earnestly that they cannot bargain if disagreements prove insuperable.[17] The goal of democracy is
equal control over the final decision.

Suppose we try to apply some of these ideas to the situation
in Smortham that was outlined at the start of the chapter. The
social services department has an old building, formerly used
as a hostel for ex-psychiatric patients, which is in the process of
being renovated for some new use. David Jackson and Sonia
Ridgeway have decided to hold a meeting, in line with their
new approach, to consult with community groups about what
purpose they would like to see it put to. They write to the local
Afro-Caribbean centre, the mosque, the temple, the churches,
the tenants' groups, residents' associations, mothers' groups,
and all the other community associations with whom they are
in touch, to invite them to a meeting. They explain that they
will try to reach an agreement about the most suitable use for
the building, but failing agreement they will put the decision
to a majority vote, with each organisation having an equal
voice.

Why should groups of such diverse forms and sizes each
count as one in the vote? Some groups may have five times as
many members as others, and some ten times as many
potential members, even though a smaller proportion actually
join. But Sonia and David reason that these are not the crucial
issues. The building has only a limited number of rooms (some
large, some small), and any use to which they are put will
involve the organised participation of groups. So it is right for

groups, who will be the department's partners in whatever the new venture is to be, to form the relevant units for decision-making. And it is the needs of their members, not their sheer numbers, that should count. If it comes to a vote, the fact that there are few or no facilities for a group with important needs should matter more than the fact that another group has larger numbers of non-needy members. So a debate about how the resource can best meet needs, followed by an equal vote for all groups if no agreement can be reached, seems the fairest system for choosing.

The meeting will be a difficult test of the new approach. They already know that the tenants' and the mothers' groups consider that the building would be ideal for a family centre, with resources for mothers and young children, and especially for single parents. The Afro-Caribbean group believe that the needs of black elders are not being properly met, and think that it would make a good day centre for them. The Muslim group are concerned about the needs of teenage girls in their community, and would like to establish a youth club for them, to be open in the school holidays and after school hours. One of the churches thinks that there is a need for a local drugs advice centre. How can these competing claims be weighed against each other?

There are two kinds of reason for doubting whether a fair and rational democratic decision can be reached in situations like this. The first comes from those who take very seriously the idea that exclusive membership groups like churches and temples have their own moral standards, which are developed within their own traditions of thought and practice. The shared values and meanings of each of these ethical communities are different from, and not commensurate with, each other; there can be no moral consensus between them, and there can be no transcendent standards of justice which can adjudicate between them.[18] According to this view, any co-operation between the groups will be purely instrumental, and a majority decision will simply reflect an *ad hoc* alliance to defeat the most disliked delegations' proposals.

It may well be true that the Christian, Muslim and Hindu accounts of moral virtues differ, and that they vary significantly in their analyses of justice. It may also be true that no abstract principle can determine which is better than the other. But that is not the issue here. The question for the meeting is not whether a Christian use for the building is better than a Muslim one, but which use will be best for the whole community in this area of Smortham. Since no such meetings have taken place before, it invites those attending to create in their imagination an idea of the collective interests of the people of the area, and to discuss the various proposals with such a notion in mind. In so far as the groups present represent all the needs of the inhabitants, the decision must take account of every group's proposal, and must try to deal with each in a way that will ensure that future meetings of this kind take place, in which similar decisions can be taken in a fair and rational way.

This, therefore, involves the creation of a new collective body, incorporating a new tradition, to make the social choices on these issues for this community. It invites the participants to invest in this meeting their common aspirations for control over their shared social environment, and to create processes and procedures through which their common interests in a good quality of life can be identified and developed. Since none previously had any say in how social services were provided in the area, and all have needs which they believe can be better met through their participation in this kind of meeting, all have a stake in its continuation. The only question, therefore, is whether they can establish ways of co-operating with each other and the department which overcome their mutual resentment and desire for competitive advantage. In fact, David and Sonia can probably expect about an hour and a half in which the only things talked about are past wrongs and injustices, before the constructive discussion begins.

There are many circumstances in which such an attempt to bring about a new, more democratic decision process in a community will fail. If the parties are so embittered by past experiences of the department, or so antagonistic and rivalrous towards each other, that they place no trust in the process and no value on co-operation, then progress will not be made. But this is a general problem, all too familiar from parts of the world where large groups have been oppressed or excluded from power for so long that they are unwilling to share power with their oppressors, and where dominant groups have become too selfish and short-sighted to recognise that the quality of their lives depends on their ability to establish trust through sharing.

The second reason for doubts about the results of the meeting focuses on the rationality of the decisions that can be made. In his famous 'paradox of democracy', Kenneth Arrow pointed out that any procedure for social choice must meet four conditions to be both rational and democratic. It must be capable of translating individuals' preferred ordering of options into an order of preference for the collective body; it must never demote an option in its order when one or more individuals promotes it in their order of preferences, and others' orderings remain unchanged; it must not take acount of irrelevant (impossible) options; and it must not always follow the order of preferences of one individual. He went on to argue that no procedure for collective decision-making meets all these conditions.[19] For example, let us imagine a majority vote over three different uses for the building in Smortham – the family centre (A), the girls' youth club (B), and the elders' day centre (C) – with three voters, the tenants' association (1), the Muslim congregation (2), and the Afro-Caribbean Forum (3). Group 1 prefers A to B and B to C; group 2 prefers B to C and C to A; group 3 prefers C to A and A to B. Under these circumstances, majorities composed of voters 1 and 3 prefer A to B, voters 1 and 2 prefer B to C, and 2 and 3 prefer C to A. So the collective decision is that the family centre is preferable to the girls' youth club, the girls' youth club to the elders' day centre and the elders' day centre to the family centre. This clearly fails the first of Arrow's conditions, that of collective rationality.

There is no way out of this paradox if we regard the participants as having fixed preferences, which take no account of others' needs, or of the arguments that will be put to the meeting. But it is much more reasonable to assume that, although all will come with their own needs foremost in their minds, they will be willing to modify their views about priorities in line with both the debate about the good of the whole community (the attempt to reach consensus over priorities) and negotiations between the participants (the attempt to bargain over priorities).[20] The aim of the meeting is not to establish procedures for reaching fixed ordering of collective preferences, but to give all the participants some control over decisions and which produces results that are acceptable to all. Since these means include both persuasion and bargaining, it is quite possible that different preferences will emerge on different occasions, as the family centre may be the consensus choice, but the second decision may rest on bargaining and negotiation. The important issue is that processes should continue to give the participants means of controlling the decisions.

So democracy, although it does not supply a magic solution to situations of mutual mistrust and hostility, does provide a model of how diverse communities can seek co-operation and fairness in decisions about their shared social environment. In the face of problems like the ones raised in this section, democracy looks for solutions through giving people more influence over their environment and more say in their lives, rather than by trying to control and coerce them, and limiting their choices. Most intractable situations of conflicting interests can be represented as 'prisoner's dilemmas', in which the parties believe they are in a zero-sum, competitive situation, because they cannot rely on others to co-operate rather than take full advantage at their expense, and negotiation is impossible.[21] The 'democratic fix' tries to reduce the constraints on the parties by opening channels of communication between them, and offering them more control. Only in this way, by participants seeing the gradual benefits of mutual trust, can a new variable-sum (win-win) game be established, in which they co-operate for the common good.

Levels of democratic decision-making

In the event, the meeting goes remarkably well. After the expected expression of pent-up frustration from groups who have experienced years of paternalism, evasion, patronisation or heavy-handedness from the department, and some side-swipes at each other, the participants get down to a very constructive discussion of the area's needs, and of ways of working together to tackle them. Agreement is reached that the main use of the building should be for the family centre, but that a room should be released for a twice-weekly drugs advice centre, and that the girls' youth club should have the use of the largest room for three evenings a week. A commitment is also made that the next available and suitable building will be used for the black elders' day centre.

Celebrating the successful outcome of weeks of hard work in a nearby public house after the meeting, David, Sonia and their colleagues are joined by Councillor Grady, who represents this ward on Smortham Borough Council. He has lent his considerable local prestige to the whole enterprise of greater participation in the social services department's work by the community, and made a very helpful opening address at the meeting. But he now wants to raise some issues which have been put to him by his fellow councillors, and by members at a meeting of the Smortham East Constituency Labour Party.

First, he wonders how these new processes of decision-making at the local level will affect the established democratic procedures at the council level. The issues to be determined by the direct democratic methods now being set up locally have been carefully defined as concerned with the development and utilisation of facilities controlled by the team, the spending of the local budget, and the priorities and practices of local staff (field, domiciliary, day care and residential). But obviously these issues have implications for the larger questions of how the borough's resources are allocated between areas, which client groups receive what resources (home help hours, day care places, residential homes), and how services are to be developed in future. Councillor Grady wonders whether the success of the meeting may result in more direct pressure on his colleagues to extend the process, with groups claiming to represent communities in Smortham as a whole bidding to participate in the council's planning and decision-making activities.

These questions are linked with other politically sensitive ones. In the Labour Party, the issue of black sections has rumbled beneath the surface for some time, and has been contained only with difficulty; the MP for Smortham East is particularly worried about this. More immediately, the Salman Rushdie affair has provoked an outburst of latest disaffection among Muslim Labour Party supporters. Although the MP's majority does not depend on votes from the Muslim community, one of Councillor Grady's colleagues' does; her seat is far from secure, and she faces a dilemma over her instinctive response to the issue (in terms of freedom of artistic expression) and the outrage of her Muslim constituents, who are demanding her support in their campaign to change the blasphemy laws. Because their local experiment in participation encourages Afro-Caribbean and Muslim communities to identify their needs and campaign for them, opinion in the party is concerned about the implications for such issues as black sections and the formation of a Muslim political movement.

Representative democratic systems and party politics do indeed have something to fear from participatory options if the latter give previously excluded individuals and groups the experience of some control over the shared social environment for the first time. Minorities who are exploited and dominated under traditional systems, and whose support means little to the major parties, can find a voice and an influence at the local level through direct democratic processes, which in turn give them the confidence to press harder on the representative structure. To this extent, Councillor Grady's colleagues have some reason to be worried.

But the principles that have been attributed to David Jackson and Sonia Ridgway do not lead logically to an overthrow of the representative democratic system by a form of direct or participatory democracy. There would be serious problems in ensuring that the groups claiming to speak on behalf of the various communities in Smortham as a whole were authorised and properly mandated to do so; these problems would be multiplied many times over in national politics. The feasible scale of the debating chamber and the practicalities of agendas and voting require some form of representation beyond the small locality. But nor do they imply that these systems should remain unchanged. There will be plenty of scope for parties and electoral systems to be modified so as to give people more control over party programmes, over the person to be elected, and over his or her actions after being elected. This suggests that previously excluded groups will use the skills and confidence they gain at the local level to press for the democratisation of political institutions, by means of structural changes and changes in the content of programmes.

However, the previous paragraph begs one important question, which David and Sonia could have put to Councillor Grady. By what principles should it be determined which decisions about the shared environment are made at the local, which at the municipal and which at the national level? Why should the town hall have the say in issues over housing, for instance, or education, while central government has those for social security benefits and defence? Could not more of the important decisions be made at the local level, and hence by a more participatory process.

These questions are by no means academic, at a time when the levels at which decisions are being made are shifting in wholesale ways. On the one hand, international groupings like the European Community are being set up, amid great controversy about the extent to which they should assume some of the decision-making powers of nation states. On the other, central government in Britain is reducing the powers of local authorities in many ways, both by taking some of them to itself (as in education particularly over the curriculum), or in giving them to private firms or voluntary bodies (as in housing), or in giving them to smaller units (as with school budgets, which will go to headmasters). And at the same time, local authorities themselves are adopting strategies of decentralisation in some of their departments, notably social services, in which budgets are devolved to areas, with some encouragement for managers to act in the ways described in this chapter to determine local needs and priorities.

One tempting answer to the questions this raises is that the more that decisions concern issues of distribution of resources, the higher the level of decision-making should be, and the more they concern quality of life, the lower. This rationale comes from the idea that exploitation (in the sense discussed in Chapter 3) is structural, and stems from features of the whole society (capitalism, patriarchy, racism) which can most effectively be challenged by redistribution of assets, or systematic abolition of the advantages associated with assets. Hence many modern writers about equality and social justice (including some who count themselves as socialists) have developed arguments for redistributive measures of taxation or expropriation which focus on the national level of decision-making, and leave individuals free to cultivate their own shared projects in their own ways – including ways that rely heavily on markets and contracts.[22] They have little or nothing to say about local government or community participation, and imply that these are of secondary importance. By contrast, writers whose critique is directed at the alienation and fragmentation of social life in modern commercial societies, and the problems of recognising common interests within a framework of choices by self-interested decision-makers, tend to focus on lack of participation and community in the workplace and the locality, and to extrapolate from these to larger-scale institutions.[23] This seems to suggest that quality of life issues about social relations can best be understood and dealt with at a face-to-face, small group or neighbourhood level.

But this distinction is unsatisfactory. In the first place, the previous chapter showed that issues of distributive justice – about equalising the benefits and burdens of co-operation – arise as much in households and social work teams as in society as a whole. While negotiations between David and Sarah Jackson would be much easier to conduct fairly if central government redistributed income and power in such a way as to abolish the advantages that at present go with maleness, this would not relieve them of the responsibility to arrange their partnership's benefits and burdens fairly. In line with my overall insistence that moral and political decisions cannot be distinguished from each other, I would argue that issues of justice arise and should be tackled as much in small groups as in wider society. Second, issues about quality of life are certainly not confined to localities. We are just beginning to recognise that the largest environmental issues (the hole in the ozone layer, the greenhouse effect) are truly international in their scope and consequences, and demand international solutions. Because many of the resources we share are global and indivisible, and because the actions of people in one community now have consequences in others far from that locality, we cannot confine such issues to the lower levels of decision-making. Similarly, world peace and international co-operation over disarmament and measures to end terrorism depend on the perception of common interests in more trustful and co-operative relationships between nation states, and hence a qualitative change in international relations. Hence the democratisation of all levels of decision-making is part of a programme for improving the quality of life and seeking the common good.

For these reasons, although David and Sonia will be engaged mainly in work in their locality, they will continue to be active within national political campaigning and trade union affairs. It is no contradiction for Sonia to promote participation in her area and to represent another as its elected councillor; nor yet would it betray her principles or work in the locality to go on to stand as a parliamentary candidate. Both distributive justice and quality of life raise issues to be pursued at all levels of decision-making.

Social workers and their clients

We can now go back to the first set of questions raised at the start of this chapter. In what sense do social workers and their clients form part of the same community, with common interests in co-operation and good relations between them? What moral bonds of mutuality or reciprocity exist between them – what if anything do they owe each other in terms of their common citizenship and membership of the same municipality? And what relevance do the efforts of the joint seniors to establish greater democratic participation in the department's work have for the quality of relationships between staff and clientele?

These questions may be put in more concrete form by quoting what one team member, Joyce Stevens, said at the allocation meeting on the Tuesday after the events described in the previous sections.

'Look, Sonia, that meeting was great, and I really enjoy the time you've made for us to go out into the community and set up all these support groups and neighbourhood associations, and work with all the other agencies, but the fact is that four days a week I'm still doing child abuse and court reports and visits to foster parents and all the rest of the statutory child care stuff. The community work really helps to keep me going, and it does wonders for our morale, and gets us working and thinking as a team, but does it really change anything? As far as my clients are concerned, I'm still the same two-faced monster – trying to help them one day, then taking their kids away the next, and always with the power to do things to them they don't like, and refuse to give them the things they need. So why should they trust me any more, and how can I treat them any better than I've been treating them these past six months?'

There are some obvious practical and pragmatic answers to these questions. Joyce is expecting a bit much if she wants results so soon from these far-reaching changes. Qualitative shifts take a long time to bear fruit in statistics on referrals or admissions to care. Moreover, the most deprived, hard-pressed people who form existing caseloads are likely to be among the last to feel the benefits of the changes. Their lives have already passed beyond their control to a great extent, and the same forces which put them into the hands of social workers will probably continue to deny them autonomy or options, at least in the short term. Like these clients, Joyce herself will probably have to wait for a while, seeing the benefits of the changes going more to people outside her present caseload, and to new colleagues joining the team.

But in the longer term, there are certain clear gains to be seen in the quality of relations with clients. We start from the same principles that inform other relationships – the ideal of co-operation based on fairness. But the fairness that is at stake in these relationships is not between worker and client, as if they were partners in a shared project – at least not initially. What brings the client to the agency is a need or a problem, or the fact that someone else sees him or her as a problem, or danger or a threat. The social worker has resources and powers that are at her disposal through her role in one of the borough's agencies. The issue of fairness concerns the relations between the client, his or her family and neighbours, and the social worker as a local government official; it may also include relations with other local or national agencies. What is at stake is fairness in the client's dealings with others (family members, fellow citizens) and in the social worker's dealings with the client. Typically, there will be concerns about what resources the client needs to be a full member of the community and to fulfil his or her social roles, and also whether the client is acting in a way that is fair to those others (being violent to family members or stealing from fellow citizens being the most common examples of unfair actions). Two types of concern are linked: often social workers will be trying to discuss and negotiate plans which involve both giving additional resources to clients and getting them to change their behaviour. In this context, co-operation and fairness will be achieved when social worker and client are able to agree that the client has the resources he or she needs to be a citizen and fulfil social roles, and that the required changes of behaviour are feasible and reasonable.

If these are the most common issues in social workers' transactions with clients, the developments in community social work and participation will help in the following ways.

1. SUPPORT

The social workers are uncomfortably aware that many of the plans they make with their clients are not fair in the above sense. The resources they can offer are not nearly sufficient to sustain the clients in a viable quality of life, or to allow a reasonable expectation that they will change their behaviour. For instance, most of the parents involved in child protection cases are single parents, many of them black, existing on income support, often repaying large debts left by absconding husbands, isolated in bleak housing, with no options in terms of employment or child minding. As with Louise in the example in Chapter 1, they are forced to rely on unsuitable friends for assistance with child care, to do risky or illegal work to try to pay off their debts, and to bring up their children under conditions they know to be against their long-term interests, and to fall short of their developmental needs. Under these circumstances, social workers cannot regard their relationships with their clients as based on fairness, and they cannot expect them to trust, confide or co-operate as if they were.

The opening of the new family centre will allow more support to be available to just this client group. The centre will allow parents, and especially single parents, a good deal of influence over how the new resource is developed, and what needs it should try to meet. It will allow them to break out of their isolation, discover some strengths in themselves, and create various options. But above all it will allow the department to share more of the tasks of child care with these parents, and to demonstrate a co-operative, supportive and helpful stance towards them, rather than always requiring change of them, but giving little in return. In this sense, it will be a step towards greater fairness in relations with this client group.

2. LEGITIMACY

In requiring clients to change their behaviour, or using power to compel them to act against their will, or to remove children from their care, social workers claim to act in the name of the community. They claim to be telling clients that they are behaving unjustly by hurting their children or stealing from their neighbours, according to standards which are accepted as binding by their fellow citizens. The rules they enforce in giving or withholding resources are similarly claimed as fair according to criteria derived from the political decisions of the whole community.

In practice, social workers know that this is a fiction. The community that elects the government that passes these laws, or the council of the borough, does not include many of the kind of people who become clients. Either clients do not vote at all, or they constitute a permanent minority, whose interests in redistribution are not reflected in any party programme.[24] The public opinion that is reflected in the press, and to which social workers are increasingly answerable, does not include their opinions. The standards of practice, of child care, of family life and of relationships generally that social workers represent are predominantly white middle-class standards, and they usually contain substantial elements of prejudice. So clients have good reasons for questioning the legitimacy of the power which is used against them, and the criteria by which they are assessed.

Developments in participation and community social work give social workers greater legitimacy. Closer contact with the community, and especially the black community, can change workers' attitudes, and allow them to recognise more strengths in their clients, and their achievements as well as their failures. It can allow them to understand patterns of behaviour, and the rationality and functionality of actions that seem bizarre or self-destructive outside this context. It can put them in touch with networks of support that are tolerant and positive, and hence create alternatives to statutory interventions. But it can also help them to discover that other actions are regarded as wrong in these same communities, and hence strengthen their resolve to act decisively to protect vulnerable people or restrain deviant behaviour. They can genuinely invoke the opinion of the community of which the client is a part in trying to persuade him or her to change their behaviour, or show that it is unjust by the standards of those they respect.

3. SOCIAL DISTANCE

Another weakness in the moral basis of worker–client relations in this area of Smortham is the fact that social workers endure few of the privations and hardships which are part of their clients' daily lives. They – like David Jackson – live outside the area, in leafier, wealthier, more sanitary, better resourced districts, in more comfortable houses. (Sonia Ridgeway is the exception to this generalisation.) They have benefited from recent government tax cuts, from mortgage interest tax relief, and from the prosperity that is now spreading through comfortable Britain, though not penetrating this area of Smortham. They drive cars and take holidays.

All these factors limit the extent to which social workers and their clients can be said to share the same social environment, and hence to be part of the same community. Living in a different locality and using different amenities implies that they do not meet face-to-face as fellow citizens or experience the same phenomena in their daily lives. Being part of the advantaged majority, albeit a subordinate and less advantaged part, social workers' interests on a range of political and

economic issues conflict with those of their clients, if these are
conceived in competitive terms. It would be understandable if
clients assumed, in the absence of evidence to the contrary,
that their social workers are content to enjoy these advantages
and have no desire to share them with the disadvantaged, or to
have any part of the struggle which is their regular lot.

The steps towards participation and community social work
do something about the social distance between workers and
clients, though they leave many of these factors untouched.
They do mean that social workers spend more of their lives in
the same social environment as their clients, rather than
remaining in their offices, or in other official buildings. They
are engaged in the same issues, and join together to work for
improved amenities and a better quality of life together – at
least during the workers' working hours. The more informal
nature of much of their interaction leads to a spontaneous
sharing of other aspects of their lives, and hence a breaking
down of the barriers which might otherwise exist between
them.

It is an irony that most social workers spend a number of
years before they go on training courses living and working in
situations where there is little social distance between them
and their clients. As unpaid or low-paid unqualified workers,
in day centres or residential homes, they usually rent accommodation which is little or no better than their clients', live on
an income which is as inadequate, ride bicycles or walk, and
incur debts. They experience claiming means-tested benefits
and endure the indignities and inconveniences that these
involve. Their working situations often allow them to be close
to clients, and to offer the kind of support and empathy that
comes from shared experiences. Once they qualify, they take
out mortgages and car loans, move into office accommodation,
keep files, and put up professional defences. It is only by
involvement in the issues which directly affect clients' lives in
their communities that some of the closeness and communication of their previous relations can be restored.

Overall, I have argued that although these changes do not
transform the moral basis of relations between workers and
clients, they do constitute an improvement. Furthermore, this
is reflected in a different, more co-operative and agreed method

of working, and in less coercive outcomes. Studies of the results of adopting thorough-going community social work methods suggest that numbers of court orders for child protection or removing delinquent youngsters from the community fall significantly.[25] Closer informal contact between the team and the community allows problems to be identified and investigated earlier, and a supportive network allows voluntary arrangements to be subsituted for compulsory orders, even when children or teenagers do need to be away from parents. Similarly, in mental health, a community-based approach reduces the numbers of referrals to psychiatrists and psychiatric day hospitals, and of new referrals to in-patient facilities.

More obviously, participation by clients in decisions about and practices within services for people with handicaps, illnesses and disabilities, both physical and mental, allows fairer, more equal and co-operative relations to develop. The democratisation of policy-making and planning that has been achieved by including service-users and carers, and the transformation of relations in homes and centres through adopting the same principles in daily practice, bear witness to the potential for change, especially in small-scale social units, once these principles are accepted.[26] Furthermore, a more participatory and democratic approach to day and residential care for these groups is also often accompanied by greater openness to and approachability for the wider community, and efforts to reach out to potential users in a preventive way, to sustain their lives as members of their households and neighbourhoods.

Conclusions

If abstract, exclusive rights and official duties cannot provide a satisfactory moral basis for social work's relations with its clientele, then we must look to the substance and context of their actual relations to supply this. This chapter started with a consideration of the community in which clients live and social workers work, and examined the sense in which it might be regarded as a shared project. Because all those who live and work there share many amenities and many aspects of their lives, they have no alternative to making collective choices about this shared social environment.

I argued that democratic theory supplies the only coherent account of how collective choice is compatible with moral autonomy, because it allows the people in any social unit to rule over themselves.[27] A perfect democracy would give all the people maximum control over decisions affecting their shared environment, and any measure to increase democracy increases their control. It also requires them to consider choices in the light of the good of their whole community, rather than thinking solely in terms of their own preferences and interests.

Democratic principles demand that members of a community try to reach agreements and co-operate over collective decisions. They also bind members to abide by these decisions, and the more democratic the process, the more morally binding the force of the decisions made. In a democratic social unit, of whatever scale, fairness demands a distribution of resources according to needs, and an equalisation of benefits and burdens. Hence a community lays down standards for the redistribution of resources to meet needs, and for fairness in dealings between its members.

Social services departments are crucially involved in all these processes at the local level. In the imaginary borough of Smortham, the team for area 4 is seen trying to increase democratic participation in decisions over communal resources, by inviting local groups to choose how a building should be used. The increased involvement of social workers in their community is seen as allowing residents to express their needs in their own terms, rather than imposing bureaucratic or professional assessments on them.

Everyday social work characteristically remains a series of transactions between deprived people who have lost control over parts of their lives, and social workers with limited resources but awesome powers to coerce. For these encounters to contain the potential for fairness, the possibility must be present for clients' needs to be met up to a standard of acceptability in the community, and for clients' behaviour to reach acceptable standards, by agreement and through support and co-operation. The chances of this are increased when social workers are trusted and seen as fair, working within criteria of justice which are set and maintained by the people for the members of their community, rather than imposed from outside.

This in turn depends on social workers being able to offer relevant and effective help and support, and demanding changes in behaviour from what is seen as a legitimate moral position – one of knowledge of the client's situation and sharing his or her concerns, rather than one of superiority, advantage and power. I have argued that all these possibilities for reaching agreed and co-operative solutions to needs and problems are increased by democratisation and a dialogue within the community about the common good.

But none of this removes from the social worker the moral responsibility for what happens between herself and the client; it merely provides the ethical framework for their encounter. The next chapter returns to those encounters, and to the examples given in the first chapter, to examine the moral dilemmas posed by casework relationships.

References

1. Barclay Committee, *Social Workers: Their role and tasks* (Bedford Square Press, 1982).
2. See, for example, King's Fund, *An Ordinary Life: Developing comprehensive locally-based residential services for mentally handicapped people*, Project paper 24 (King's Fund Publishing, 1982); R. Blunden and D. Allen, *Facing the Challenge: An ordinary life for people with learning difficulties and challenging behaviour*, Project Paper 74 (King's Fund Publishing, 1987); S. Ramon, 'The value and knowledge bases of the normalisation approach: implications for social work', *International Social Work*, vol. 32, no. 1 (1989), pp. 1–17; A. Brandon and D. Brandon, *Consumers as Colleagues* (Mind, 1987); Nigel Malin (ed.), *Reassessing Community Care (with particular reference to provision for people with mental handicap and for people with mental illness)* (Croom Helm, 1987).
3. See, for example, Ann Richardson, Judith Unell and Beverly Aston, *A New Deal for Carers* (King's Fund Informal Caring Unit, 1989).
4. See, for example, DHSS, *Mental Handicap: Progress, problems and priorities* (HMSO, 1980); DHSS, *Care in Action: A handbook of policies and priorities for the health and personal services in England* (HMSO, 1981).

5. Peter Beresford and Suzie Croft, *Community Control of Social Services Departments* (Battersea Community Action, 1980); *Towards a Social Strategy* (Battersea Community Action, 1984); *Whose Welfare?* (Lewis Cohen Urban Studies Centre, Brighton Polytechnic, 1986).

6. A. Sutherland, *Disabled We Stand* (Souvenir, 1981); P. Thomas, *The Experience of Handicap* (Methuen, 1982); M. Oliver, *Social Work With Disabled People* (Macmillan, 1987).

7. Green Paper, *Punishment, Custody and the Community*, Cm. 424 (HMSO, 1988).

8. Lena Dominelli, *Anti-racist Social Work* (Macmillan, 1988); Vivienne Coombe and Alan Little, *Race and Social Work* (Tavistock, 1986); A. Ohri, B. Manning and P. Curno, *Community Work and Racism* (Routledge and Kegan Paul, 1982).

9. See, for example, Peter Singer, *Practical Ethics* (Cambridge University Press, 1979), ch. 2.

10. Tariq Modood, '"Black", racial equality and Asian identity', *New Community*, vol. 14, no. 3 (1988), pp. 397–404.

11. Joseph Schumpeter, *Capitalism, Socialism and Democracy* (1943, reprinted by Allen and Unwin, 1961), pp. 250–85.

12. Steven Lukes, *Power: a Radical View*, Macmillan, 1974.

13. This was the dominant view in western liberal circles, following Schumpeter's *Capitalism, Socialism and Democracy*.

14. Keith Graham, 'Morality, individuals and collectives', in J. D. G. Evans (ed.), *Moral Philosophy and Contemporary Problems* (Cambridge University Press, 1988).

15. Frank Cunningham, *Democratic Theory and Socialism* (Cambridge University Press, 1987), pp. 26–7.

16. *Ibid.*, p. 32.

17. *Ibid.*, p. 38.

18. Alasdair MacIntyre, *After Virtue: A study in moral theory* (Duckworth, 1981).

19. Kenneth Arrow, *Social Choice and Individual Values* (Wiley, 1951), ch. 3.

20. Wulf Gaertner, 'On some concepts of distributive justice', paper given at the Conference on the Welfare State, Welfare Economics and Justice, Zentrum for interdisziplinaire Forschung, Bielefeld, W. Germany, 15 June 1989.

21. Robert Axelrod, *The Evolution of Co-operation* (Basic Books, 1984).

22. For example, John Roemer, 'Equality of talent', *Economics and Philosophy*, vol. 1 (1985); Robert J. van der Veen and Philippe Van Parijs, 'A capitalist road to communism', *Theory and Society*, vol. 15 (1986), pp. 635–55; Hillel Steiner, 'The natural right to the means of production', *Philosophical Quarterly*, vol. 27 (1977), pp. 41–9; Ronald Dworkin, 'Equality of resources', *Philosophy and Public Affairs*, vol. 10 (1981), pp. 283–345.

23. Carole Pateman, *Participation and Democratic Theory* (Cam-

bridge University Press, 1970); Ann Richardson, *Participation* (Routledge and Kegan Paul, 1983).

24. Bill Jordan, *The Common Good: Citizenship, morality and self-interest* (Blackwell, 1989), chs 6 and 7.
25. Mike Cooper, 'Community social work', in Bill Jordan and Nigel Parton (eds), *The Political Dimensions of Social Work* (Blackwell, 1983), pp. 146–66; Bob Holman, *Kids at the Door: A preventive project on a council estate* (Blackwell, 1982).
26. See for instance David Towell (ed.), *An Ordinary Life in Practice: Developing comprehensive community-based services for people with learning disabilities* (King's Fund Publishing, 1988).
27. Keith Graham, *The Battle of Democracy* (Wheatsheaf, 1986). For an account of the relevance of democratic theory to decentralisation of local government services, see Paul Hoggett and Robin Hambleton, 'The democratisation of public services', in Paul Hoggett and Robin Hambleton (eds), *Decentralisation and Democracy: Localising public services* (University of Bristol, School for Advanced Urban Studies, 1987), ch. 4.

7

MORAL REASONING AND JUDGEMENT

It is time to go back to the examples of moral dilemmas for social workers and their clients set out in Chapter 1. They were all situations in which people were choosing between courses of action involving their obligations towards or responsibilities for others in their family or community, and their social workers had powers (over resources or to compel) which were relevant to those choices. We are searching for a method of moral reasoning which will allow both to discover what they should do, and to agree on how to do it.

The issues at stake in those particular examples, and in a great deal of present-day social work, are serious ones. They contain the possibility of some people losing their liberty for several years of their lives, of marriages or families breaking up, and even of avoidable death. These people are at turning points in their lives, and the consequences of their decisions are likely to be far-reaching. Their social workers and probation officers have considerable potential influence over their choices, and power to overrule them if they consider them to be wrong. So how can both parties discover the right thing to do?

My argument so far has been concerned mainly with providing an ethical situation or setting for this question. I have put a case against the notion that morality is all about abstract principles. Ethical reasoning takes place within groups and communities, with shared resources and shared conceptions of their common interests. It provides a way in which individuals can relate their own good to the good of others, and debate about what is for the good of all the community's members. In this way, individuals can have reasons for choosing certain actions which are not derived from their own ('internal')[1] sets of preferences or sympathies, but which are derived from the social choices of the collective of which they are part (i.e., they are 'internal' to the collective preferences and sympathies of the social unit). But these 'external' reasons both move individuals, and have some moral force, because as members they play a part in making collective decisions, and are therefore jointly responsible with fellow members of the good of their community.

This has an important bearing on questions about what these clients and their social workers should do. I want to claim that the standards which apply to their deliberations are *objective*, in the sense that they come from outside these individuals, but not *absolute*, in the sense of rationally unquestionable, applying without exception, and answering every moral question.[2] The reasoning that will be applied to these examples is not intended to be that of a strictly neutral outside observer, but that which seems relevant to their situation in modern British society.

But it has also been argued, especially in Chapter 3, that ethical standards cannot just be derived from the way actual communities do things. There are plenty of real-life communities with the most objectionable institutions and practices, and present-day Britain is, on my analysis, a clear example of an unjust society. So we also need some way of criticising and discriminating between communities, to judge which are good and just, and which are not. I have argued for standards of justice which allow all citizens a share of rights and resources that gives them equal autonomy, and a share in a good quality of life. This involves an appeal to human rights – the idea of the whole of humanity as a community with common interests, and of what is due to each member of the human race.

So I am arguing that clients and social workers meet as fellow citizens, to reason together about the ethical decisions that confront them. This means that they meet in the real context of relations not only within their society – its laws, conventions and values – but also within a wider context of human relations. Social workers must take seriously clients' commitments to the culture and practices of which they are members; clients must take account of the laws and procedures under which social workers do their jobs. But both must also be willing to reason with each other in terms of standards which transcend these, and refer to the better and more just society which theirs could become.

For example, the facts that a client holds racist attitudes, lives in a racist community and has commitments to racist groups may clearly be relevant to his or her encounter with a social worker, especially if the social worker is black; the concept of equal citizenship provides a standard against which to challenge such allegiances. But the facts that a social worker holds coercive power, belongs to a department that has policies of using it against certain groups and has been identified with the implementation of these policies in the neighbourhood may also be relevant. A social worker who is a well-adjusted member of an oppressive agency is no more ethically justified than a well-adjusted member of a racist district.

If we accept this view, then much of social work, and much of the work required in the case examples, will consist of ethical reasoning, including disagreements about moral principles and how to apply them. These disagreements leave open the possibility of reasoned persuasion; each party argues that the others, if they were to consider the problem in a reasonable manner from what is claimed to be the appropriate perspective, would come to the same conclusions.[3]

The point of arguing in this way is to persuade others to adopt certain principles as their own. This can operate at several levels. Take the situation of David Jackson proposing to share his senior's post. When he first suggests this to the team, he may only need to point out that this is an example of the sharing of power and resources which they all in principle endorse; in this case, the argument will be about whether it is an appropriate example, and whether some other principle overrides it. Alternatively, it may be that the team has never discussed sharing (even though they practise it in various ways among themselves), so he needs to urge them to accept it as a general principle of their working life, and then press his job-share as an example. This is likely to be a longer and more far-reaching argument, taking more aspects of the team's relations into account. Lastly, it may be that the team has a strictly individualised system of responsibility, with hierarchical accountability through David as senior, to which they are strongly committed, in principle and in practice. In this case he has a much more protracted and difficult set of discussions and disputes on his hands, trying to convince them that an entirely different structure would produce fairer relations and better social work. David is required to challenge the team's rules, and propose that it adopts new principles, new definitions of rights and roles, and a new conception of the good team. To do this he must appeal to standards outside the present culture and practices, and show how these would be better and more justifiable ones.

There is still something missing from this analysis, though: something extremely important for the case examples we are about to consider. One of the reasons that David might use in his debates with an individualistic, hierarchical team would be that its present structure provides a distorted situation for moral reasoning about individual cases. If social workers are themselves part of a structure in which there is no sharing and co-operation, there are great inequalities of income, power and responsibility, there are no black people in positions of authority or influence, women are all subordinates, and so on, then each one of them is likely to reason about their cases in a way that reflects this structure. As part of a team with unequal, unjust relations, they will be more prone to accept standards of practice which reflect similar relationships – clients excluded from any control over decisions, the use of coercion, rationing of resources, discrimination against black clients, and so on. David can argue that a more egalitarian, co-operative team structure would promote the principles of democracy, sharing and negotiation in all their work.

Yet this leaves something out of the account. Even under the individualised, hierarchical structure, not all the social workers would practise in the same way. Some might well have strong principles of their own, derived from working elsewhere, from training, or from personal experiences. A personal commitment to a more democratic, shared, negotiated style of practice could be just as important an influence on how this particular social worker handled situations like our case examples as the structure of the team. Conversely, even if David succeeds in persuading all the team to adopt the new principles to their relations with each other, not every member will apply them to her work in the same way. Each will have to try to accommodate them to her previous principles and practices, and the results will differ a good deal from one social worker to another.

The same, of course, is true for clients; they will not all apply principles in the same way, and the process of absorbing them into one life may yield very different results in another. The missing something that we are seeking in this chapter is an analysis of how individuals come to make ethical principles their own, and use them to guide their choices. The point about the case examples is not to ask what it is right for clients in general to do, but what these particular clients should do in their situations. Michael's choice should not just be right, it should be Michael's.[4]

Ethics in the middle ground

As was pointed out at the end of Chapter 1, the Smortham story and the case examples serve rather different purposes. The clients in the case examples have real-life problems; the workers in Smortham have principles. For the latter, I have provided only the briefest of biographical detail; we know the minimum about the private lives of the social workers, for example. Even David and Sarah Jackson, about whom we know slightly more, remain essentially shadowy. Why, for instance, did David suddenly get uncomfortable about the balance of his role and Sarah's? Was it a book he read, a conversation in the pub, the break-up of a friend's marriage, or the tired, sad look of Sarah last Friday evening? What effect, if any, will it have on his liking for football, or his consumption of beer? His new principles have origins and implications. Moral reasoning takes place somewhere between a person's experiences and the standards to which they subscribe.

To be able to reason about what is the right thing for an individual to do, we must know about, and take account of, his or her projects and commitments – plans and purposes pursued over time, relationships, associations and beliefs. David and Sarah have other options which we have not discussed. They could sell their house in West Smortham and move to an area where housing is cheaper. This would allow him to work for a voluntary agency, where his pay would be lower, but the policies and structures would be more in line with his principles. Sarah too could transfer to a housing charity, and do campaigning or advocacy work on behalf of homeless people. Unless we know more about them, we will not be able to say whether these options would be better or worse than the one set out in the story.

But this implies that ethical reasoning is not just a matter of discovering the relevant principles for a given set of circumstances, and then drawing a conclusion that would apply equally to any individual who was in those circumstances. It suggests that what is right for one person to do in this situation is not necessarily right for another. David is right to share his job and the housework, but that would not be right for Daniel or Desmond. They could find equally valid moral justifications for making other choices, given that they are themselves, and not David.

This sounds dangerous. It seems to imply that moral judgements depend on subjective factors (preferences, tastes), and are quite arbitrary. What is right for me depends on my point of view, and the principles I happen to choose; if I think you are wrong to take a certain action, and you think you are right, we are not even disagreeing, because we are merely stating our own perspectives on that action.[5] This puts social workers in a very awkward position. Suppose Michael's probation officer wants to try to persuade him to accept an offer from his father to have Michael home again. Michael says no: he will go his own way. If Michael's choice is consistent (he is being 'true to himself') then there seems little left to say.

This does not necessarily follow from the idea that one course of action is right for David (or Michael) but not for Daniel or Desmond. In reasoning about the decision which is *his*, each of these individuals must consider all the factors mentioned in the previous section (the human rights of the other people involved, his commitments to them as a member of the same family, group, neighbourhood, community, etc., and the standards of behaviour by which the good of those social units is upheld), but also the shape and direction of his own life, and how he reconciles the sometimes conflicting requirements of his projects and relationships. This tries to capture the idea that someone's principles are not just the ideas that they share with others who bind themselves to similar rules of conduct, or join the same clubs; they are the ways in which that individual shapes and steers his life, and – having decided how he should live it – gives expression to his identity through his choices.[6]

These same considerations apply to the social workers in the case examples. How they respond to their clients' dilemmas will depend substantially on the culture of their teams, and the action-guiding standards that these have generated.[7] In most social work settings, these include sensitivity, courage, resilience, humour, and a refusal to be panicked. More fundamentally, they will include ideas about why they became social workers in the first place (for instance, about the worth of each individual, or the possibility of meaningful communication). But underpinning even these general principles is each social worker's moral direction, including the commitment to try to do the right thing as often as possible. This last level of ethical energy and purpose is far broader and deeper than the role of social worker; it both informs and integrates all the person's roles. It also allows some distance and room for manoeuvre between the person and the role being played.[8]

Researchers often report that social workers seem inanely eclectic and unprincipled in their practice; they seldom relate their methods or decisions to theory, and say things like 'it just feels right for me'.[9] This may not be as unreflective and uncritical as it sounds. In the last resort, social workers have to do things that they are prepared to stand by – often to stand by in the witness box, because they involve the use of compulsory power to override clients' wishes. Moral commitment to these choices cannot come only from general principles or rules of good practice; it has to come from themselves as moral actors, playing a role which is necessarily underscripted, and requires the exercise of personal judgement and hunches as well as professional knowledge and skill.

This also helps to explain why social workers often learn most from their mistakes, and from breaking what they took to be inviolable principles. The rules we give ourselves to guide our actions and decisions are seldom ultimate; they are subject to amendment or even radical alteration. Sometimes this process comes from reflection, but at other times it comes from the shock of realising that we have broken a cherished maxim. My analysis suggests that this is because in the last resort the resolve to try to do the right thing in each individual situation, and to make choices we are willing to claim as ours, is stronger and more persuasive than our adherence to general rules.

Relationships and moral reasoning

So far this chapter has argued for a discussion of the ethical issues in the case examples which is both objective, in the sense that it relates to standards external to the client and the social worker yet makes moral claims on both, but also relative, in the sense that it acknowledges that each must choose not only what is right but also what is right for him- or herself. This is a case for ethical reasoning in the 'middle ground', between the absolute demands of universal principles, and the subjective wants and emotions of individual people.[10]

This sounds as if it fits quite neatly with my emphasis on negotiation and dialogue in the previous two chapters. The analysis of morally justifiable social choice has been in terms of democratic participation and debate towards decisions which are acceptable to all, by individuals and groups who meet on terms of membership of a community which recognises common interests in a good quality of life, and gives each a fair share of rights and resources. This implies that my account of how people should choose and act is located in something like the real world rather than on a hypothetical desert island, or behind a veil of ignorance, as in the theories of many modern political philosophers.

But my borough of Smortham is not the real world, it is an idealised and stylised one, where people not only make remarkably moral decisions but also get optimistically generous responses for doing so from others. David Jackson and his colleagues appear somewhat magically to have preferences which are 'refined' (in the sense of taking account of others' needs) rather than 'brute' (in the sense of being crudely self-interested). Even though they use everyday language and arguments to reach their ethical conclusions, under everyday circumstances, they seem nonetheless to be more consistently and determinedly moral and self-improving than people in the real world.

The case examples set a sterner test of the arguments developed so far. There is no reason to suppose that the clients will always act morally, or have any special interest in ethical or political issues. Like most people, they can be assumed to regard large areas of their lives as spheres in which self-interested decision-making applies. What is more, their circumstances are unpromising ones for moral deliberation. In the first place, the clients are in rather highly-charged or desperate situations, in various states of emotional distress or crisis. Although the circumstances do – in most cases – involve commitments to others, their feelings run against reflective consideration of these commitments, and towards choices that are survival orientated. In this sense, their emotional turmoil (including feelings of guilt, resentment and confusion) leads them away from decisions which take account of others' needs and towards a kind of selfishness which stems from the need for self-protection. They are likely to be in a state of mind which is not so much immoral or amoral as no fit state for moral reasoning and choosing.

Second, if we are to see the social workers' role as in any sense one of a moral coach – someone who helps clients reflect on the ethical implications of their situation, reason about it, and act morally – then we must examine their credentials for this role. Some of these are not very satisfactory. Unlike other moral coaches – such as confidants, confessors and gurus – they have not been chosen by the client; indeed, the client probably does not immediately want any form of moral coaching from anyone. Unlike those others, they have powers to enforce their advice, or to withhold helpful resources if they disapprove of the client's choices. And they may well also have a history of antagonistic relations with this client, or another family member, or a neighbour, to contend with, or simply be part of a department with a record of unpopularity because of high-handedness or seeming indifference towards this client's or others' needs. For all these reasons, the social worker is often not the obviously best person to create the atmosphere for reflective consideration in which the kinds of choice I have outlined are likely to be made.

This, of course, applies both to the direct conversations between the client and the social worker, and to any family, group or neighbourhood meeting the social worker might try to arrange, in which the issues might be debated and negotiated according to the proposed principles. In either situation, some of the social worker's formal characteristics (as a middle-class official or as a power-holder) work against moral deliberation. These arguments strengthen the case for community involvement because this allows some of these formal attributes to be softened and the social worker to emerge more as an ordinary person sharing in many of the issues of the client's world than as a remote official.

These adverse factors also help explain why social workers consider it important to 'build up a relationship' with a client and to continue contacts over a period of time. The idea behind this is usually expressed in terms of the need to develop trust and empathy, so that clients feel safe to explore painful issues, and gain sufficient support to envisage the challenge of change. None of this is inconsistent with the view being developed here. If social work is concerned with reasoning about fairness in relationships, as argued in the last chapter, then it is essential to create a climate of security and trust in which co-operative and reciprocal thinking can flourish.

One school of thought emphasises clarity about the goals and the terms of the relationship as a basis for trust and co-operation. This school looks to contracts which specify the tasks and the duration of the work that they will undertake together to avoid the vague, open-ended nature of much social work.[11] The psychodynamic and interactionist literature emphasises the importance of regular and rewarding interviews, in which the client experiences a sense of goodwill, and an accurate understanding of his or her feelings.[12] In this way the relationship itself becomes an important element in the atmosphere for this kind of thinking and choosing to emerge. Words like 'genuineness' and 'empathy' in accounts of successful and effective practice indicate a moral dimension to the encounter, where the issues are serious, and involve values and commitments which are central to the clients' beliefs and hopes about themselves and their relationships.

Negotiation and counselling

In the previous two chapters I have tried to make a case for a definition of fairness in relationships between members of a shared project (including a community) which rests on equal control (voice) and equalisation of benefits and burdens (within a context of differing abilities and needs). I have also argued that social work is part of a system (ideally a democratic one) by which people with special needs seek resources to meet these, and people who have suffered wrongs, or have perpetrated wrongs, can discover agreed ways of righting them. This implies that social work is crucially concerned with fairness, both in redistributing resources to people in need (especially the needs associated with physical and mental handicaps, mental illness and old age) and in negotiations over problems in relationships in families, neighbourhoods and communities.

But social workers are not arbiters or judges – they do not claim to be disinterested adjudicators on legal or moral issues according to strict interpretations of rules. Nor are they bureaucrats, in the sense that they dispense standard rations of services or benefits according to written regulations. Rather they are officials who assess people for discretionary benefits and services (mostly given in kind), where the assessment involves negotiations about fairness and need (for example, how does an old person's need for day care relate to her carer's need for a break). They are mediators or conciliators too in crises and disputes in people's relationships, where negotiations about fairness have some chance of resulting in an agreement between the parties.[13] The compulsory power they have usually takes the form of an authority to refer people to an official (legal) arbiter – a court or tribunal – or to another professional body – such as a psychiatric hospital – rather than to impose their own authoritative solution on the situation, and an authority to supervise people's performance of their obligations after such a decision has been given.

This is a deceptively simple description of a complex activity. The examples of clients' situations indicate the range of desperate or dangerous situations that can present themselves to social workers, with someone (often not the person identified as having 'the most serious problem') demanding that a resolution (often requiring a major change) must be found. It is all too common for these situations to present themselves to social workers only at the stage when all the parties have despaired of finding an agreed solution or one which allows their previous relationships and commitments to continue – a stage, in other words, at which the standards of fairness which govern the relations in that particular group or community have already been so seriously breached that someone is demanding either an end to their mutual commitment as members, or the imposition of some external, compulsory control or punishment. Although to describe what is required as 'negotiation' may do justice to much of what goes on in everyday social work – checking out an old person's need for home help or a home adaptation, calming ruffled feathers after a family row or a teenage outburst – this description hardly fits the difficult processes demanded by the examples, or the skills required to resolve the moral dilemmas and the interpersonal conflicts they pose.

What is especially difficult about these situations is that the choices to be made seem so all-or-nothing – to have such potentially drastic long-term consequences – and that the clients are trying to make them under pressure of extreme material adversity or emotional pressure. In this sense they are not ordinary situations; they are just the kinds of situation we would all hope never to be in ourselves. Furthermore, as ordinary people, we would hope never to be called on to try to resolve such situations; and if we were, we would probably look for the first opportunity to hand the responsibility on to someone else, usually a social worker. In this sense social work is, as someone once remarked, about being ordinary in unordinary situations[14] – about introducing and maintaining ordinary standards and behaviour like fairness, consideration, patience, forgiveness, courage and kindness in circumstances of high conflict, fear, confusion or despair. The most skilful social workers are able to get people who have recently been violent, terrified, bizarre, mute or manic to talk and eventually to act in ways which put them back in touch with those ordinary standards and qualities of their life, and to reason with others about what should happen next.

The willingness and ability to tackle such responsibilities are what social workers are paid for; after all, plenty of others (and especially plenty of women) spend a great deal of their lives patching up ordinary quarrels, consoling ordinary sadnesses, and reasoning with ordinary over-reactions, without being paid to do so. Social workers' professional skill is in creating the conditions for negotiation from these very difficult initial situations and fraught feelings, and sustaining negotiations which are always threatened by this background. These skills in handling deep rage, hurt, shame, ambivalence, melancholy and euphoria within a framework of ordinariness (rather than an aura of expertise) has gone by various names – none particularly pleasant – in social work literature. It used to be called 'casework', but associations with complacency and conservatism caused it to be changed to 'counselling'. Service users do not particularly like that word either, since they tend to regard it as implying manipulation and mystification, often disguising the real (unfair) intentions of the worker. But at its best, counselling which consists in getting people back in touch with the coping strengths that can allow them to survive crises, to negotiate conflicts and to move forward in their lives is indeed a skill, and one which is valuable precisely because of its connections with ordinariness.

In another sense too, social workers' skill lies in their ability to be effective in unpromising situations. The ancient professions – medicine, law, teaching – are all very concerned with the same range of issues (meeting special needs, resolving conflicts and sustaining reasoned discussion), but they set about their tasks in very different ways. First, they lay claim to exclusive professional expertise, and often use a largely private professional language which they do not share with their clienteles. Second, they take pains to practise in special (and often especially formal and imposing) settings like hospitals, courts and schools, where they are at an advantage and their clienteles are at a disadvantage. Third, they reserve for themselves powers to impose their decisions on their clienteles, as expert solutions to their problems. Although social work has sometimes tried to ape these aspects of those professions, its best traditions are surely quite different. Social workers are willing and able to work in informal and chaotic settings, like people's homes, community centres or clubs; they should be able to explain what they are doing in ordinary language, and hence to expose their thinking to critical scrutiny by their clients; they seek agreements rather than imposing solutions by the use of power, except as a last resort. Their expertise is therefore shared with their clients in a far more transparent way, and within a more equal relationship, which means that they can be called into question more readily, and are more vulnerable to criticism. If the basis for their work is fairness and co-operation, the discomfort this brings seems worthwhile.

This account of social workers' professional skills is certainly not orthodox. Most theories of counselling emphasise the ability to solve problems and accomplish change, rather than skills in negotiating and reaching agreements (the exception here being writings about conciliation in custody and divorce). I have suggested that the ability to listen in a special and creative way, to communicate understanding and support, to elicit deep fears and feelings, and provide constructive feedback, are all means to an end which involves negotiation and agreement. Solving problems and changing are outcomes of a process in which clients choose how to live their own lives and how to share with others. Counselling is not a way of getting people to make particular choices but a way of reaching the point where they can reason about these choices and make them in a particular way – reflectively and, if possible, after discussion and agreement. This may be the end of a long process, in which the client takes much time to express hurt, anger, remorse or loss – raw feelings that overwhelm the possibility of moral reasoning. But the point of the counselling process is not to purge these feelings (as if they were an illness) but to reach a point of readiness for choosing actions and commitments with realistic assessments of their own and others' needs. Thus there are two processes of change – one which restores some kind of reflective equilibrium, the other in which the clients embark on the next stage of their life. (This is even more marked in work which can properly be described as 'therapeutic', in which the first stage often takes place under very artificial conditions and 'rules' – as for instance in psychodrama or gestalt therapy – and prepares participants for actions and choices which they may never even report back to the therapist or the group.)

One of the commonest problems in social work is that there is no time to go through these two stages consecutively. When social workers complain that they get no chance to do the 'real' work (counselling), and that they are constantly dealing with crises, this seems to be what they usually mean. In fact, of course, it would be surprising if their caseload did not include a high proportion of situations which are experienced as crises by their clients, in the sense that they feel stressed, frightened or out of control. But this only becomes a crisis for the social worker if an important decision has to be made straight away, before there is time to use counselling skills to try to re-establish a reflective equilibrium, or to make space for discussion by reducing stress or giving some of the parties supported 'time out'. Under pressure for instant action, social workers feel that there is no opportunity to reach the point where proper negotiations about the real issues can take place, and real agreements be struck. Instead there are instant decisions to be made (whether to admit a child to care, whether to take proceedings for breach of probation, whether to apply for compulsory admission to hospital) which do not address the fundamental, underlying questions for the client. Often these actions further obscure the issues and postpone consideration of the really relevant choices. When social workers then have to rush off to yet another crisis in someone else's life, involving yet another pressured yet tangential decision, these real issues may never actually be tackled. This takes its toll on social workers' morale, and develops one side of their skills – managing crises – at the expense of their ability to create conditions for addressing long-term patterns in relationships and behaviour.

Crises and moral dilemmas

The examples in Chapter 1 were chosen so as to introduce an

element of pressure from time and the rush of events into the dilemmas facing clients and social workers. Michael, the black youth, is likely to get into trouble again soon if nothing changes. Donna, the runaway teenager, is acting in such a way as to force a decision, and her parents are insisting on the opposite choice. Louise, the single parent, has the offer of a job and her children's needs are pressing. Brian, the ex-offender, is up against the hostel's time limit on his stay there. Samantha must decide whether she is going to return to Nigel when she leaves hospital, and the staff are already saying that she is really no longer ill. Joan the carer is near the end of her tether, and feels unable to care for her mother much longer. George, the old man with the heart condition, must leave hospital in one direction or other in the next couple of days, and his life is at stake.

As we have seen in Chapters 2 and 3, their social workers can find ways of responding to these pressures which appear to discharge their moral responsibilities for these clients, either by putting the full burden of the decisions to be made squarely back onto them, or by taking matters right out of their hands, by making a purely procedural decision to do something for them or to them, without any real attempt to discuss or agree on the underlying moral issues. Much social work done under pressure takes one or other of these forms. But the complaint that this is not 'real' social work, although it is ostensibly one about job satisfaction ('my work would be more rewarding if I had the space to do much more counselling'), seems to be as much about the moral discomfort of leaving clients with far too little support in some cases, and imposing unconvincing, unilateral decisions on others, so that every crisis evokes a pseudo-resolution which is in fact no answer to the issues it raises. Not only is this unsatisfying in itself, but also its consequences tend to come back to haunt the social worker, as these false solutions soon break down, and the clients return with another crisis.

Even in the best-organised and best-resourced agencies, social workers will sometimes be faced with situations of this kind. If we recognise that our discomfort in them stems at least in part from the difficulty in handling moral issues under these pressures, it is important to analyse both what is most problematic for the worker, and how some space can be made to address these matters. It seems that the hardest thing is to make some connection with that part of the client's thoughts and feelings which is also dimly aware of the issues that are being evaded, of the futility of the proposed solutions, and of the moral surrender that is occurring. It is far easier to assume that no such thoughts and feelings exist – that the client is so hell-bent on self-destruction, so mad, so terrified, so drunk or so angry that nothing will deflect him or her from a pre-set path; and that the social worker's only choices are to go along with it or to oppose it with unilateral compulsory force. If the social worker allows the moral issues to enter her conscious-ness at all, they weigh all the heavier on her because of the belief that they cannot be discussed or shared with the client in the high emotion of the crisis, and therefore that she must handle them alone.

Yet most experienced social workers have on some occasions felt brave and inspired enough to communicate just these despairing or disconsolate thoughts to a client in such circumstances, and have known the relief and the moral uplift it has given them to see the significance of their confession recognised by the client, and reflected in a change of mood and tone in the encounter. Janet Mattinson and Ian Sinclair recount how Mrs Yates, a long-term client with serious marital problems, violently challenged a worker's decision not to give her money for the weekend, and threatened to abandon her children in the waiting room.

> The area officer and I needed each other for support to withstand the fury and obstinacy with which we were confronted. In desperation I asked Mrs Yates why she had to make us behave like such bastards towards her. She screamed that we were bastards and rather wearily I agreed that maybe we were. Almost at once she began to soften and decided to leave with the children. She left us drained and shattered.[15]

In my own early social work experience, the guilt and self-disgust I felt about ducking out of situations, in which I felt intimidated or inadequate, by taking courses of action I strongly suspected were evasions of the real issues, led me to a radical reassessment of my own practice. I reached the conclusion that the clients I found most alarming or undermining were those who were most frightened of their own primitive feelings, and that they communicated this fear to me in such a way that I felt compelled to protect them or others from them. Determined to put this right, I looked for ways of withstanding the pressures they put on me in crises, mainly by seeking the chance to feed back to them my own worst feelings, and suggesting that perhaps they felt these themselves, and feared that they would be overwhelmed, or become murderous, mad or suicidal.

This simple method of sticking with people under extreme pressure, refusing to be panicked, but acknowledging fear, uncertainty and hopelessness and their disabling effects, seemed to work; people who previously had insisted that the only answers to their problems were to move away (with a cash handout), to separate from spouses, to put their children into care or to enter psychiatric hospital gradually found other ways of dealing with the crises which had become a feature of their lives. Eventually most of them stopped having crises. The ideas which inspired these ways of working provided the basis of my first two books about social work,[16] and remained fundamental to my own practice for twenty years.

Here is an example of a crisis in a mental health setting, taken from *Invitation to Social Work*.[17] At the time I was working in a peripatetic interdisciplinary team, which used a church hall in a small seaside town as its base once a week. The team aimed to give low-key preventive assistance to individuals and families under stress, and had no psychiatrist among its members; there were therefore rather strict limits to our ability to handle serious mental illness.

Reg, aged 70, and frail-looking, was referred to us as depressed and lethargic. At first he could say little about himself or his problems, but with encouragement he revealed that he had been a highly skilled engineer in his working days, and a brilliant if eccentric amateur inventor, a charming man whose council house and garden were stocked with novel devices of his creation. Reg had been seriously ill ten years previously, had had to leave his life-long occupation, and had become depressed and rather dependent on his forthright, no-nonsense wife May. She was mainly concerned about one problem – Reg had fairly recently committed an offence of shoplifting and had a court appearance, and she was terrified of a recurrence of this.

We worked with Reg and May for a time, and he became much more cheerful and active, and left the clinic. But one day Reg arrived unexpectedly, and in a terrible state. He was almost mute with distress, weeping and holding his head. It emerged that he had been shoplifting again, that although he had not been prosecuted this had come out, and May was beside herself with fury, threatening never to let him see his grandchildren again. He hinted at suicide, and also at the need to be admitted to hospital; my colleagues were alarmed at his condition, and thought an admission was indicated, but I suggested an alternative course. I walked home with Reg, and we waited until May returned from shopping. She was as distressed as Reg, but it all came out in angry rejection – with Reg mainly, but also with us and the doctor for not listening to her, and for not taking his shoplifting seriously. Reg listened in frozen alarm as she described his intolerable behaviour – his obstinate and rather manic activity up to the offence, his self-destructive depression since – and said that either he must be admitted or she would leave, perhaps to hospital herself. I acknowledged our fault in not listening well enough to her, and her real distress. But I tried to reach the sadness and fear behind her anger, pointing out that they were near the end of their lives, had had a good – if sometimes stormy – marriage, and how Reg, if he went into hospital at this stage, might well die there. Eventually May burst into tears, and went and embraced Reg, so that they were weeping together. I visited again that evening and several times during the week, keeping in touch by telephone between visits. The general practitioner was very supportive and concerned, and a home visit was paid by a psychiatrist. Reg was put on a new medication, and gradually the storm died down. In weeks normality was restored. I kept in touch with them by regular visits until Reg's death, some two years later, and I still see May now. Although his final years were difficult, they were together, and May's memories of him are happy ones.

In the next chapter, I show how the same methods might be used by the social workers faced by the crises in the lives of the clients used as examples in the first chapter.

Criteria for non-manipulative negotiation

Social workers often feel in a weak and vulnerable position,

but clients do not always see them that way. They do in fact
have formidable compulsory powers, and they gatekeep for
various resources which can represent the difference between
surviving or succumbing for clients. We have already noted
that clients often see social workers' methods as a form of
clever manipulation to achieve their covert ends. Even the
ability to feed back feelings or marshal arguments about the
wider implications of choices can be powerfully influential on
the outcomes of such situations. In a series of role plays
performed with a colleague and chosen to illustrate ways of
working in crises of this kind, my colleague remarked that my
methods made him feel 'cornered' or 'trapped' into facing issues
that he did not really want to face.

But manipulation is a two-way street. Social workers often
describe their most difficult clients (the ones who are most
prone to these crises) as 'manipulative'. Although the word is
somewhat over-used, what is being described is a feeling that
there is something wilful and not quite spontaneous about the
way a crisis is presented, orchestrated and choreographed. The
timing is just a little too professional, the one-liners a touch too
glib. After several such performances, the social worker begins
to be familiar with the script, and to recognise the cues for
lights, music, action, tears and laughter. The suspicion of bad
faith creeps in, disbelief is no longer so easily suspended, and
the worker begins to resent the rather gullible and collusive
role that she is being invited to take. Far from feeling a moral
obligation to uncover the underlying issues by exposing her
own vulnerability and ethical perplexity, she wants to even up
the scores; she may even be tempted to resort to some dirty
tricks of her own. The famous 'paradoxical injunctions' of one
school of family therapy (advising clients to do just what they
are doing already in an even more exaggerated and stagey
way) might be seen in this light; so might one or two of my own
descriptions of my responses to what seemed like over-
rehearsed and excessively long-running performances by some
of my more jaded mental health clients.

I would argue that social workers and clients are both bound
by the same standards for ordinary human conduct that people
can reasonably expect of each other in their particular
community. Under normal circumstances, politeness, consider-

ation and reliability are part of this reasonable expectation –
but these circumstances are not normal. Clients are under
great stress, and even if this is of their own making it is
nonetheless destructive or debilitating. Social workers too are
under stress, from the crisis itself, and from pressure of other
priorities. Often the physical conditions in which they meet are
far from relaxing or reassuring. So one or other of them needs
to appeal to those ordinary standards in an extraordinary
situation; usually it is the social worker who is in the better
position to do so. Sometimes she has to resort to unusual
methods to achieve this, as in this example from Janet
Mattinson and Ian Sinclair. The project worker had called to
offer Mr and Mrs Mothersill regular appointments, but on
gaining admission to their dark basement flat, and asking
them whether they wanted these, an argument broke out
between the couple.

> In the response they began to shout at each other at the tops of their
> voices. I could not understand what they were shouting about, so I
> repeated my question. They continued to shout, and again I
> repeated my question, and again they went on shouting, the noise
> they were making getting, if anything, even louder. Eventually I
> shouted above the din that what they seemed to be asking me was
> whether I could *stand* coming once a week to discuss their marital
> problems. At once they fell quiet, and Mr Mothersill then said 'in a
> manner of speaking' that seemed to be what they were asking.[18]

My own rather more theatrical method of conveying a similar
message is described in *Helping in Social Work*.[19] A middle-
aged woman patient in the psychiatric hospital requested an
appointment, commenting to her fellow patients that I should
'turn on the tape recorder'. As soon as she sat down, she shut
her eyes and launched into a rambling, flat monologue about
her problems, scarcely drawing breath. After staying silent for
some time, I quietly got out of my chair, and sat behind my
desk, where I could no longer see her. After a while I shouted
'Stop' in the middle of one of her sentences, and then pointed
out that this was what she made me feel like doing, since she
was neither behaving like nor treating me like a human being.
After becoming angry and tearful, she said she knew she drove
people away from her, and began a rather successful process of

getting to grips with the fundamental problems in her relationships.

The appeal to these ordinary standards of behaviour seems to me to be an implicit attempt to create conditions for reflective deliberation on the fundamental issues at stake, and for negotiations in which neither side will manipulate the other. Once these negotiations begin, the implicit principle which governs them is once more that of fairness. But the issues at stake are usually intimate and complex personal ones, and the process of uncovering and clarifying them may be protracted. Past wrongs, injustices, hurts, abuses and exploitations; old confusions, evasions and self-deceptions; former fantasies and frustrations; all these will need to be expressed, explored and examined. Crude judgements cannot be applied to such questions as are raised by these experiences.

Take two of our examples. Brian, the ex-offender, has been abused by his parents, wronged by past foster parents and care staff, neglected by an indifferent series of social workers, punished by the courts and bullied by his fellow prisoners. He in his turn has been secretive, stubborn, obsessive, deceptive and, above all, dishonest; he has cultivated an unlovable defence against the rejections and abuses that have been heaped upon him since his early childhood. But since he came to the hostel, Brian has been trying to be more open, more spontaneous and authentic, more willing to express his feelings and be vulnerable; in particular, he has tried to be like this with Sandra, and has benefited from her encouragement and support. It is typical of Brian, of course, that when he felt the plan to move him on from the hostel as a threat to reject him he should write this in a diary (but leave it out to be seen) rather than tell Sandra directly. But is this mere 'manipulation'? It would be easier for Sandra if she could tell herself it is, but she really knows that it is just what he is feeling.

On her side, Sandra wants to bring the discussion of his leaving and his threat to reoffend out into the open, and to help Brian express his feelings of hurt and fear in words and actions so they can communicate about the decision. But she is uncomfortable over the implication that his feelings for her include sexual attraction and emotional possessiveness, both because of the inappropriateness of these responses, and because she fears the obsessive, intense side of Brian's personality. She would far rather evade the personal issues raised by this part of the message, but she knows they are not incidental, or irrelevant to his future chances of living independently and staying out of trouble. In this sense, it would not be fair to pretend that she had not grasped this element of the diary entry.

Joan presents quite a different problem for her social worker. Since she was young, Joan has always helped others in her family – first her younger sister, who was mildly spastic, and needed practical assistance; then her husband's father, who was a widower and lived with them for many years; then her husband, who had a serious accident at work, and eventually died of a brain tumour ten years ago; and lastly her mother, whose rapid deterioration during the three years she has been living with Joan has caused the present crisis. Joan is only too willing to accept more than her share of the burdens of her commitments, and to forgo the benefits. Her social worker suspects that Joan's mother has always somewhat dominated her and taken advantage of her kind, tolerant and giving nature.

Day care resources are in short supply, and it will be extremely difficult to get what Joan's mother needs, and what will allow Joan to take the job she yearns for. The social worker has recently spent much time fighting on clients' behalf for just these resources, and this has taken its toll. Even if she can succeed, she suspects that the old lady will be very difficult and make as much fuss as she can to stop Joan working. She rather dreads having to negotiate the whole thing with her. So the social worker is strongly tempted to persuade Joan to go on coping for a little longer – something she suspects she could, without too much difficulty, achieve. But this would involve a form of manipulation, playing on Joan's sense of duty, rather than allowing her sense of fairness and her assertiveness of her own needs to gain in strength.

These examples help to explain why good listening and empathy have so much prominence in the literature on social work practice. The social worker needs to be able to tune in to what the client is saying on several different wavelengths, getting messages from body language, from silence, and from the emotional tone, as well as from the words being said. Only by an accurate appreciation of all these elements can she really hear what the client is saying about the situation, and be in a position to help him or her deliberate on choices of action.

But it is not only the client that she needs to listen and attend to. Her own responses, and especially her less rational and appropriate feelings, will be important clues about what is going on. If she feels strongly protective or sympathetic, as much as if she feels angry, impatient or cool towards the client, this will indicate something about the interaction, and be evidence of the client's unexpressed needs as well as her own responses. A non-manipulative negotiation of the moral issues will not be a dispassionate, disengaged, cerebral investigation, carried out between two super-rational people. In matters of close personal relationships, or of individual identities and life-plans, strong primitive feelings and mutual emotional influences are inevitable; reflective deliberation will be achieved only through acknowledging and using these positively. They help both sides to understand the significance of events, their impact on relationships, and their implications for commitments. The criteria for non-manipulative negoti-ations are more about a shared understanding of these factors than about their elimination.

The nature of obligations

Once the crisis is contained, the conditions for deliberation and negotiation achieved, and the issues at stake explored, the question that the client has to answer can be simply stated: 'What should I do?' If the social worker's response to the crisis and its aftermath has been successful, the question may be better posed as: 'What should we do?', in acknowledgement of a sharing of responsibility between them, and the support being offered to the client. In this sense, the decision-making process may have become more of a shared one, but the question remains essentially the same even with this modification.

In the Kantian view of moral exploration, the outcome should be the discovery of an obligation, such as the duty to perform a certain action in obedience to the requirement of an ethical principle. In any strict interpretation of the notion of an obligation, it is morally binding; it serves to discriminate between individuals, picking out one as having this duty; it excludes some options; and it indicates an action to be chosen. So the uncovering of the relevant obligation should indicate to each client what he or she should do.

But obligations are not the only kinds of ethical consideration that should enter the dialogue between social worker and client. As Bernard Williams has pointed out, moral philosophy since Kant has tended to deal in a form of morality which focuses on obligations, and sees the morally binding force of an obligation as being overruled only by another (usually more general) obligation.[20] But this is misleading. An obligation (for instance, to keep a promise to visit a friend) can be overruled by the urgent and immediate needs of a complete stranger (such as the victim of an accident) even though we have no commitments to this person. And an obligation can also be overruled by the importance – rather than the urgency or immediacy – of the issues facing someone. For instance, the decisions to be made by the clients in these examples – especially Louise, Samantha and Joan – are likely to affect the whole future course of their lives for the next several years. These issues demand an approach to ethical reasoning which transcends their specific obligations. It is more important for Joan to make time to talk about her future with the social worker than it is for her to respond to her mother's repeated questions about who the social worker is, or when it will be time for her tea, even though Joan has an obligation to reassure and help her mother. It may be more important for Joan to take a job than to go on being a full-time carer, even though she recognises an obligation to look after her mother.

I have described obligations as arising from commitments to shared projects (including communities). In joining these, people commit themselves to sharing resources and working co-operatively, according to certain principles; they bind themselves to abide by decisions made by agreed processes. But families, in particular, involve such close relationships, and such personal forms of sharing, over so many tasks and resources, and in such a range of situations, that the scope for unfairness (domination and exploitation), for hurts and for wrongs is enormous. If attempts to renegotiate fail, and communications break down, then a great deal of damage to trust and goodwill may have occurred before the matter reaches the social worker, and a long list of unresolved issues and unexpiated injuries accumulated. The task of reviewing the client's commitments, and analysing the rights and wrongs of these relationships, is inevitably both painful and painstaking. Obligations are by no means obvious, and principles have often been applied as part of a process of managing complex on-going messes.

In addition to these factors, people also of course belong to many different groups and communities, and their obligations to other members of these can conflict. They can find themselves in situations where the obligations and values that are part of belonging to one shared project clash with those of belonging to another. They must therefore decide which principles and commitments take priority, and what demands are those that are most binding on them.

I have argued throughout the book that moral reasoning is not just a matter of applying rules, but also of exercising judgement. In the process of deliberation, clients must recognise those features of their situation which call for the exercise of the standards they are committed to, and make their choices according to these. Some obligations – like keeping promises – are easy to recognise, though difficult to prioritise; others, like those associated with loyalty, forbearance and forgiveness, make strong claims in certain relationships (for example, when the other person has shown many examples of these towards us), but are imprecise, and do not always come to our minds at the time when their exercise is most appropriate. Moral reasoning is about sorting out the features of situations which should call forth responses that stem from our commitments, giving them their proper weightings in making our decisions. It is far more likely that we can do this in a dialogue; if our communications with the other members of our family or group are stuck in a rut, or have broken down completely, a social worker may be able to help us sort out these issues.

Clients in extreme versions of these moral messes are usually not short of consciousness of their obligations and principles; they are just torn between conflicting ones. Often they have not resolved a burning sense of injustice about past wrongs or failures in relationships, or other similar situations in which no satisfactory answers have been found. The guidance they need is dialogical rather than dogmatic, but one which is based on the notion that there are some choices that are better than others, and some actions that are clearly wrong, even if none can be perfectly right.

Consider the example of Louise, the single parent. Her unreliable husband Gordon (now in prison) introduced her to a wide circle of his disreputable friends, who still form her network of support. Her own family live far away, and have preoccupations of their own. Although they have got her into all sorts of trouble (for instance, by being drunk in charge of her children) Gordon's friends provide Louise with her only adult support, without which she would probably have been driven to prostitution or stealing to try to clear the debts Gordon left behind him. They drop in and sit around her house, they take her out for rides on their motorcycles, and one of them, known as Ferret, calls her up on his CB radio for long and incomprehensible conversations which Louise seems to experience as a kind of counselling. Admittedly some of these were overheard by the girlfriend of one of the others, who threatened to knife Louise for defamation (her children nearly had to come into care over that incident), but on balance the support, friendship and escape she gets through these men probably outweighs the problems they generate. It is through Horse, another one of them, who acts as a bouncer at a night-club, that Louise has the offer of the bar work there. The moral claims of these relationships may seem dubious to pious middle-class eyes, but for Louise the bonds of friendship are strong, and make calls on her which sometimes conflict with her genuine if scatty concern for the children. Living on such a low income, with such large debts, so few inner resources, such frail coping abilities and such a yearning for company and excitement, it is upon these relationships that her quality of life depends, and within them that her moral qualities will be developed.

It would be foolish and counter-productive of Louise's social worker to ignore the claims of these relationships, to treat them as distractions from or obstacles to her moral reasoning about the real issues. For Louise they are the social context in which she must learn to reason and exercise judgement, in which she will acquire virtues and standards (if anywhere). It is no more enlightening to regard Gordon's friends as a bunch of deviant ruffians than it is to see the characters of Homeric epics and Icelandic sagas in the same ethical light. Louise's moral education can only come through motorbike sagas and night-club epics, just as that of the Greeks and Norsemen came through the voyages and battles of their ruffian heroes. If the social worker is going to help her weigh the claims of the children against those of the members of this group, and try to find ways of reconciling them, then she must see these relationships as a serious testing ground of Louise's sense of obligation and principle, and regard Ferret and Horse as morally earnestly as she would Ulysses or Agamemnon.

I am arguing here for a kind of ethical analysis which sees the commitments acquired in people's actual relationships as morally binding, and hence understands obligations objectively, but regards their implementation as contestable. In fact, Louise and her social worker do not disagree about the priority to be given to the children's claims, they agree that their dependence and vulnerability give them the highest weighting in any attempt to balance the account. But Louise does not regard her request for them to come into care as a sign of irresponsibility or fecklessness; exactly the opposite. Sentiment and her consciousness of local opinion would strongly counsel her to keep them with her, even if she cannot do justice to their needs; but a calm and rational assessment of their chances of reaching their full potential if they remain in her care for the next few months or years leads her to believe that she is acting as a good mother in asking for them to be fostered. It is simply a fact that no-one would be approved as a foster parent who could not provide for them better – emotionally and materially – than Louise is at present able to. She knows that, given the opportunity, she will keep closely in touch with them, and if things go well she will be in a position to have them home sooner rather than later. For her, it is quite simply in their best interests to go into care, much as it upsets her to acknowledge this. If her social worker wants her to question this choice further, the way to do so is not to attack the moral basis of her reasoning (since this is not where they would disagree), but to see whether she has thought about every possible option, and every implication of her request, and to ask herself whether she has offered Louise all the support available to give her and her children a fair chance of a decent life.

In situations like this, the social worker's ability to offer the client a number of different perspectives, and her capacity to consider the circumstances from those various perspectives herself, are crucial to the process of moral reasoning. She must somehow bring into the reckoning Louise's position as a member of the community (claimant of income support, in heavy debt, isolated except for Gordon's friends and some local teenagers); as a woman (single parent, abandoned by her husband who treated her with no consideration or respect, and in effect also by her family, without labour market skills or experience, and with no female network of support); as a parent (her children are quite demanding and difficult, and her own emotional and practical resources are currently over-stretched); and as a client with a longstanding relationship with her department (repeatedly dealt with on a short-term basis, and receiving no effective support, either moral or practical). All these are relevant to the assessment of how Louise should act, and how she should act towards (or with) her. Ideally, these are not just matters relevant to fairness in their relationship which she weighs up at the office, or with colleagues at a case conference, but ones which are debated with Louise as they reflect on what to do about her situation and her request.

This is why I disagree with those authors who suggest that the theoretical perspectives associated with psychodynamic, behaviourist, client-centred, humanistic, radical and Marxist practice are mutually exclusive, and that social workers should choose between them, and make their theoretical assumptions more explicit. This view has been strongly and influentially advocated recently by David Howe, who regards clear, theoretical commitments as a necessary condition for purposeful practice. But at the end of his book, Howe does concede that perhaps this is not so desirable – that new developments, such as feminist reassessments of psycho-

analysis, and Marxist re-examinations of individual personality, reflect a more creative pathway for practitioners. He
comments: 'As relationships [political and moral, economic and
technological] between the individual and society become more
complex, multi-faceted and contentious, so the theoretical
expressions of these relationships become more varied. Each
theory seeks to capture a key feature of social reality'. 'On this
basis theories will have elements in common as well as
elements in opposition. ... By its very nature, in its very
position between the state and the individual, social work is
bound to be buffeted by the full force of the tides and the
tensions that comprise social reality. There are no simple
models of social work any more'.[21] Social workers need to
employ all these perspectives to make creative sense of the
messes they encounter. They do some violence to the theories
in applying them to clients' situations, but through offering a
number of views, clarifying the moral dimensions of their
problems, they can help them negotiate or even master their
messes.

Injustices and defections

The final matter to be considered in this chapter is how wrongs
– breaches of obligations and unfairnesses – are best righted or
dealt with in some other way if they cannot be repaired or
atoned. This is no simple issue, since it covers a whole range of
instances, from careless failures to observe a duty to severe
and systematic domination, abuse and exploitation. We must
find some way of assessing the seriousness of wrongs as well as
deciding which response – from forgiveness to punishment – is
appropriate.

There has been plenty of instances of such breaches and
defections in the examples I have used throughout the book.
We considered hypothetically the possibility that David Jackson might refuse to share the household work with Sarah, or
that she might unilaterally refuse to do any more paid work.
One of the community groups might go back on its original
agreement over priorities for new resources in Smortham.
Michael looks as if he is going to refuse to abide by the

conditions of his probation order. Brian is threatening to commit an offence. Samantha is considering ending her marriage to Nigel. How should the social workers and others affected by these decisions respond to them?

The difficulty with these questions is that not all social relations are equally co-operative, or conducted on the same terms. We live our lives in a number of social spheres; in some (among friends, family and some local communities) we have reason to trust and rely on others' responses; in others (among strangers) we are more on our guard; and in a few we may have grounds to fear systematic exploitation or consistent hostility (because of past wrongs and quarrels). So it is impossible to generalise about how to respond to a single breach or defection, since different responses may be appropriate in different social environments.

It seems an obvious rule of ethical conduct that we should always start our relationships in such a way as to seek co-operation, and to assume that the other person will do likewise until or unless given evidence to the contrary. Once a form of co-operation is established, any breach or defection should be dealt with in such a way as to restore this pattern as quickly as possible. Where co-operation breaks down altogether, then the aim may be damage limitation and the avoidance of a cycle of mutual recriminations.

Some experimental evidence on this issue is available from the work of the American political scientist Robert Axelrod.[22] He organised two computer tournaments between programs, entered by academics and gamesters, designed to test which strategy (in a two-player game involving two hundred moves representing co-operation or defection) was the most successful. We should be cautious about drawing conclusions from Axelrod's tournaments for a number of reasons; they were competitive, all against all, and aimed to measure success in terms of individual scores (and hence self-interest). Even so, it was surprising that the most successful program in both tournaments was a simple one called 'Tit for Tat', which always followed the other player's previous move, thus reciprocating both co-operation and defection. It therefore always maximised the rewards of co-operation, but punished defection in a way which showed it was not willing to be 'played for a sucker'.

Tit for Tat could be represented as a kind of Old Testament morality of 'an eye for an eye and a tooth for a tooth'. Although it lost to some thoroughly nasty programs, it was much more successful than these in an overall environment with some nice (co-operative) and other nasty ones (the nasty programs scored very lowly against each other, and hence finished bottom of the league). In the first tournament, where most of the programs were opportunistic occasional defectors, a more forgiving program, which allowed one defection without retaliation ('Tit for Two Tats') *would* have won, if it had been entered.[23] In other words, a New Testament morality of turning the other cheek would (given that we only have two cheeks) have been even more advantageous for the player than the Old Testament one. But in the second tournament several entrants, knowing that Tit for Tat was the program to beat, submitted ones which were specifically designed to take advantage of it if they could. This meant that Tit for Two Tats, which was entered the second time by one contestant, fared quite badly, because it suffered at the hands of programs which were geared to exploit forgiveness. Tit for Tat, by contrast, was again the most successful, because it robustly withstood attempted exploitation.

The point about these findings is that they indicate that different levels of forgiveness are appropriate for different social environments. In a group or community in which relations are occasionally opportunistic, a New Testament morality is the best way of maximising co-operation in relationships. But in one where more systematically exploitative individuals are operating, a more guarded, Old Testament response is best. In other words, individuals could expect to get the best results for themselves (even in terms of self-interest, and in circumstances in which no reasoning and negotiation with the other are possible) by tolerating one-off lapses in fairness and co-operation in those relationships which they judge not to be calculated to take advantage of this level of forgiveness; but as soon as they find themselves in relationships which are exploiting this tolerance, they should revert to an Old Testament response. Another way of looking at the same findings is to suggest that individuals should follow a New Testament morality among people they have reason to believe they can trust (friends, family, local community, all with a few known exceptions) but a more guarded stance among strangers who are known to be potentially hostile or exploitative, always starting with co-operation, but reserving retaliatory powers. The point about the latter is that they should always be proportional, and never escalatory, since the greatest danger to co-operation comes from an endless round of mutual recriminations, and the aim is to restore good relations as quickly as possible.

We should remember that Axelrod's game allowed each of the players to have equal powers on each move; an advantage gained on one move was accumulated in the player's score, but not in terms of extra power over the other in the next move (as it is in a game like Monopoly, for example). Real life, and especially real economic life, is more like Monopoly: successful exploiters gain cumulative advantage over the exploited, and power breeds power. As we saw in Chapter 3, this gives some players an interest not just in minimising their disadvantages, but also in trying to change the rules of the game. The argument of this book is that disadvantaged people (the poor, women, black people, people with handicaps) should indeed struggle to change these unjust rules, and redistribute the assets that give the overdogs their advantages. But they are unlikely to succeed in doing this by persuasion unless they can show that in the subsequent, more co-operative system of relations, there will be gains for all. Axelrod's findings are encouraging on this point. Underdogs who take a tough line on injustice, insisting that overdogs should share more fairly, can promise that the consequence can be harmonious and fair co-operation in which it pays the participants to be tolerant of minor infractions.

We have, then, three rationales and strategies for individual choice over injustices and defections – one for face-to-face and communal relations (Tit for Two Tats); one for impersonal stranger relations in an environment of moral indifference (Tit for Tat); and one for an environment of structural injustice, domination and exploitation (Struggle to Change the Rules). These seem to provide broad guidelines that may help clients, help social workers to counsel clients, and help social workers to decide what to do about their clients' defections and breaches of obligations. The difficult judgement to make is which environment one is occupying; the wronged individual has to decide whether to treat an infraction as a lapse, an attempt at systematic exploitation, or evidence of structural injustice.

This is obviously particularly difficult for disadvantaged people in face-to-face relations. For example, women are systematically disadvantaged in society as a whole, but in their relations with individual men (in the family and at work) they have to try to negotiate a viable, fair, democratic means of co-operating, for the sake of a good quality of life. Hence everyday wrongs have extra significance, since they raise issues about exploitation and injustice in wider social relations. In the same way, black people are sure to be more conscious of the injustices associated with racism in their daily relationships with white people, and to suspect this factor of contributing to casual thoughtlessness or inconsiderable actions. And disadvantaged clients will be suspicious of advantaged and powerful social workers, especially the white male ones, even when they are trying to work in a spirit of co-operation and fairness. Trust will take longer to establish, and actions will have to speak before words are given much heed.

Social workers can provide useful counsel for people in moral messes by helping them to distinguish between these kinds of wrongs, and decide what level of action they are contemplating – retributive or rule challenging. They may be able to assist them by putting them in touch with groups which are organised to challenge the rules – women's groups, black people's groups, claimants' groups, groups of people with handicaps – while at the same time helping them to be more assertive in resisting exploitation and insisting that their needs are met in their personal relationships. This is another example of the importance of keeping several theoretical perspectives simultaneously in social work practice. Social workers cannot help clients operate on more than one level or distinguish between the responses appropriate for each unless they can themselves understand the principles that apply to each kind of relation, and can judge the best way of applying them to the various aspects of this particular situation.

Much work with family members over the wrongs they have

done each other will use many of the principles of conciliation. Social workers in disputes over custody and access in divorce have developed methods which focus on reaching agreements over these issues. Instead of trying to arbitrate between conflicting parties with the welfare of the child as their criterion, they have sought to define a territory of limited co-operation in the mutual interests of the parents. The skills that are needed for this work are ones of allowing the parties to get their feelings about past wrongs in proportion, to clarify their own needs, and their perceptions of those of the children, and to reach fair agreements over which they themselves have control. Negotiation and mediation are hence the methods, with counselling as a means of preparing the parties for this process if trust has been badly damaged, and arbitration as a last resort if agreements are not achievable, or are breached by one side or the other.

Contracts are also a way of working by agreement which owe something to this way of thinking. The main purposes of a contract are to spell out clearly the goals of the work, the steps to be taken, and the obligations of worker and client. But by binding themselves to tasks in this explicit way, both sides also provide a framework in which the terms of co-operation are defined, and hence the necessary (often limited) degree of trust can be established. The focus can be on what can be achieved within specific areas of the client's life, rather than on past wrongs or a general sense of injustice. Research suggests that poor people use systems of informal justice rather in this way, to specify to other family members the boundaries of acceptable behaviour, and gain a secure territory for conditional co-operation.

In the final chapter we shall see how these methods, among others, work out in practice. The social worker's most valuable skill lies in being able to discriminate between wrongs which are serious violations of trust and fundamental breaches of the terms of the relationship, and wrongs which are incidental infractions which do not threaten these basic moral elements. This applies to wrongs in the client's shared projects, and wrongs that clients do to her – breaches of their commitments to each other, both implicit and explicit. And clients, of course, also monitor these commitments, and voice their own criticism, or even moral outrage, if social workers seem not really to care, or to be 'two-faced' in relation to their power and authority. Moral reasoning works in both directions, and social workers can expect plenty of comments on their own ethics and the propriety of their decisions, especially when they take action in respect of breaches of agreements.

As we saw in Chapter 4, the ultimate powers of social workers (for example, in child protection) have their moral basis in a failure to establish trusting co-operative agreements, or in breaches of such agreements where they have seemed to exist. Where there are identified risks to children or others, it is the social worker's responsibility to monitor these agreements, to check that the situation has not subtly changed, and to test out any covert shifts which might represent gradual or secret defections by the clients. In such cases, while trust may be a necessary condition for effective work, it is not a sufficient condition; the social worker has an obligation to prove to herself over and over again that the child is properly protected, and to follow up the slightest emotional or material hints that things may not be quite as they formerly seemed. These are clear cases where overlooking lapses cannot be policy, because it is not her life that is at risk of being lost.

Conclusions

This chapter has been a rather ambitious and wide-ranging exploration of moral reasoning and choosing in relations between individuals. Even so, there are some decisions that I have not attempted to investigate, such as the decision to become a social worker, and some situations that are beyond the scope of this book, such as emergencies involving groups of strangers who are not members of the same community. If the examples of the first chapter can be taken as at all definitive of the scope of ordinary ethical dilemmas in social work, then the aim of finding a rationale for analysing these should suffice for the purpose of the book.

First, it was argued that we could hope to provide good reasons for recognising one particular choice as the right one, or the best one, in all these examples, and that we could reasonably expect the social worker to be able to agree this with the client, if they were able to deliberate on the issues in a calm way, trying to consider them in an impartial manner.

Second, it was suggested that a trusting and co-operative relationship was the best one in which to reflect on these issues, to discuss and negotiate over choices, and make decisions. But people in moral messes are not calm, and many clients are unlikely to trust social workers' judgements. Hence there are skills required of workers (counselling skills) which enable them to reach clients' moral consciousness, and create the conditions for this deliberation, even in pressurised, crisis situations, such as those of several of the examples.

Third, it was suggested some criteria for fair (non-manipulative) negotiation between people engaged in a moral dialogue. They include ordinary standards of politeness, consideration and reliability, but these are often too much to expect of people in a mess or a panic. Hence it may be up to the social worker, aware of strong emotional pressure in a certain direction, to clarify this by making it explicit. But social workers must also expect to be called to account if clients think they are being unfair or pressurising.

Fourth, it was argued that obligations arise from our commitments to shared projects and are often imprecise in their demands, or in conflict with each other. Hence moral judgement is required for decisions, and is best exercised in a dialogue where a number of perspectives on relationships and their wider implications are debated. Hence a variety of theoretical perspectives on human relations and social justice are of value to a social worker, and she should be encouraged to offer insights from several or all of them to clients who are trying to decide what they should do in a morally messy situation.

Fifth, three rules over the question of how to respond to breaches of obligation and unfairness in relationships were proposed. These different levels of forgiveness of defections and injustices apply in more and less co-operative social environments; but the rule of struggling to change the rules applies in all situations where some people have assets which give them cumulative advantages over others. Moral deliberation can help clients and social workers judge how to respond to specific wrongs.

The final chapter describes, with a change of style, how matters proceed in the seven examples, trying to use the ideas of this chapter as the framework for my account.

References

1. Martin Hollis, *The Cunning of Reason* (Cambridge University Press, 1988), ch. 5. This is a retort to Bernard Williams, 'Internal and external reasons', in *Moral Luck* (Cambridge University Press, 1981).
2. James Fishkin, *Beyond Subjective Morality: Ethical reasoning and political philosophy* (Yale University Press, 1984), pp. 45–81.
3. This is what Fishkin, *op. cit.*, p. 140, calls a 'minimal objectivist' position.
4. Bernard Williams, *Ethics and the Limits of Philosophy* (Fontana, 1985), pp. 201–2.
5. Fishkin, *op. cit.*, p. 145.
6. Martin Hollis, 'The shape of a life', in J. Altham and R. Harrison (eds), *World, Mind and Ethics* (Cambridge University Press, forthcoming).
7. Williams, *op. cit.*, p. 140.
8. Hollis, 'The shape of a life'.
9. Phyllida Parsloe, 'Some educational implications', in Phyllida Parsloe and Olive Stevenson, *Social Work Teams: The practitioner's view* (HMSO, 1978), ch. 14, especially pp. 339–42.
10. Hollis, 'The shape of a life'.
11. W. Reed and M. Shyne, *Brief and Extended Casework* (Columbia University Press, 1969); J. Corden and M. Preston-Shoot, *Contracts in Social Work* (Gower, 1987).
12. Charles B. Truax and Robert R. Carkhuff, *Towards Effective Counselling and Psychotherapy: Training and practice* (Aldine, 1967); Gerard Egan, *The Skilled Helper: A model for systematic helping and interpersonal relating* (Brooks-Cole, 1975); Philip Priestley and James McGuire, *Learning to Help: Basic skills exercises* (Tavistock, 1983).
13. Bill Jordan, 'Counselling, advocacy and negotiation', *British Journal of Social Work*, vol. 17 (1987), pp. 135–46.
14. Donald Houston, Seminar in Department of Child and Family Psychiatry, Yorkhill Hospital, Glasgow, 1973, quoted in Jill Ford, 'Negotiation (counselling and advocacy): initial thoughts in response to Bill Jordan', 1987, unpublished.
15. Janet Mattinson and Ian Sinclair, *Mate and Stalemate: Marital work in a social services department* (Blackwell, 1979), p. 139.
16. Bill Jordan, *Client–Worker Transactions* (Routledge and Kegan Paul, 1970); *The Social Worker in Family Situations* (Routledge and Kegan Paul, 1972).

17. Bill Jordan, *Invitation to Social Work* (1984) (Blackwell, 1988), pp. 172–3.
18. Mattinson and Sinclair, *op. cit.*, p. 182.
19. Bill Jordan, *Helping in Social Work* (Routledge and Kegan Paul, 1979), pp. 17–18.
20. Williams, *op. cit.*
21. David Howe, *An Introduction to Social Work Theory* (Macmillan, 1988), p. 169.
22. Robert Axelrod, *The Evolution of Co-operation* (Basic Books, 1984).
23. *Ibid.*, p. 120.

8

CONVERSATIONS

Michael

Defeated, he slumps down on one of the plastic chairs that circle the pool table. A youngster with a leather cap perched jauntily over his ear shapes up for a pot, and knocks the pied ball spinning into the corner pocket, to a rapturous response from Michael and his friends. Watching their exuberance, the probation officer feels old, boring and very white.

Of course, Michael has a point: the local hostels are run by white staff, and although one of them is quite constructive, open and supportive, its success rate with black teenagers is not impressive. As for the YTS, the programme that would suit him is full, and there is a waiting list of others like himself, but who are really keen for places. Seeing him with his friends, it is obvious that Michael is popular, humorous and socially skilled. No wonder he mistrusts all attempts to separate him from this group, and treats the offer of hostels or lodgings as little better than custody. Yet many of his friends have themselves been in trouble, and Michael's chances of staying out of court seem negligible.

Perhaps there isn't any answer. At least he isn't going to think of one sitting here, watching them play pool. Maybe Michael is right, and he should just go back to his office and wait for whatever happens next – if he can just find a half-dignified way of leaving, without this appearing to be a total rout of the forces of law and order. Clients 23, Probation Service 0: about average for this season.

A self-protective thought crosses his mind. He has supervision on Monday, and his senior is bound to check his caseload; she is a stickler for clearing up loose ends, and Michael is a looser end than most. With the Home Office inspection coming up, she's

bound to press for breach proceedings, unless there is a clear
action plan.

Why not breach Michael? He's made no effort to comply with
his order, he is rude, dismissive, contemptuous – why take
time when there are others asking for help? Two reasons,
maybe, thinks the probation officer. First, Michael is in one
way typical of so many black teenagers; if I can't help him,
what am I doing in this job, especially working with black
youngsters? I should admit I'm useless and resign. Second,
there is something about Michael himself as an individual.
He's not just average stroppy, he's *extra* stroppy, defiant,
angry. If he could channel that in some direction, he'd be really
good. He seems to challenge me, because although he's typical,
he's different also – an original.

So, what next? How to get back into the game, so to say?
Literally, perhaps. Never could play pool, but in this job you've
got to be prepared to make an idiot of yourself from time to
time.

He catches the eye of the youth in the leather cap. 'I'll play
the winner, if you'll let me.'

They snigger and glance at Michael. He looks slightly
embarrassed, and pretends it's nothing to do with him.

'Okay.' The lad in the leather cap performs the *coup-de-
grâce*, and the probation officer rises from his chair and holds
out his hand.

'Ian Clarke. How do you do.'

'Paul Thompson. Pleased to meet you.'

His opponent scores steadily, but eventually Ian flukes a pot.
The onlookers raise a slightly mocking cheer. 'Luck,' someone
mutters.

'Skill,' he rejoins unconvincingly.

'Do you know Mr Prendergast?' asks Paul.

'Yes, his office is next to mine. Do you?'

'He's my probation officer.' Paul sinks another ball; he has
almost won. 'He reckons I'm a worry to him.'

'Why's that?'

'I dunno. Ask him.' A snigger goes round the group.

'We probation officers are all worriers. Perhaps you guys
should teach us how to relax.'

'It's just a matter of staying cool, man,' says Paul, to a gale of laughter. With a flourish, he ends the game, and shakes hands.

'You could come and give us lessons – in pool and cool – at our day centre.'

A murmur of dissent goes round the group.

'No way, that place stinks. We're not coming there for a load of abuse and harassment.'

'Such as what?'

'Everything. Look, you probation officers think that you're so great; Mr Prendergast told me how you're against racism and all that. So how come these white kids run that day centre? And how come they get away with about twenty fights and robbings, and we just do one thing and we get nicked?'

They're angry, and they have reason to be angry, he thinks.

'All right, you've had bad experiences – you feel there's one rule for white, and another for black . . .'

'We know there is.'

'. . . and you don't see the probation service doing enough to challenge that injustice for you, or with you. I recognise your anger, and your disappointment with us.'

There is a pause. It feels like an opportunity.

'Is there somewhere we could get a cup of coffee, to talk about this?' he enquires tentatively.

They look at each other and nod. 'Yeah, in the next room,' says Paul.

They insist on paying for his coffee. The room is empty, except for a couple of older women at a table in the corner. Michael remains on the outside of the group as they draw up their chairs.

'So you think that black people get a bad deal from the probation service?'

'That's obvious, isn't it. You're on the side of the police, and the judges, and all the rest. You don't see a lot of black judges, do you?'

'So it's you against the white authorities?'

'Look, we're only asking them to leave us alone. Just . . . you know, when we're standing on the corner talking, and this big police car pulls up, and they start asking what we're doing, where we've been . . . And they come smashing into our club, they don't care who they hurt, what they break . . .'

'Why do you think those things happen?'

They all talk at once. Eventually someone who hasn't spoken before has his say.

'They just think if you're black you must be a criminal, you know. We're guilty unless we can prove we're innocent.'

'They don't want to listen to our side of the story,' adds another. 'They always believe a white person's story against ours.'

'So you reckon that we're the same, we probation officers?'

No one answers. Michael looks away.

'You think we should do more listening to you.'

'When you go in that office,' says Paul, 'it's like you're being ... inspected or something ... scrutinised, all them questions: Where you been? What you done? Why you done it? It's like school, only much worse – there's someone checking up on you for everything, you can't even move without someone's watching you, you know, writing these reports about you, "Paul has an anti-social attitude, Paul has a problem with authority, Paul doesn't wash his hands after he goes to the toilet ...."'

The others laugh in agreement.

'So the office is the wrong place for you to talk, and us to listen?'

They nod in assent. 'We don't feel right there, you know. Okay, so we've got to go there every two weeks or something, because that's part of our punishment and everything. But don't expect us to tell you all about ourselves, what we feel about our families and all that stuff, not in that place. It gives us the creeps.'

'So, where would you be willing to talk?'

There is a short silence. 'What about here?' says someone. It is Michael.

'Fair enough,' replies the probation officer, being careful not to look directly at him. 'Would you rather see your own probation officers, or meet like this, as a group?'

'Like this,' they say in unison.

'Well, I'll discuss it with my colleagues. Perhaps Mr Prendergast and I could meet you here.' He's sure Max will like the idea – the rest of the team might have some reservations, but they can probably be talked round. They certainly wouldn't veto their clients attending anyway. 'Shall we aim for this time next week?'

There is a murmur of agreement.

'Just one other thing. I know you don't like being scrutinised and questioned about everything, but we can't just ignore the fact you've been in trouble. We'll agree to talk about what it's like to deal with the white law system, if you'll agree to talk about how you get into trouble. I think that's fair, isn't it?'

'Not if you're just going to come here lecturing us about all this "offending behaviour" stuff.'

'Did I say that?'

'It sounded like it.'

'What I said was, let's talk about what both sides are doing wrong. What the law system's doing wrong, and what you're doing wrong. We'll try to put ourselves right if we can, but that works both ways.'

A muttered conversation in the group, then. 'Okay, fair enough.'

'Next week then . . .'

Donna

Donna stares glumly out of the window. The silence hangs heavy between them, and like a fog it seems to pollute the air she breathes and stick in her throat. The social worker collects herself to try to say something that may clear the fog of mistrust and anger, soften Donna's dismissive replies, and relieve her own feelings of useless irrelevance.

It is a very risky thing to say, and she is not at all sure she can handle what follows, but it seems like the only way to stop going round in circles.

'When girls of your age keep running away from home, it sometimes comes out later that they have reasons,' she says, deliberately pausing. Donna is still looking out of the window. 'Good reasons,' she adds, pausing again, and watching her carefully. 'One good reason is if they've been sexually abused at home,' she adds finally, as neutrally as possible.

Donna turns immediately and looks straight at her. Their eyes meet for a moment, and then she glances down. In that moment Donna communicates her recognition that she has been offered a way out of the impasse. She understands what is being asked, and its significance. She only has to say that her father has done one thing, perhaps even said one thing, and the trap is sprung. But it is a trap that can catch all of them, Donna as well as her parents. Does she see that? How much understanding did that look convey?

The social worker looks at her intently, trying to read every line of her posture, her gaze, her movement. There must be a terrible temptation to point a falsely accusing finger if there is nothing true to tell, to allege. The resentment against her parents is already so strong, and now she is being offered the perfect way to hurt them, perhaps to destroy them. It is a lot of power to hand to someone so young, and a lot of responsibility.

How will she know whether to believe Donna, either way? Professional wisdom is so fickle and changeable on this point. For years no-one asked children, no-one believed them if they spoke out. Now the experts believe, but selectively. They believe when the context seems right, when the evidence points in that direction, or when other professionals believe. She must try to read Donna's whole response, not only her words, but how she says them – and listen to her as a person, without making assumptions about someone of her age.

'No,' says Donna at last.

She says it directly, looking up briefly.

'That's not your reason?'

'No.'

It sounds true. There is nothing to indicate fierce conflict in Donna, or a raw suffering uncovered. It is fairly matter-of-fact. But at least Donna has treated it seriously, as important. There has been real communication.

Another pause.

'Because if not,' adds the social worker, slowly and quietly, 'it's difficult for me to find a good enough reason to see my job as protecting you from your parents. Do you see what I mean? If you were being abused, then that would be my job. To make sure that you were protected, that it stopped, and everything got sorted out. But if not, then somehow we've all got to reach some kind of agreement about where to go from here, if that's at all possible. It's my job to help you and your parents get through the next year or so, till you're in a better position to make your own choices, and find your own way of life.'

'You'll have a job getting any sense out of them.' Donna is

back on her old tack, but somehow the tone is slightly modified. She has acknowledged that the social worker takes her seriously – maybe even that she took a risk in asking the questions, in that she too had something to lose if the answer was yes. Something important has been shared, perhaps, and this can be the basis of a rather different kind of discussion.

'What's it really all about then, this fierce battle?'

Donna tugs at the chain round her neck and pulls a face. 'They don't really love me. They want to run my life, to know everything about me, to make me into someone just like themselves. Jackie'll find out when she gets to my age . . .'

'Your sister?'

'Yes. They're always saying how good she is, how perfect. But I know what she really thinks, and when she's my age she'll be just the same.'

'What does she say about you running off?'

'Oh, she takes Mum and Dad's side, or she says she does. That's partly because she doesn't want to be left on her own with them.'

So Donna sees it as a power struggle, in which her parents have all the advantages. She sees her parents as denying her any autonomy, and unable to let their daughters grow towards independence.

'Where does John, your boyfriend, come into all this?'

'Dad hates him. He won't let me bring him home. He's like that with any boy I've known. He sort of puffs himself up, as if he's trying to pick a fight with them, before they've even said anything.'

'What's that about?'

'Treating me like a little kid, who's got to be sheltered. Treating me like I belong to him and Mum.'

'He seems to disapprove of John in particular.'

'Just because he's a labourer – that's all he knows about him . . .'

'What about the fact that he's 19?'

'Oh yes, he brings that up all the time, and Mum does. What difference does that make?'

'Well, he's left home, he's got his own place . . .'

'No he hasn't, he's in lodgings, because he's working for the contractors on that new hotel.'

'And you keep running away to his place.'

'Where else can I go, when they're shouting at me, and threatening to lock me in my room?'

'I don't know, Donna, but it certainly makes your parents very angry that you go to John's place.'

'They just jump to conclusions about him and me. You ask the police where I was when they picked me up. I wasn't even with John – I was having a cup of tea with his landlady, in the kitchen. She's more like . . .'

'More like what?'

'Well, more understanding – like parents should be.'

Donna sees her life as a prize to be won in a fight with her parents. Can she think of what she'll do with it, if in the end she wins?

'Just for a minute, try to imagine what you'll be doing when you're 16. That's what – just over a year from now? Imagine you've left school. What sort of life will you be leading?'

'I don't know. I want to have my own flat, that's for sure. And a job, I suppose.'

'What sort of job?'

'In a shop, something like that. Or looking after children.'

'And how would you like things to be between you and your parents?'

'How do you mean?'

'Would you want to see them?'

'They wouldn't want to see me if I left home.'

'Just think how you would like things to be.'

'Well . . . being able to call round and see Jackie, I suppose, and not have any rows when I see Mum and Dad. I expect Mum would want me to visit. See her in my dinner break one day each week – meet her in town, or something.'

'So that's what you're aiming for by next summer. You've got your own flat, and a job, and able to see your sister and your mother, and possibly your father, without a fight breaking out.'

'Yes, but . . .'

'At least we can start from an idea of what you're aiming at. So we can agree that you don't want to do anything that'll stop you getting to that situation. Whatever arrangements we try to make for the next year or so should be steps towards that, and you shouldn't do things that make it less likely to come about.'

'Yes, but they won't agree with that.'

'Hang on, don't jump ahead yet. They aren't going to agree with you leaving home before you're 16, that they've made quite clear. But after that, it's not really within their power to stop you. So if that's what you want, to be in charge of your own life when you leave school, the only way you can lose it, can chuck it away, is by getting yourself in a real mess between now and then. For instance, by coming into care under a court order . . .'

'What do you mean?'

'Well, if things got so bad, with your parents making allegations about you and John, and the police involved, and the rows and running away, there could be care proceedings on the grounds that you were beyond their control, and in danger of harm . . .'

'That's all wrong,' says Donna, glowering at the social worker.

'Things can go wrong, terribly wrong, for girls of your age, when you push everyone too hard. What I'm trying to do is stop that happening.'

Donna scowls at the floor. There is a long silence.

'So now I've got to meet with your parents again,' continues the social worker, 'and try to calm things down a bit, so we can all talk it over – probably after a night's sleep.'

Donna doesn't reply. Shuttle diplomacy in the police station at 2 a.m. is a strange job, thinks the social worker. The best that can be negotiated is a truce – a breathing space, in which the conflict can perhaps be contained for a while.

'Eventually, we're going to have to talk about school, about you seeing John, and about preparing for your independence. None of that's going to be easy, and I don't look forward to it either. But it's worth trying, if the only other end to the battle we can see is a court case and a care order, don't you think?'

Louise

The small boys tug at Louise's skirt, demanding her attention. She wipes Sean's nose in an abstracted, automatic way, scolds Patrick for being noisy, and takes another drag at her cigarette. She looks pale and tired, like so many of the single parents on this estate. Her expression speaks of debts and deficits – of food, heat, energy of all kinds, resources, patience, stamina.

I need a holiday too, thinks the social worker: this much deprivation and misery, day after day, can endanger health. If mine, how much more hers? She's well entitled to a break from all this, week after week, month after month. And she isn't really asking for a break exactly, just a chance to 'get herself straightened out'.

Yet Louise's request for the boys to come into care sets alarm bells ringing in her head, and will cause worried expressions in the team. So many children of single parents have come in this way, in what seems to be a short-term crisis, and have stayed on for years, sometimes for the rest of their childhood. It's not that the mothers are cynical or irresponsible, just shuffling off their children onto the department. Their lives are so impoverished and joyless with the kids that without them they fall straight into some new relationship, usually a mess involving other children, sometimes violent. Often they see their kids doing better in the foster family, and believe that it is not in their interests to return – they have toys, warmth, food, order and something like security there.

Of course it's only in a small minority of cases that this happens, but they cast a long shadow over every request for care. A shadow that has even influenced the legislation, so that kids who come in voluntarily in situations like this will be given 'accommodation', to distinguish them more sharply from the ones who are admitted compulsorily for 'care'. But renaming things does not solve fundamental problems. Sean and Patrick need much more than accommodation, just as Louise needs much more than a break.

The real issue is whether their needs are best met separately or together. It's not an issue that the department can sort out on its own, by rules or procedures. Somehow Louise must be part of the reasoning, and part of the decision-making. That won't be easy, thinks the social worker. Seeing them together, it isn't about a risk to the children, not immediately anyway. But Louise can't see her way forward with the children, or their way forward with her. She doesn't really want to discuss it any further, because it is all so painful and hopeless. Putting them in care seems like the only way out of her trap.

'Let's just think about this for a minute, Louise. You say you want the boys to come into care until you get yourself straightened out. Could you say a bit more about what you mean by straightened out. Suppose they were in care for six or eight weeks. What would you do in that time?'

'Well, for a start they might be better, you know, in their behaviour – more controllable, like . . . when they come back.'

'You mean, being away with foster parents would get them to behave better, to be easier for you to control?'

'Well, you see what they're like now. And I'd be able to sort my debts out, and get the money straight . . .'

'How would you try to do that?'

'Well, working at the club, like. It's about £10 a night, and then there's tips on top of that of course.'

'And that's for how many nights a week?'

'As many as I can. Up to six I suppose.'

'Hold on a minute. Is that on top of your money from social security, or instead of it?'

'Well, I don't know. On top of it, I suppose – until I know how much I'm earning. I'd have to declare it in the end, I know, otherwise someone'd tell them.'

'And after that? Even on six nights a week that's only £60, plus a bit for tips.'

'I could get that family credit.'

'Not if your kids are in care.'

This is all missing the real point, thinks the social worker.

'It sounds as if I'm trying to put a dampener on all your ideas,' she says. 'I don't mean to do that. All I'm trying to say is, because of the rotten rules of income support, and I don't agree with them, as a single parent you'd have to earn a hell of a lot, probably nearly £100 a week, to be able to pay your rent and be better off than you are on benefits. And when the boys come back, you'd either have to give up the job again, or pay someone to look after them properly, which would mean earning nearer £150 to be better off.'

Louise looks defeated and close to tears. She shouts angrily at Patrick, who is poking at an electric socket with his toy gun, and takes Sean onto her lap.

'It's good that you want to sort out your debts, and that you've got the chance of a job. It's quite important to you, isn't it?'

'I'll go mad if I have to stay in here all the time much longer. They took Linda next door away to the nuthouse last week. I reckon I'll be next.'

'So, what do you most need to keep you sane?'

'The company, I suppose. Someone to talk to that isn't tied down by kids, and moaning about being broke, the same as me. A bit of life . . . chance to let off steam. Have a bit of a laugh . . . That's not a crime, is it?'

'You do have some friends . . .'

'Oh yes, I expect the neighbours have reported them. *Men* friends. Who *visit* me. On *motorbikes*. It's all on the files.'

The social worker says nothing, and sits back in her seat. Louise continues. 'Yes, it's them that got me this job. And they're the only ones that are any help, that try to help anyway. They're quite good with Patrick and Sean – a hell of a lot better than their father was.'

'Suppose you did two nights a week, and kept £15 on top of your income support money. Suppose we could arrange for someone to look after the boys those nights, and your mother took Vickie?'

'What, you mean not take them into care at all?'

'Not if the main reason is so that you can get out, have some company, and earn some money. Only if there's a real risk that you'll hurt them, or they really need something you can't give them, or you really need a complete break from them.'

'Well, they do need proper looking after, and some discipline. Better than I've been able to do these last few weeks, anyway.'

'But would you be able to give them enough, do you think, if you were less depressed, about yourself and the debts?'

'I might, I suppose. Who'd have them those two nights, though?'

'Well, I thought I might be able to find someone quite near here, who could take them from, say, 6 in the evening till noon the following day, so you could have a lie-in. Would that be any good, if we could pay for it?'

'What if they play her up?'

'Well, it's a couple, and they've plenty of experience of

children. Really they're no different from the kind of people who'd be foster parents if they came into care, except that they live a lot closer, and you'd be able to get to know them a bit better.'

'I expect they'd tell me all the things I'm doing wrong, like everyone else round here does.'

'They might have some useful hints.'

Louise falls silent again. 'It still won't sort the money out,' she says eventually.

'So are you saying that it might help get things better here at home, if we can also tackle the debts?'

'It might, I suppose. At least they'll soon tell you – the people who'll be looking after Sean and Patrick – they'll be able to tell you if I'm not looking after them properly, won't they?'

'That's not the main idea. It's meant to help you and them, and to give you all a fair chance of getting on as a family, instead of getting in each other's way. But yes, it will mean that someone whose judgement we respect can tell us if things don't seem to be working out. And perhaps they'll be able to help you too.'

'Hmm.' Patrick and Sean are playing together quite quietly now. A hopeful sign, perhaps, that Louise feels some real relief about the plan.

'What about the debts then? £15 a week won't go very far – two of them want over £100 straight away. They're threatening all sorts.'

'I suppose you've thought about trying to get another loan from the social fund?'

'What – that? No way. I'd rather borrow from Jaws!'

'Who's Jaws?'

'The loan shark, you see him waiting outside the Post Office when the women pick up their child benefit money.'

'Any other ideas?'

'I thought your people sometimes help out. It sounds a bit cheeky I suppose, when you've just said you'd pay for Sean and Patrick to be looked after, and that. But it's cheaper than having them in care, isn't it?'

'Well, yes. I can't promise anything. Our budget is pathetic. But I'd better take down a few details.'

'Well, first there's the clothing club. I've only just finished paying off Gordon's leather jacket; and there's still the kids' Christmas . . .'

Brian

'You meant me to see it, didn't you, Brian?'

He blinks bleakly, his shut-away expression hardly changing. If anything, he seems to retreat a little further inside himself.

'Yeah, I suppose so.'

'So it was meant to be . . . a kind of threat.' Sandra knows that isn't quite fair. Brian isn't really threatening, certainly not in the way some of the other residents are. 'Well, not exactly a threat. Maybe a sort of cry for help.'

'Yeah, I guess so.'

'And you meant *me* to read it.'

There, she's said it. Sandra has acknowledged the personal message in Brian's note, the one that was especially for her. She's been struggling with whether or not to do so, veering between resentment that he should presume to involve her in this way, by making claims on her as a person that go far beyond her work role, and guilt about her strong impulse to evade the implications of these claims, or pretend she hasn't noticed that he is making them.

Brian makes no reply, looks bleaker than ever.

'Because you wanted to tell me that you were keeping out of trouble, keeping going here and in your job, for my sake. And that was something . . . personal.'

Still no reply, no change of expression.

'Which makes me feel bad – and it's meant to, isn't it?' She tries not to make it sound too much like an accusation, even though she was angry at the time she read it. 'It's meant to make me feel bad that you don't matter to me, you aren't important to me, in the way you say I am important to you.'

'Sorry,' he mutters, by now a tiny bleak thing deep inside himself, and shrinking faster all the time.

'Sod it, Brian, it's not a matter of "Sorry",' she bursts out, and then feels terrible. Now he's just like he was when he first came to the hostel, scared, secretive, locked away with his obsessions; and she is left feeling that it's her fault. 'What I mean is, you can't just take over someone like that. You can't just say that's what your relationship with me means to you, without giving me any say in it.'

'I won't do it again, Sandra.'

This isn't how this conversation was supposed to go at all. She is beginning to bully him, to hurt him, to retaliate. She's been encouraging him to allow himself to show feelings, to be more vulnerable, and now he has shown what's really there inside him, she is punishing him for it.

'I'm sorry to hurt you, Brian. I didn't want to do that.'

It doesn't touch him, she knows. She must acknowledge that it has been hard for him to shed his defences, to be more open.

'You've been brave about a lot of things since you came to The Laurels, Brian. You've shared your thoughts and feelings with lots of other people, not only me, and it hasn't been easy. But this is different. You're trying to take me over, and have me to yourself. You're saying that I'm special to you, so you want me as ... well, as a sort of possession, as yours. And you're threatening ... you're saying, anyway ... that if you can't have me, then you'll go back into prison.'

No comment from Brian.

'Which is really trying to deal with your problems like you used to do. To try to take something or someone, or a feeling, and lock it away inside you. Which didn't work, did it?'

No answer.

'After all, it has been better here, since you learnt more about sharing ...'

'Which is why I don't want to leave.' Quite a sharp answer from Brian, and very much to the point. Sandra pauses to reflect, but Brian continues.

'You say that I mustn't go back to being inside myself, on my own. That I must try to go on sharing things with other people. Okay, so how am I going to do that, living by myself in a bedsit? Where's the sharing in that? And how can I keep my job? The pay's not enough for lodgings. So I'll end up even more on my own. I'd be better off in nick, wouldn't I?'

'Okay, fair point,' says Sandra, and pauses again for thought. Brian is shaking slightly, but has come to life again. He is not going to burst into tears – not yet, anyway.

She needs to get this conversation onto a different track. 'We're getting two different things mixed up here, aren't we? There's the question about you leaving The Laurels, and there's what you wrote about me. We've been talking about what you wrote about me, and I've had my say about that. I've said it wasn't fair on me. Now you want to talk about leaving The Laurels, and you're saying that isn't fair on you.'

'It isn't, is it? I know everybody's got to leave sometime, but most of them have got somewhere to go . . . and someone to go to. They're always talking about their family in Darlington, or their girlfriend in Walsall, or something like that. I haven't got anyone.'

'Hmm . . .' says Sandra, thinking about confidentiality, but deciding that this issue needs to be tackled as one that isn't just Brian's. 'Nobody likes to admit that they haven't got anybody. There's probably more of them in a position that's a bit like yours than you think. That's the way it is here – the guys talk about their families and their plans and their worries with their key workers, and they use the groups to talk about what's going on in the hostel. People feel defensive about their outside life, and they certainly don't like to admit that they're worried about leaving. You didn't talk about it in the group, did you?'

'No, I suppose not.'

'So, I think the issue you've raised – about whether it's fair to expect someone who's learnt to share more with a group to go and live alone in a bedsit, on very little money – is a very real one, an important one. But I don't think it's just an issue about you, about what's fair on you alone. I think it affects other people too.'

'I'm not going to talk about it in the group, if that's what you're going to say.' Brian is one jump ahead of her.

'Well, I wasn't going to say that you should raise it in the group, no. I was going to offer to talk to the warden about it, to say that I think it's a real problem, not just for you, but for several others as well. And I was going to offer to try to raise it in the group myself, to see whether I can get some discussion going about it.'

'What good will that do? I don't want to be funny, Sandra, but I don't see what good that would do me.'

'Well, I can't promise anything. But at least it would be trying to take your point seriously, and try seeing whether we could tackle the whole business of people leaving here differently.'

'How do you mean?'

'I mean, if several people have the same problem, it may be possible to find some kind of shared accommodation, for a start.'

'Yeah, but ... it might not be the ones I get on with. I certainly wouldn't want to share a place with Eric, or Geoff. No way ... Not in a flat, not getting your own place ... If that could work out, people would do it of their own accord already, wouldn't they?'

'Not necessarily. It may be that the staff aren't letting it happen. Not stopping it exactly, but talking about people's plans individually, never looking at what they have in common. I think that does happen.'

'I don't think it would work out for several guys together without any staff. You lot keep this place going, don't you? Whatever they say, they'd be lost without you. There'd be fights, and stuff nicked all the time. It'd be anarchy, know what I mean?'

'I'm not so sure. I think sometimes we set it up to seem like that. And in any case, this place is supposed to prepare you for living in the big wide world, not to be hermits and loners.'

'Mmm ... well, I'm not going to talk about it in the group.'

'Not even if other people do?'

'Not if it means having to share a place with Eric or Geoff.'

'The fact that you keep on about them makes me think that there must be others you wouldn't mind sharing with.'

'I don't know. I haven't thought about it.'

'Well, think about it, Brian. Because it can't really be a choice between here and prison, can it?'

'I suppose not.'

'And I'll talk to the warden. I won't bring it up in the group until I've discussed it with him, and I'll see you again when I can tell you what he says.'

'I expect he'll say I've got to go.'

'Just the same as I have, you mean?'

'No ... but he still won't let me stay, will he?'

'No, not indefinitely and unconditionally. But that was never the contract, was it? At least we're talking about how to avoid chucking away all the progress you've made.'

'That's something, I suppose.'

Samantha

'What have you said to Nigel so far?'

Samantha's blonde hair flops across her eyes, and she traces patterns on the table-top with her manicured fingers. It is hard to believe that she is over 30.

'Nothing much,' she says lethargically. 'He wouldn't understand.'

Mary tries to clarify what Samantha's dilemma is doing to herself, as a woman and social worker. She feels for her, as a wife caught in her husband's image of womanhood as pretty and protected. But she feels angry with her for so willingly accepting the material rewards of that status. Samantha too readily acknowledges that she is a coward and a hypocrite. Such an easy confession is a cop-out.

Mary knows that Samantha may see her as a threat and a reproach. Even though Samantha knows nothing about her private life, the fact that Mary is a woman of her own age who has worked her way into a professional job is probably enough. In a way, Mary can't help feeling that Samantha *should* feel bad about the discrepancy between them. Not that she should feel guilty about having done so little about making a life for herself so far; more about her unwillingness to start now, even though she says she knows that she should. Perhaps Mary can act as a sort of goad to Samantha, or a model. But if she seems too much of a threat, Samantha will become defensive and discouraged, and may just give up.

'Imagine the kind of person who *would* understand you. What would she or he be like?'

'How do you mean?' asks Samantha, a bit startled.

'The kind of person you could tell about your yearnings to be different, to have a life of your own, to take a pride in yourself, and to be valued by other people as somebody worthwhile, instead of being Nigel's beautiful but mixed up and unhappy wife.'

'I don't know really. I'd never really thought about it ... someone like you, maybe,' she adds as an unconvincing afterthought.

'Or maybe not. Perhaps you feel I don't understand either.'

'No,' protests Samantha rather weakly. 'You've been really nice to talk to. It's the first time I've told anyone these things.'

'But now you've told me them, the question is what to do next. And I'm not sure you feel much further forward with that.'

'Well, no, not really. But that's not because of you. I just don't seem to have any energy or courage.'

'Who would understand about that, do you think?'

Samantha pauses, her brow wrinkled in puzzled thought. 'The doctors?' she suggests hopefully.

'Perhaps. Who else?'

'Well ... umm ... some of the other women here? Dolores took an overdose, and she seems fed up with her life, and her marriage.'

'And how would that help? Talking to other women with similar problems?'

'I'm not sure. It's ... well, it's the sort of thing you do in these places. Anxiety management groups, and that kind of thing.'

'Anxiety management?'

'Well, I'm not the expert,' says Samantha with a laugh. 'Surely you know what groups are for? Don't set me these hard questions, Mary. You'll give me a headache.'

'I just wondered if you could see any difference between, say, a relaxation group, and a group of women talking about what they have in common, what it's like to be a woman.'

'Well, I expect there is a difference. You wouldn't have to take your shoes off, for a start,' Samantha giggles. 'No, sorry, Mary, I mustn't be facetious ...'

'Have another try.'

'All right ... um ... well, finding out there's always someone worse off than yourself?'

'Does that help?'

'Not much, no.'

'Keep going then.'

'Er . . . this is really hard. It's like exams at school or something. Ask me the question again, Mary.'

'How would it help to talk to other married women about what it's like to be a woman, a wife, a mother?'

'Yes. It would help because . . . because I suppose every woman has to sort out this thing over how to be a person of her own, have her own life. Only . . .'

'Yes?'

'Only the ones who end up here are either the ones whose husbands won't let them, or the ones who haven't been able to, for some reason.'

'And which would you say you are?'

'Oh, the second. Except that Nigel does stop me in one way. In the kindest possible way.'

'Well, there might be plenty of ways for men to make it difficult for women to have a life of their own, some of them kindly meant. You mightn't be the only woman here with a kind husband.'

'I hadn't thought of that. I suppose I wouldn't feel so guilty if I talked to other women with kind husbands who are fed up with themselves and their marriages. But I've got less excuse, because we're quite rich, and most of the other women here aren't, are they?'

'What difference does that make?'

'It gives me a stronger reason for staying with Nigel, because I'd find it hard to cope with less.'

'Is that your main reason?'

'Not the only one, no.'

'And the others?'

'Cowardice about being on my own. Not wanting a fight over the children. Not wanting to hurt him. Not being sure what I want.'

'Do you think you're the only woman here with those feelings?'

'No, I guess we all feel those things. So I suppose it would help to talk about them with the others, to get them in some proportion, to try to make sense of them. But I still don't see how that would help me decide what to do. Surely each person's case is different? My situation is like Dolores' in some ways, and unlike in others. What's right for her isn't necessarily right for me. I don't know, I couldn't do your job, Mary.'

'Stay with the similarities and the differences for a moment, Samantha. Suppose you found out that your situation was *exactly* the same as someone else's?'

'How do you mean? It isn't the same as Dolores'. Her husband is far older than her, that's part of the trouble . . .'

'No, not Dolores necessarily. Imagine someone else – Susan – who's not you, but is in exactly the same circumstances as you. Should you do the same as her?'

'No, no, I don't think so. Not always.'

'Why not?'

'Because . . . well, because she's had a different life from mine up to now, she's got different ideas and things. And anyway, her husband's not Nigel, he's Henry or something. She might be able to work something out with him. Or he might change even.'

'But Susan doesn't want to discuss it with Henry.'

'Well, I think she should.'

'Unlike you.'

'Look, I know I should talk to Nigel, but I know what he'll say, and I just can't take any more of it . . .'

'That wasn't a trick question, Samantha. I actually agree with you that, even if your situation was just the same, what's right for you isn't necessarily the same as what's right for Susan. But I also agree that we can't be finally sure about what's right for Susan – or for you – until it's been discussed with Henry – or Nigel.'

'I can just see his face. All hurt and not understanding anything.'

'So what you mean is that you want to protect him?'

'In a way, I suppose, yes.'

'You're so sure that he can't change, and you aren't sure you want him to change?'

'He was brought up to see everything like that. It's the only way he knows. His parents had that kind of marriage. He thinks his mother's blissfully happy – perhaps she is. He couldn't imagine any other kind of marriage.'

'Maybe he's as much trapped in his rules about how marriage should be as you are.'

'How do you mean?'

'Well, what does he think about your suicide attempts?'

'He thinks I'm ill.'

'And how does that affect him?'

'It makes him unhappy, of course.'

'So his rules don't make him happy either?'

'No . . . but you can't just change the rules, can you?'

'Why not, if they don't benefit anyone?'

'Nigel's very conventional. He hates new ideas.'

'Even when the old ones make him miserable?'

Samantha clutches her head. 'I don't understand what you're saying, Mary. First you say I should talk to other unhappy women – but that might upset me even more. Then you say I must talk to Nigel – but that might upset him even more.'

'Talking to other women might help you decide how you want to change the rules – what you want the rules between husband and wife to be, what rules would be fair on both. And you can't change the rules unilaterally. You have to discuss it with him if you want to change them.'

'But what if he can't change, or won't change?'

'We're talking about changing the rules, not him. You're probably right, neither of you can change with your relationship as it is. You do need to start again, in a way – to agree new terms. If you can't, then it will be time to think again.'

'He'll be terribly upset.'

'You say he isn't happy as it is.'

'Yes, but . . .'

'We could discuss it with him in the context of where you go from here. You said yourself that you're afraid it will happen again.'

'I couldn't tell him that . . .'

'Would it help if I offered to see you both together?'

'Could you? I'm not sure . . .'

'The offer's there, Samantha.'

'I'll have to think about it . . . perhaps . . .'

Joan

'It's just so unfair, Joan. You've spent your whole life, almost, caring for members of your family. First your sister, then your father-in-law, then your husband, and now your mother. And you've never had much support from anyone, especially not the social services. And now you're asking for something perfectly reasonable, a bit of help you certainly have a right to expect, and I can't give it to you. Not in a way that's really what you need, anyway. I feel terrible about it.'

There, she's got that off her chest anyway. She wanted to express outrage on Joan's behalf, and now she has.

'Oh, it's not as bad as that really, dear,' says Joan, instinctively comforting the social worker, and trying to make her feel better about it all. 'You're doing your best, I'm sure. It's not your fault.'

'Not my fault personally, perhaps; but the fault of a rotten system that I'm part of.'

'Well, you said it was all changing soon. Perhaps it will be better then, and you'll be happier working in it.'

'No, I don't think so really. I can't see it changing all that much for people like yourself. Because you really need almost full-time day care for your mother, on weekdays anyway, to make it possible for you to work. And I don't think that's going to be available, not for a long time anyway. There just won't be the resources.'

Joan's mother wanders in from the next room, asking about tea, and who this lady is. Joan leads her patiently back, and tries to get her interested in the television programme, which seems to be about uranium mining in Australia. Joan reminds her mother that she had an uncle who went to Australia, but her mother cannot remember him.

'Mother wouldn't want to be at a day centre for that long every week anyway,' says Joan, returning. 'I don't think it would be right for her. She needs me really.'

'But you need a life of your own.'

'Yes, but I suppose I've got the rest of my life. If I can just survive this. I got in a bit of a state last week, that was all. It's not quite so bad now. Not to upset yourself about, anyway.'

'I'm upset about you, and about the way my department treats other people like you. I think we should all feel bad about that.'

'Well, I probably wouldn't have been able to find the right job anyway – not many organisations want people of my age. I'll just have to sort out something for myself, and not make too much fuss.'

Oh Lord, she's feeling guilty about bothering me now, thinks the social worker. I obviously overdid my outburst. Now she's embarrassed, and wants me to go away.

'I'm getting angry on your behalf, Joan, because I think you have reason to feel angry, or at least critical of the service you're getting. But you had every reason to ask for help, and you do need help. If you hurt yourself, or became ill, you wouldn't be able to look after your mother like this. It's a full-time job in itself, and there's no breaks from it.'

'Yes, I do worry about falling ill. I thought I might be going to have a breakdown or something. Just . . . everything got on top of me . . . out of proportion. I was quite scared at the time . . .'

'So, how are things going to get better?'

'Well, they aren't, I suppose. But I'll just have to put up with them, if there's nothing you can do . . .'

'I didn't say there was nothing. Just that we couldn't give your mother the day care that would let you take a full-time job.'

'I thought about working part-time, but I'm only supposed to earn £20 a week. I've looked in the paper, and the only daytime jobs round here for just a few hours are cleaning or looking after old people . . .' She laughs, in a tired way. 'I've got enough of those to do already.'

'What would you want from a job?'

'Oh, a bit of company. Someone to talk to about ordinary things. A change of scene. Being treated as an intelligent, a reasonably intelligent person, with something to contribute. Something different to think about.'

'Have you thought about a group, meeting with other carers?'

'No, not really. Is there one?'

'Yes, one of my colleagues organises it. It's for people who are looking after a spouse or a parent with Alzheimer's disease.'

'You mean to compare notes, and talk about what it's like to . . .'

'Yes, that's the starting point, anyway.'

Joan looks thoughtful for a while. 'I don't want to sound ungrateful, but no, I don't think that's for me. I think I'd get more depressed, hearing others talking about the same

problems. That sounds awful, I know, but I'd really rather not
...'
'Is it that you don't think you'd get on with the other carers?'
'No, it's not that. I expect a lot of them would be . . . well,
more or less like me. It's just . . . I don't think it would help to
talk about what we do all day, about how the disease has
affected the person we're looking after, about how distressing
it is. I found it helpful to talk to you, but I don't think that's
what I want to talk about if I meet other people.'
'So you want to talk to other people, possibly even other
carers, but not about being a carer?'
'Yes . . . but I've got so little to say nowadays, I suppose that's
stupid . . .'
'No, I think that's important. You want to meet people and
establish some common ground that isn't to do with looking
after confused old people. You want to build up your links with
people and activities that aren't to do with caring, and to
remind yourself that you aren't just a carer, you're someone
with ideas and skills and interests of your own.'
'Yes, that's why I wanted to get back into a job.'
'But that shouldn't be the only way of someone like yourself
being an active member of the community. There should be
lots of other ways that you can join in, and belong to
organisations.'
'Perhaps. I've never had much chance to join in things. When
I haven't been looking after someone, I've been earning a
living.'
'And would you like to join something?'
'Yes . . . well, I don't know. I've never really thought about
it.'
'What about classes? Have you ever thought of studying, or
joining a craft class or something like that?'
'I did think once about studying for the Open University. Not
that I'm clever enough, I don't expect. But anyway, it would be
hopeless here – I'd never read more than a page without an
interruption . . .'
'But suppose that we aimed at giving your mother day care
at a time that would allow you to join an adult education class,
or become a part-time student at college?'
'Yes, that sounds quite . . . actually, I'd be terrified, I expect,

if it came to the time . . . but it sounds quite a nice idea, if there was something that could be fitted in. Aren't all the classes in the evening?'

'Some, not all. Suppose you telephone the college and ask for a full prospectus of all the classes and courses? Then we could look and see what might interest you, and how to arrange things for your mother.'

'Mm, all right. Though thinking about it, I'm not sure I'd be brave enough to go on my own. It's been such a long time since I did anything like that.'

'Would any of your friends be interested?'

'Not in a daytime course, no. They've got jobs themselves, or . . . no, I shouldn't think so.'

'There might be another person who's caring for a parent who'd like to go with you. I've been thinking, quite a few carers don't want to join the group, but do want to do something that gets them away from their homes. It might be possible to form a new organisation, a sort of club . . .'

'I see what you mean.'

'Perhaps you could back each other up, in taking up new activities, either by going together, or maybe even sitting for each other from time to time.'

'Yes, that sounds quite good, doesn't it.'

'So if you'll find out about the courses, I'll see if I can find out who else might be keen on joining this club, and finding somewhere you could meet.'

'I quite like the idea of a club. When you're stuck at home like I am, you get to think you're so far outside things that you'll never belong to anything again. Yes, that sounds quite good. And it might have a gardening group; I like that. And funnily enough, that's one thing that still interests Mother. She likes to sit out in the garden, and she can still remember the names of the flowers . . .'

George

'What you're really saying is that you're prepared to take a chance on it. That you'd rather die at home next month than die in a home next year. Something like that, isn't it?'

George doesn't answer. Maybe he thinks that by making it

explicit he will make it impossible. He wants to do a deal, but
he thinks the only possible deal is an unspoken one. A nod and
a wink, a handshake, we both know what's what, but I leave
him to get on with it. Dying, that is. His business, not mine. A
death of his own.[1]

'I'm not trying to get you to say something that I'm not
allowed to hear. George. Actually, I think people should be
given a say in where they die. But we do need to talk about it. I
can't just assume that you mean something like that. Because
it would be completely wrong if I just sent you home, knowing
there was a real risk, without even checking out that this is
what you're saying.'

George has been looking at him intently, but now looks
away. He is thinking about it.

'You're not saying much,' says the social worker.

'I'm listening. You keep talking, boss.'

'I'm *not* saying that if that's the way you want it, then it's
your decision, your responsibility, and I wash my hands of it. I
can't say that, because of my job, and I don't want to say that,
because I don't believe that's how life should be. That's not how
people should treat each other. But I'm not saying that I'm
going to stop you going home because there is a risk, and
because there isn't enough social services help available to get
rid of the risk. What I'm trying to say is that I think we should
try to reach an understanding about the risk, and how to share
responsibility.'

George looks puzzled. He has been trying to say too much,
talking to himself really, to clarify the position.

'Let's take it in stages. You'd rather be at home, even if there
is a risk that you'll have another stroke, or a fall, and no-one
will be there for several hours, or even a whole day and night.
Is that about right?'

'That's about the strength of it. When I had the first one, I
lay there for twelve hours, something like that, wasn't it?'

'So I've been told, yes.'

'Well, I've had the practice, like. If I done it once, I can do it
again, sort of thing.'

'And if you die before someone comes?'

'You've got to go some time, haven't you? Better like that, in
your own place, than put away in a home.'

'But you've never even visited one, have you? You don't know what it's like.'

'Yes, I have. My other neighbour, Mabel, she's in one, Broadmead, quite close by. I've been to see her. Not bad, really, as far as cleanliness is concerned, and the staff are quite friendly. It suits her, I think she's happier there. But it's not for me. I couldn't stand it.'

'Why not?'

'Hard to say really. I feel sorry for the blokes there. Some of them try to make themselves useful, poking about in the garden or sommat. Others just give up and sit there, switched off. It's just not my style, I suppose.'

'What is your style then?'

'Me? Oh, scratching about for myself . . . just as long as I can take a few steps, out into the kitchen, and the back yard. What about one of them walking frames? I'm not proud.'

'And your shopping?'

'The milkman's very good. He delivers stuff . . . don't eat much nowadays.'

It's no good asking these questions, the social worker thinks, he's only going to tell me the good news, the things that make it sound feasible. He'll leave out the snags – like the fact that his neighbour is herself disabled, and the step down into the kitchen. It's pointless to expect him to be 'realistic' or to 'come to terms with his loss'. His is a different kind of realism, that knows that for him a residential home would be a way of staying alive, but not of living.

'You're just fobbing me off, aren't you? I know it's going to be much harder for you than you're making out, and you know it.'

He takes it as a rebuke. 'No, I'm not. I know what I can do.'

'Could do, before this.'

'I can walk.'

'A bit, with help.'

'I'll improve. The physio lady said it was just a matter of practice. She said I was doing well.'

Is George unconsciously deceiving himself, wonders the social worker, or is he consciously trying to deceive me? Has he no insight, in which case these questions run the risk of taking away his cheery defences against despair, or does he see clearly, but want to let me down lightly? The assessment of

George's realism is part of the assessment of his needs, and of whether it can really be regarded as his choice (in his interests) to go home. Unless George can acknowledge at least part of the problem, he cannot take part of the responsibility, and the social worker is left with the full moral burden of the decision.

'Were you ever a betting man, George?'

'I used to do the horses a bit when I was working, yeah. Just a few bob, now and then.'

'And what odds would they be offering on you surviving on your own then?'

'What, competely on my own, with no help at all?'

'Yes, if you like.'

'For how long?'

'Say, three months.'

'Oh . . . 25 to 1, I guess.'

'Against?'

'Yeah, of course. 25 to 1 on would be a dead cert. Or, I suppose, a live one in this case.'

The social worker breathes an inward sigh of relief. George has indicated that he is cheerful and positive in spite of the odds, not because he doesn't know them.

'So what we've got to do is see how we can improve those odds. That's my job.'

'You'll let me go home, then?'

'Hang about, I didn't say that. I'll try to get the social services department, my lot, and the health service to give you the help and support you need to get those odds down to something more manageable. But if the odds are still against, then you and I are going to have to talk about that.'

'I thought you said that the services aren't there, not enough of them.'

'I can try to get you as much home help as possible, for the first few weeks at least, and one meal a day. And you'll be coming into the day hospital for physiotherapy once or twice a week. But that leaves the weekends completely uncovered . . .'

'Dorothy, my neighbour, she'll see to me then. She can check up on me.'

'Which still leaves the odds at . . . what would you say?'

'Oh, near enough evens, I'd guess.'

'And how much better if you went into a home?'

'I dunno. But that wouldn't be living for me, like I say.'

'It could come to that, as you know, if you had another stroke, or a fall . . .'

'But it hasn't come to it yet.'

And you don't want it to, thinks the social worker, you'd rather that next one, when it comes, is final.

'So how will you feel about having a home help, if I can get one for you.'

'Fine, good.'

'Because it's part of her job to make sure that you are safe, and coping. If not, she has to tell her manager, who'll tell me.'

'Kind of part-time spy, sort of thing.'

'Because I'd want to talk to you again about how it's going. Not just wash my hands of it when you leave hospital. I wouldn't be able to come often, because of all the things I have to do here. But once a month, for a time at least, to make sure you haven't changed your mind.'

'I won't.'

'And you won't tell me to mind my own business?'

'No, of course not. It is your business in a way, isn't it?'

'I'm glad you see that.'

'That's a deal then.'

Yes, thinks the social worker, and I hope we both now understand the deal, and everything it implies.

'It may not work out the way both of us want.'

'Oh well, you can't win 'em all.'

Reference

1. The example of George is loosely based on Martin Hollis, 'A death of one's own', in J. Bell and S. Mendus (eds), *Philosophy and Medical Welfare* (Cambridge University Press, 1989).

INDEX